UNFORGOTTEN IN THE GULF OF TONKIN

UNFORGOTTEN
in the **GULF** of **TONKIN**

A Story of the U.S. Military's Commitment to Leave No One Behind

EILEEN A. BJORKMAN

Potomac Books

AN IMPRINT OF THE UNIVERSITY OF NEBRASKA PRESS

Library of Congress Cataloging-in-Publication Data

Names: Bjorkman, Eileen A., author.
Title: Unforgotten in the Gulf of Tonkin: a story of the
U.S. military's commitment to leave no one behind /
Eileen A. Bjorkman.
Other titles: Story of the U.S. military's commitment to
leave no one behind
Description: [Lincoln]: Potomac Books, an imprint
of the University of Nebraska Press, 2020. | Includes
bibliographical references and index. |
Summary: "Unforgotten in the Gulf of Tonkin is the
thrilling true story of Navy pilot Lt. William Sharp's high-
speed ejection from his F-8 over North Vietnam and
escape."—Provided by publisher.
Identifiers: LCCN 2019045347
ISBN 9781640121911 (hardback)
ISBN 9781640123632 (epub)
ISBN 9781640123649 (mobi)
ISBN 9781640123656 (pdf)
Subjects: LCSH: Sharp, Willie Dean, 1940– | Vietnam
War, 1961–1975—Aerial operations, American. | Fighter
pilots—United States—Biography. | Vietnam War,
1961–1975—Search and rescue operations—Vietnam. |
Crusader (Jet fighter plane) | United States. Air Force—
Search and rescue operations. | United States. Navy—
History—Vietnam War, 1961–1975. | United States.
Navy—Officers—Biography.
Classification: LCC DS558.8 .B595 2020 |
DDC 959.704/348—dc23
LC record available at https://lccn.loc.gov/2019045347

Set in Scala by Mikala R. Kolander.

The views expressed in this work are those of the author
and do not reflect the official policy or position of the
Department of Defense or the U.S. government.

To our missing warriors and all those who continue to search

CONTENTS

ILLUSTRATIONS

ACKNOWLEDGMENTS

I thank Willie Sharp for the dozens of interviews he sat through and emails he patiently answered as I pieced his story together, along with the many pilots, aircrew, and others who told me stories and answered my questions (see the bibliography for a complete list). I also must thank DeeDee Slewka, who helped turn my manuscript into what I hope is a compelling story; my literary agent, Leah Spiro, for taking on my project and pointing me in the right direction; and Tom Swanson, my Potomac Books editor, who understood the significance of Willie's story. In addition, I thank the numerous personnel at both the Naval History and Heritage Command and the Air Force Historical Research Agency who provided me many reports and other historical documents during my research. Finally, I thank the many people who reviewed my manuscript and made helpful suggestions along with catching small errors and inconsistencies.

My special thanks to the following people who agreed to be interviewed for this book, whether in person, by phone, or by email: John Borry, Miles Burd, John Christianson, Arnold Ebneter, John Glenn, Rabbi Jem Golden, Joseph Isenberg, L. David Lewis, Carol Leitschuh, John Miller, Rick Millson, John Miottel, Tom Saintsing, Willie Sharp, Bob Shumaker, Daryl Strong, David Wendt, and John Whitesides.

UNFORGOTTEN IN THE GULF OF TONKIN

Introduction

I DISCOVERED THE STORY OF WILLIAM SHARP'S EJECTION BY accident. A magazine editor asked me to write a story to mark the sixtieth anniversary of the first flight of the U.S. Navy's F-8 fighter jet. I knew nothing about the F-8, but I jumped at the chance to expand my aircraft repertoire outside of air force planes.

During interviews several F-8 pilots and maintenance personnel mentioned a distinctive howling made by the F-8's jet engine in flight. Hoping to describe that sound in my article, I searched for F-8 videos on YouTube one evening. After an hour of viewing that didn't satisfy my curiosity, I spotted a video titled "The Ejection of Lieutenant William Sharp."

I've always been fascinated by aircraft ejection stories, a fascination born from the possibility that I might have to eject from one of the military jets I once flew in as a flight test engineer. Ejections are rare enough events nowadays that they often make front-page news. But in the 1950s and 1960s they happened almost daily and were common even in the 1980s, when I flew in the rear seat of jets at Edwards Air Force Base in California. From those days I knew dozens of pilots and other aircrew members who had ejected. I once was at a dinner party where all three of the pilots seated at my table had ejected—one from a jet on fire and the others when they lost control of their fighters. I worked with a test pilot who had retired to a desk job after ejecting from three different airplanes. He walked with a pronounced limp.

Because ejection was a realistic possibility, I spent many hours wondering how I would react if it ever happened. Our survival instructors told us we would probably go into shock right after we ejected, partly from the violence of the ejection itself but also from the instantaneous extraction of our bodies from a warm cockpit into the hostile atmosphere above the earth, which at thirty thousand feet is freezing and oxygen deprived. The repetitiveness and detail of our training was supposed to make our actions instinctive so that even while in shock we didn't have to think.

With all my fascination about ejections, when the video preview of William Sharp's ejection popped up on my laptop, it took me one nanosecond to click on it. For the rest of the evening, I forgot about the F-8 engine.

The video, since deleted, had audio and photos from Sharp's ejection and subsequent search and rescue mission. The ship that launched a rescue helicopter recorded the radio transmissions of all surface and airborne participants, providing a rare peek into the intensity and confusion of combat. Another pilot on the mission snapped photos of the ejection sequence with a 35 mm camera he carried. I went through two glasses of wine as I watched the twenty-minute video repeatedly over the next two hours.

According to the video, William Sharp had later been a pilot for a major airline. The airline bubba net is small and active on the internet, so it didn't take me long to determine that he was probably a member of a retired airline pilots association. I sent an email to the secretary of the association asking if he would mind passing my contact information to Sharp.

I didn't plan to put Sharp's ejection into my story—I already had three ejection anecdotes—but I thought the story might be a good second article, if he would talk to me.

One evening, a few days after viewing the video, my cell phone rang with an unfamiliar number on the caller ID.

"This is William Sharp. I hear you're looking for me."

He told me he preferred "Willie," and over the course of two interviews, I realized his shoot-down and aftermath had too much angst, uncertainty, ingenuity, and heroism for me to capture it all in an article limited to three thousand words. By the time I hung up after our second interview, I knew I had a project on my hands.

Piecing together the story of Willie's shoot-down was more difficult than I expected. I thought that the audio recording would make it easy to re-create a timeline of events. But the transcript I created and my interviews with Willie left me with many questions, such as the locations of different players and the actions of the players involved. Much of the recording was inaudible or too scratchy to be useful. Pilots and controllers didn't always use call signs during radio transmissions; some had distinctive voices, but at other times I guessed at who was talking.

Luckily, I discovered several other references that helped me assemble the puzzle. Deck logs from several of the ships involved helped to refine some locations. The rescue report and combat loss report disagreed on some items but still helped to refine locations and contributed information about the actions of pilots and controllers. Many of those involved in Willie's mission have passed away, but I found two pilots who added significant details. Another pilot and a navigator who were in Vietnam in 1965 but not flying that day helped me to further paint the picture of what the rescue aircraft were likely doing. The discrepancies I found among sources were mostly minor, such as times that disagreed by a few minutes. In other cases mistakes were obvious, such as a wrong location in the combat loss report. Despite faults in the audio recording, I considered it the gold standard for events, and it served as a tiebreaker on a few occasions. The finished story is like a jigsaw puzzle with a few missing pieces that don't detract from the overall picture.

One last note: In 1962 the navy switched to a new system for designating aircraft. For example, the F-8 was called the "F8U-1" when it first flew in the mid-1950s. Many Vietnam era navy aircraft also changed designations. Rather than confuse readers with different nomenclatures, I use the newer designation for all Vietnam era aircraft. Also, unless the specific model of an aircraft is important (e.g., F-8D vs. F-8E), I refer to aircraft by their basic designation (e.g., F-8).

1

The Hit

NOVEMBER 18, 1965, ABOUT 9:45 A.M.

Navy pilot Willie Sharp sat in the bubble of his fighter jet, hazy blue skies above, a sea of clouds below obscuring the path to the target of this morning's bombing raid, a North Vietnamese rail yard. The clear plastic canopy overhead, along with his helmet and oxygen mask, muffled the hellish howl of his jet engine. After one hundred combat missions over enemy territory, bombing a set of stationary boxcars was about as routine as anything can get in combat.

As if on cue, the clouds parted to reveal the rail yard and boxcars that U.S. intelligence suspected of running supplies down the Ho Chi Minh Trail to Viet Cong soldiers.

Other pilots on Willie's mission unleashed their bombs, and an antiaircraft artillery site on the ground began firing at the jets. Willie fired two Zuni rockets at the enemy emplacement, and then, as he flew back around for a pass at another set of guns, he felt a jolt, as if he'd run over a speed bump in a parking lot. Thump, thump. It didn't seem like much. Then, a dull shudder and a sound as if the life was being sucked out of the jet. But the jet kept flying.

Outraged that his jet was damaged, furious at the North Vietnamese who had nailed him, and mad at himself for letting this happen, Willie retaliated. He jammed his control stick forward, aimed his aircraft at the guns below, and unleashed his remaining ten rockets. A satisfying series of explosions mushroomed below.

As Willie pulled away from the target, a glance at his instruments told him that two of the jet's three hydraulic systems had failed. The remaining system would keep the F-8 fighter flying for now, but this could be a lethal hit. Could he make it back alive to his aircraft carrier floating thirty minutes away in the Gulf of Tonkin?

An artillery shell smashed through the right side of Willie's cockpit. The oxygen tank behind his seat exploded with a resounding bang. Metal fragments shot into his legs. He glanced up; there was a hole in his canopy. At two thousand feet he didn't need the oxygen, but things were going from bad to worse.

Willie's instincts kicked in. He slammed his throttle fully forward to ignite the F-8's afterburner. He turned east, accelerating to nearly supersonic speed back toward the relative safety of the Gulf of Tonkin. He had survived a hit to his left wing a few months earlier, but that damage had been minor and he had made a normal landing on the carrier. Today he knew he would not be so lucky. He doubted his jet would hold together long enough to land on the carrier's flight deck.

He had no idea how bad things really were until another F-8 pilot, "Cactus Jack" Buckley, called over the radio, "You're on fire."

The flight leader that day, Cdr. John Tierney, also caught up to Willie. He confirmed the flames shooting from the bottom of the jet and said, "You'd better get out."

Willie believed the other pilots, but he swiveled his head left and right at the parts of his wings and fuselage he could see: no smoke, no fire. He glanced into the rearview mirrors attached to both sides of the canopy—still nothing. No fire warning light in the cockpit either, and the engine was running fine.

With Tierney three ranks above him, Willie would normally have concurred with his commander's suggestion to eject. But Willie was the master of his own airplane. He had to make his own decision. He looked down. The clouds that had parted just in time for the attack on the target once again blanketed the earth below. Not yet, he thought. I might still be over land.

Eject too early, and he would parachute to the ground among

the enemy. The North Vietnamese were sure to capture him. A pilot in his squadron had ejected the previous month and was presumed captured. There had been no further news of him, and Willie did not relish sharing that destiny.

Wait too long, and the F-8 might explode around him. Eject at the right time, and he would splash into the Gulf. Even then, a lot of things could go wrong. Many pilots died during ejections; they were, after all, screaming through the air at hundreds of miles per hour. If he landed alive, a North Vietnamese fishing boat might pick him up. A rescue aircraft might not find him. He could drown if his equipment malfunctioned. Other American pilots flying in Southeast Asia had succumbed to all these fates.

Parachuting into the water was his best chance if he could live long enough to get past the coast, but he wasn't sure how far the gulf was. He had followed the rest of the aircraft in his flight, and now he was too busy to look at his map long enough to figure out exactly where he was. He decided he would be safely over the water if his crippled jet held together for even five more minutes.

Willie prepared to eject. His six-foot-two frame was shoehorned into the cockpit. Now it felt as tight as a coffin. To increase his chances of clearing the cockpit without injury, Willie ran his seat down as low as it would go and pushed the rudder pedals all the way forward. Taking his hand off the stick, he removed his knee-board and stowed it so it wouldn't fly up and hit him in the face. He grabbed the stick back with his right hand and clutched the ejection handle at the top of his seat with his left.

The minutes seem to last forever, especially for Tierney as he watched the flames streaming from the F-8's belly. He suggested Willie make a distress call. Everyone in radio range would know what was happening.

This time Willie heeded his commander. He pushed a button on his control stick and called, "Mayday, Mayday, Mayday. This is Feedbag One-Zero-Eight." Feedbag 108 identified him and his airplane that day.

Then two seconds of silence as Willie gathered his thoughts. Suffused with static from crappy radios, the silence permeated the helmets of pilots in nearby jets. It also sounded through the headsets of radio operators aboard the USS *Strauss*, a nearby ship that helped to coordinate airstrikes.

No one spoke during those two seconds. The pilot in distress has the right-of-way over everyone else in the sky. Willie could say anything he wanted and go anywhere he wanted. Pilots who could see him would stay out of his way. Air traffic controllers would estimate his path through the air and move other airplanes away from him. They would do whatever was needed to keep Willie safe.

Willie paused. He could not remember *Strauss*'s radio call sign, "Fleet Fox." He glanced down at his TACAN radio navigation receiver. It was tuned to *Strauss*'s TACAN, channel 25, and reported the direction and distance to the ship. I'll use that, he thought.

Sounding as matter-of-fact as if he were ordering a cheeseburger at a drive-in restaurant back home in California, Willie continued: "Presently heading zero-nine-five inbound to channel twenty-five. Fifty-three miles out. I'm on fire." Knowing where he was relative to the *Strauss* didn't help with his ejection decision since he had no idea where the ship was.

Willie still could not see the flames. He called to Tierney, "Still no fire warning light."

But Tierney could see that it wouldn't be long before the fire burned into Feedbag 108's only engine. He suggested again that Willie eject.

"Roger, I want to stay here a *little* longer, try to get as close as I can." Willie's voice squeaked a bit on the *little*. With the F-8 eating up a mile every eight seconds, even a few seconds could make a huge difference.

"Okay. As soon as I see any more action there, I'm going to tell you to eject."

"Okay," Willie agreed.

"That's up to your decision." Tierney seemed to back off his suggestion a little, perhaps remembering Willie was still in charge of his own aircraft.

An air traffic controller on board the *Strauss* reminded Willie to set his transponder to the universal emergency code. Willie took his gloved right hand off the control stick and twisted a knob on the right console until the word *Emergency* aligned with an arrow. Feedbag 108 blossomed into a bright green blob on the controller's radar. The airplane now stood out from the dozens of small dots depicting other aircraft on the controller's screen. The controller could now more easily keep track of Willie and call out his position to rescuers.

Crown Alpha, an air force amphibious search and rescue aircraft, checked in twenty-two miles southeast of Willie's position. With Willie still above the clouds, Crown Alpha's crew couldn't see him yet, but the air traffic controllers on the *Strauss* pointed them in the right direction.

Twenty seconds later Tierney called, "Try opening the speed brakes once to see if that will affect the flames."

"Ah, negative. I have no hydraulic pressure."

"Ah, roger. You had better go—the flames are getting worse. I'd . . . I'd go now."

A controller asked Willie for his altitude.

"I'm at eleven thousand, five hundred now."

Just then the fire burned through Feedbag 108's lower fuselage. The right landing gear fell away.

Tierney, his voice rising, called: "You've got to get out of there now. It's going to blow. Go now! Go quick!"

There was no more time for arguing.

Bracing to hit a wall of air at five hundred miles per hour, Willie yanked his ejection handle.

The statistics for downed combat aircrew are stark: in the first hour after ejection or crash landing, chances of surviving and being rescued are about fifty-fifty.[1] Death or capture is very real. This was the case for Sen. John S. McCain III, who as a U.S. Navy lieutenant commander landed in a North Vietnamese lake after ejecting from his stricken A-4 Skyhawk in October 1967. Taking advantage of McCain's shock and injuries, villagers pulled the pilot from the lake and turned him over to North Vietnamese soldiers. He subsequently spent more than five years in captivity.

After the first hour, if a downed aircrew is alive and not in enemy hands, their chance of recovery and survival drops very close to zero. They almost certainly will be killed or captured.[2]

John, chapter 15, verse 13, in the *Bible* says, "No one has greater love than this, to lay down one's life for his friends." It would be hard to find anyone who takes that dictum more seriously than combat search and rescue (CSAR) personnel, whose motto is "That Others May Live." (Although the military did not use the term *combat search and rescue* [CSAR] to describe rescue missions until after the Vietnam War, I have used CSAR throughout the text as shorthand for search and rescue missions performed under combat conditions.) In particular, U.S. military commanders have an unspoken agreement with their troops: if you get into trouble in enemy territory, we will do everything possible to bring you back, including sending others into harm's way. This implied contract is more than the right thing to do; it also increases morale and confidence in the young people the United States asks to fight our wars.

The ethos of "leave no one behind" isn't always possible, even with modern technology, given the uncertainties and confusion of combat. But with the state of technology in the 1960s, finding and rescuing a downed aircrew member in that precious first hour was daunting. And even when pilots and other crew were located, that information was useless if there were no CSAR aircraft nearby. CSAR capabilities during the early days of the Vietnam War were limited and ad hoc. Aircraft and techniques developed and refined during the Korean War had been largely abandoned as military strategists turned to nuclear deterrence. The idea of CSAR during a nuclear war was ridiculous—there would be no one left to rescue. But Vietnam was not a nuclear war, and the air force struggled to relearn everything about CSAR it had previously learned in Korea.

By the time Willie Sharp ejected in November 1965, the navy and air force had recovered some of their CSAR techniques, but they still had only a handful of rescue aircraft designed specifically for combat conditions. No aircrews were trained for rescues under fire. However, both services had set aside specific aircraft for combat rescues, and controllers coordinated with each other to direct the nearest aircraft to a downed aviator, regardless of his parent service. Throughout the war CSAR capabilities continued to grow.

Today it's difficult to determine how much we spend each year on CSAR capabilities, given that only a handful of aircraft have CSAR as their primary mission and CSAR funding has waxed and waned over the years along with rising and falling conflicts and defense budgets. But based on publicly available data regarding recent contract awards and the number of aircraft in the CSAR fleet, it's likely that, during the next decade, the United States will spend about two billion dollars each year buying and operating CSAR aircraft and other equipment. This might sound like an outlandish amount of money, until you consider that it is about the cost of a Subway sandwich for every U.S. citizen.

For the United States, leaving no one behind also doesn't stop at the end of a war. The U.S. military continues to search for the nearly eighty-three thousand personnel who remain missing in action from World War II, Korea, Vietnam, and other conflicts. With perennial debates on how much defense spending is enough and what wars our nation should be prepared to fight, some may consider funding for MIA searches an extravagant expense that only fuels our obsession with bringing back all our war casualties and dead.

But cold statistics and numbers alone do not tell the value of U.S. practices regarding downed and fallen personnel. That story can only be told by the men and women who have rescued someone, been rescued themselves, or had a loved one returned to them. Thousands of stories exist; most will never be told beyond a circle of family and friends. Some, like Willie's, live on, cautioning us to never forget the cruel realities of war and the sacrifices of our warriors.

2

Leave No Man Behind

WILLIE HURTLED UPWARD THROUGH THE SKY, STILL STRAPPED
to his ejection seat. All the requisite timers and tubes had opened
the canopy, snapped his legs against the seat, and thrust him out
of the jet. When he slammed into the atmosphere, his left arm
wrenched back so hard that he thought the limb was gone.

In twenty seconds he fell through six thousand feet. Then his
parachute opened and slowed his descent.

As he sank toward the earth, Willie was cut off from radio contact, but his fellow pilots didn't abandon him. John Tierney circled above, still in charge. Younger pilots in other jets swooped
about like angry gnats, the deafening roar from their engines
oddly comforting. Some of the pilots saluted Willie with their
middle fingers. He returned the salute in his mind and shouted,
"Fuck you!" They couldn't hear the insult, but the joshing made
him feel better.

He had about five minutes before sinking into the clouds below.
He still didn't know if he was over land or water, but he was con-
fident that rescue aircraft were probably already looking for him.
Propeller-driven aircraft and rickety helicopters made up much
of the rescue fleet, but Willie didn't care what aircraft pulled him
to safety. He was a fighter pilot without a plane, a knight who'd
been tossed from his horse. It was time to be humble.

After he plunged into the clouds, he lost sight of his fellow
pilots. He couldn't yet see what awaited him below. Still, he had
faith that friendly pilots were anxious to help. He most likely had

never met the rescue pilots searching for him, but he knew they would never willingly leave him behind.

Willie's confidence that help was coming wasn't available to World War I pilots. They didn't wear parachutes, and no one was going to rescue them if they survived a crash. Downed World War I pilots were largely on their own, relying on their wits and sometimes on the ingenuity of fellow aviators for rescue.

On March 20, 1917, British and Australian biplanes swarmed a few hundred feet above the ground as they dropped howitzer shells on an enemy train near Gaza.[1] One of Lt. Frank McNamara's shells exploded upon release. Metal fragments blasted through the flimsy wood and fabric cockpit of his Martinsyde and embedded themselves into the Australian pilot's thigh.[2] Although McNamara was injured, his aircraft was only lightly damaged.

At the same time, Capt. Douglas Rutherford's British BE 2 was hit by ground fire and developed engine trouble. McNamara watched the pilot land his plane near some Turkish cavalry troops.[3] Forgetting his own predicament, the wounded aviator spiraled toward the downed pilot. The Turks fired furiously at McNamara and other friendly airplanes as they raced to the crash site. McNamara arrived first and landed about two hundred yards from his British compatriot. They needed to get out of enemy territory, and fast. But there was a problem: the Martinsyde had only one seat. The other pilot climbed onto the lower of the two wings and grabbed a strut.[4]

McNamara added full throttle and tried to take off, but with the other pilot's weight on one side of the wing, the nose of the airplane swerved off course. McNamara couldn't push his injured leg hard enough on the rudder pedal to straighten the airplane. Instead of lifting into the air, the machine flipped upside down. The rollover damaged the craft beyond hope, but neither pilot was seriously injured.[5]

They struggled from the wreckage of the Martinsyde and then set fire to it, to prevent the plane from falling into enemy hands. Their only recourse now was the damaged BE 2. It was a long shot, but if they could restart the engine, the airplane should fly;

the rest of the aircraft had only minor damage to the fuselage and struts from the crash landing. McNamara was still heavily bleeding, but the two aviators ran to the BE 2. Rutherford tinkered with the engine while McNamara climbed into the pilot's seat. As the Turkish cavalry approached at a gallop, McNamara shot his revolver at them. Rutherford swung the four-bladed propeller around, and the engine started. He jumped into the observer's seat, and the two pilots lifted off over the heads of the soldiers and their mounts and flew seventy miles back to their aerodrome.[6]

World War I pilots who went down over water didn't need the heroics of fellow pilots to be rescued. A pilot who landed in the sea often had some sort of flotation equipment that kept him alive long enough to be picked up by a passing steamer.[7] But a rescuing ship might belong to the enemy and take the aviator prisoner. On December 14, 1914, two British seaplanes, each carrying a pilot and mechanic, took off in the late morning near the seaside French town of Dunkirk. Flying along a foggy North Sea coastline, the pilots navigated about forty miles northeast toward a German submarine factory near Bruges, Belgium. The crews dropped their bombs onto the docks surrounding the factory; then one aircraft developed a mechanical problem. The pilot and mechanic continued flying northeastward, following the Belgian coastline for about fifteen miles until they crashed inside the Netherlands, a neutral country. Following the Hague Convention regarding the laws of war, Dutch authorities detained both airmen.[8]

In the meantime the pilot of the second aircraft became confused by the fog and turned west instead of south back to Dunkirk. He almost made it across the North Sea to England, but engine problems forced the crew down a few miles from the coast; the pilot likely ran out of fuel. The aviators were lucky—the ship closest to them was Dutch. The crew from *Oranje Nassau* quickly plucked the men from the gray waters and allowed them to return to England. Two British ships later spotted the abandoned seaplane bobbing in the North Sea. A navy destroyer was dispatched to recover the aircraft so the British military could repair it and return it to service.[9]

McNamara's dramatic rescue was the exception during World War I. Early advocates of airpower had focused on how to use their new instrument of war, without much thought for the risks to the pilots, observers, and others who flew them. The idea of rescuing downed aviators apparently just didn't occur to early war planners. Neither did wearing parachutes.

That early military pilots flew without parachutes seems especially egregious, given that Leonardo da Vinci had proven three centuries earlier that parachutes could lower someone safely to earth from a great height. One reason for the lack of parachutes was practical: early designs were too bulky for cramped aircraft cockpits. The other part was ignorance: many erroneously thought that jumping from an airplane would cause a pilot to black out.

Early parachutes used rigid frames that worked for jumping from balloons but were too large for an airplane. The next generation of parachutes evolved to silk canopies stuffed in knapsacks, but military leaders still balked. The knapsacks required the user to pull the ripcord manually during free fall, and many aviators thought a person could withstand a free fall for only a few seconds before blacking out. Georgia "Tiny" Broadwick safely demonstrated free fall jumps in 1914, but her jumps had no effect on how early fighter pilots were equipped.[10] Until the early 1920s the only option for a military pilot in a disabled craft was to ride the airplane to the earth below. It often wasn't much of a choice.

"Going down with the ship" usually proved fatal for the aircrew of an aircraft spinning out of control from catastrophic battle damage—say, a lost wing or disintegrated tail feathers. Pilots could often safely land airplanes that had been hit in the engine, fuel system, or an area not critical to controlling the aircraft. World War I airplanes were small and light enough that they could land in open terrain smaller than a football field, but since there were no rescue services, the enemy detained most pilots who survived a crash away from friendly territory.

Even if World War I planners had the idea to rescue downed aviators, it's hard to imagine how a rescue might have worked, given that airplanes and pilots weren't equipped with radios. If no one saw a pilot go down, he had no way to call for help and tell someone where he was. After the war, newer technology shrank radios to a size that fit in an airplane cockpit. Also, a series of demonstrations at Wright Field, Ohio, in 1919 finally convinced the military that free fall was possible.[11] In addition, military planners figured out that the cost of a parachute was tiny compared to the cost of training another pilot, even with the added expenses of maintaining the parachutes, training pilots to use them, and finding somewhere to store them. Even so, it took several years before parachute use by military pilots became common. Some of the lingering reticence was from pilots themselves, including famed aviators such as Jimmy Doolittle, who thought wearing a parachute was for sissies.[12]

However, it didn't take long for the new equipment to prove its worth to these early aviators, given the alarming frequency with which they crashed their airplanes. On October 20, 1922, Lt. Harold Harris, a test pilot at McCook Field in Dayton, Ohio, nearly left his parachute on the ground when he discovered the chute's bulk made it hard to fasten his harness. For some reason he changed his mind. While maneuvering during a mock dogfight with another aircraft, Harris's plane disintegrated. As bits of airplane swirled around him, he released his lap belt, and g-forces tossed him into the air. He pulled the parachute's ripcord and alit in a grape arbor in the backyard of a nearby home. Harris gathered the parachute and carried it a half-mile back to the base. From then on all test pilots wore parachutes on every flight.[13]

Not long after Harris's bailout, the Irvin Air Chute Company formed the Caterpillar Club, an informal club that still exists. The only membership requirement is that someone parachute from a disabled aircraft to save their life.[14] Many famous aviators soon gained membership in the Caterpillar Club, including the most famous of them all, Charles Lindbergh.[15]

Parachutes got pilots on the ground alive, but during combat, that solved only half the problem. If a downed pilot was captured, his expensive-to-create skills were still lost for the rest of the war. The British also recognized the morale-building value of rescue; pilots more willingly flew into dangerous situations if they knew someone would try to find them and bring them back if they got into trouble. In 1925 Royal Air Force flying boat crews started carrying inflatable dinghies, and during the late 1920s crews practiced rescue operations.[16] By the beginning of World War II, the British had developed rudimentary rescue capabilities, which were further honed during the Battle of Britain in 1940.[17] But even the British had not figured out how to rescue pilots from behind enemy lines. Nearly all rescues during World War II were performed over water, and the mission became known as air-sea rescue.[18]

While the British honed their rescue skills, the U.S. military largely ignored rescue equipment and procedures, focusing instead on further developing the doctrine of strategic bombing. When the United States entered the war in late 1941, the Army Air Force (AAF) leaned heavily on British rescue services in the European theater.

Early in the war, U.S. crews received little training on what to do if they bailed out or crashed into the sea. On March 4, 1943, a B-17 returning to England from a raid on Germany ditched into the sea after German fighter pilots damaged three of the bomber's four engines with their guns. The inexperienced crew landed into a swell instead of the preferred practice of landing parallel to the waves. The aircraft broke into four pieces, but the crew of ten was unhurt. They slid into the water, along with the rescue dinghies. But the crew hadn't been trained in how to use the dinghies; three of them drowned while several other crew members spent thirty minutes inflating a single dinghy. The seven survivors found a radio floating nearby and called for help. A minesweeper picked them up eight hours later.[19]

Problems like those experienced by the B-17 crew and the increasing demand for air-sea rescue pushed the AAF to improve its rescue capabilities. In August 1943 the army established an office in Washington DC to develop rescue tactics and training and to determine where best to station rescue forces. But squabbling among the U.S. Army, Navy, and Coast Guard over rescue

FIG. 1. An OA-10 Catalina used during World War II.
(Courtesy Wikimedia Commons, U.S. Air Force)

responsibilities delayed the establishment of dedicated rescue units. The Joint Chiefs of Staff didn't help matters, concluding that the best solution was to let each service rescue its own aviators.[20]

A few months before standing up the army's new rescue office, the AAF dispatched a handful of OA-10 amphibian rescue aircraft and crews to Malta.[21] These first aircraft and crews formed only an interim rescue capability; the aircrews sent with the amphibians had no formal rescue training. The OA-10 Catalina had a boat-like fuselage, retractable landing gear, and a high wing that held two engines, each a few feet away from the cockpit (fig. 1). The aircraft carried several .50 caliber machine guns for self-defense. On a runway the Catalina landed with the landing gear down, on the water with the gear up. The aircraft was designed for endurance, which proved valuable for a rescue aircraft. In 1935 a navy crew flew a Catalina nonstop for 3,281 miles in about thirty-five hours to establish a new world distance record.[22]

In August 1943, not long after the base in Malta was established, an OA-10 landed in the water to pick up twenty airmen who had survived two separate B-17 crashes. All twenty survivors climbed aboard the Catalina, but it had been damaged during the landing, and the pilot couldn't take off from the water. Not to worry: the pilot elected to taxi back to shore. During the taxi they encountered several high-speed launches that took the passengers and towed the oa-10 back to port.[23]

Damaged oa-10s soon became the norm. The oa-10 was technically the same aircraft as the successful Consolidated Aircraft Corporation pby Catalina design that the navy used primarily for bombing submarines. But the aaf's Catalinas were built by a Canadian company, Vickers, that altered the design in a way that weakened the fuselage.[24] Inexperienced pilots flying the weaker structure produced inevitable results: popped rivets and damaged fuselage plates that maintenance crews had to replace or repair after almost every water landing.[25] Taxiing and towing became common tactics during oa-10 rescues.[26]

The aaf's first purpose-built and trained rescue unit, the First Emergency Rescue Squadron (ers), was finally established on December 1, 1943. The unit's aircrews trained for about ten weeks on the oa-10 in Boca Raton, Florida, before moving to Casablanca and then on to Italy, France, and India as the army tried to figure out how to best use the airplanes.[27] In addition to the oa-10s, the squadron had a few l-5 liaison aircraft, along with b-25 and b-17 bombers. The b-25s weren't much use; they could drop a few pieces of equipment to survivors, but couldn't rescue anyone. The b-17s couldn't do much either; the aircraft had been modified so they could drop large lifeboats to survivors, but no one ever shipped any lifeboats to the squadron.[28]

The First ers had plenty of work. A little over a month after arriving in Casablanca, an oa-10 took off in poor weather to look for a British Wellington bomber that had crashed. Skimming one hundred feet above the water to stay beneath a cloud deck, the oa-10's crew spotted not the bomber but a lone survivor in a dinghy, bobbing on top of fifteen-foot waves. The waves alone would make a water landing difficult, and a strong wind made things worse. The oa-10 was too low for the crew to call for help on the radio. No one wanted to climb back above the cloud deck; they might never find the survivor in the sea again. The five Catalina airmen decided to make a water landing. They pulled the survivor on board. But then, as expected, the damage to the Catalina was too severe to try a takeoff. The crew taxied the OA-10 toward land until they ran out of fuel. A high-speed launch found them and towed them to shore.[29]

Despite the slow start to building rescue forces, once the United States committed to rescue as a dedicated mission, airmen quickly developed new techniques and systems, adapted older ones, or borrowed ideas from the British. The most difficult part of any air-sea rescue operation was finding the survivors—specks bobbing in a vast ocean. Crews carried all manner of signaling devices—whistles, flares, yellow life vests, yellow rafts, yellow dye to drop into the ocean, and even homing pigeons to carry a note from a survivor back to shore—but the best signal was a radio.[30] However, the radio caused a new headache: false alarms caused by equipment failures or misuse of the equipment. In late 1944 more than half the alert signals heard by rescue units turned out to be false.[31]

U.S. rescue crews adopted the use of "spotter planes" to augment searches. The spotters were fighter aircraft that could speed toward a crash site and locate survivors more quickly than the lumbering OA-10s. The fighters couldn't rescue anyone, but they could drop additional equipment to survivors and relay their position to aircraft or ships that could complete the rescue. In 1944 a spotter squadron was tossed together using twenty-five "war-weary" P-47s. The Americans maintaining and flying the spotters soon outfitted the aircraft with smoke bombs for marking survivor positions, dinghies to drop to survivors, and an extra fuel tank so crews could fly nonstop for five hours.[32]

Spotter crews also figured out optimum search paths and tactics to overcome the P-47's limited radio range at low altitudes. Pilots learned to fly in pairs, one at low altitude to better spot survivors and the other at a higher altitude to get better radio coverage for relaying positions to other rescue aircraft.[33]

Rescue in the Pacific theater was very different from Europe. Since the army couldn't rely on the British for search and rescue in the Pacific, the AAF developed rescue forces earlier than they did in Europe. In early 1943 the Fifth Air Force Rescue Service was established to support operations in the Southwest Pacific, primarily New Guinea. The unit initially had only three people, who directed search and rescue missions using any aircraft or ship they could find. The AAF's Second ERS, nicknamed the "Snafu Snatchers," arrived in the Pacific theater in July 1944 complete with organic aircraft, boats, and personnel.[34] Given the vast area of the Pacific, other rescue squadrons soon followed. Equipment eventually included B-17s, OA-10s, and L-5s, small liaison aircraft that were mounted on floats.[35]

The AAF's trained rescue forces in the Pacific developed tactics somewhat different from their European counterparts. As in Europe, passing ships and boats augmented rescue forces, but submarines were also available in the Pacific. When combat aircraft flew inland for bombing missions, rescue aircraft and boats trailed the bombers and remained near the coastline, waiting for returning aircraft that might be in distress. Other aircraft waited on standby at their bases in case the forward aircraft needed help. During one airstrike on Balikpapan, Indonesia, on October 10, 1944, that resulted in several downed aircraft, rescue forces saved forty people—twenty-four with aircraft and sixteen with submarines.[36]

Upon hearing an SOS, an OA-10 or other rescue plane immediately headed for the crash site and began searching. Once it located the downed aircraft, the Catalina landed and picked up survivors, if sea and weather conditions allowed. If the OA-10 couldn't land, the crew dropped a dinghy and other supplies to the survivors. The crew then circled above the scene and radioed for a pickup by a ship or submarine. As in the European theater, the OA-10s were often damaged by water landings. In early 1945 B-17s with large lifeboats became available. The lifeboat was dropped instead of landing the Catalina. In theory the survivors could rescue themselves with the equipment and supplies in the lifeboat. In reality most of them were still picked up by ships or submarines.[37]

On March 4, 1945, Tech. Sgt. Ed Matthews, a B-25 radio operator and waist gunner, woke at 5:00 a.m. on the Indonesian island of Morotai. That day he was assigned to one of eighteen bombers for an attack on a Japanese-held airfield at Zamboanga, an island in the Philippines.

Each of the bombers carried a crew of three officers and three enlisted men.[38] As Matthews ate breakfast, 1st Lt. Frank Rauschkolb and his crew were already airborne in their Catalina, call sign "Playmate 42." The Catalina rumbled toward an orbit point over Manalipa Island, a few miles east of the bombers' target area. The copilot, Capt. Willis Helmantoler, outranked Rauschkolb, but the younger pilot sat in the left seat, making him the aircraft commander. He would make the final decisions that day.

The B-25s, cruising at twice the speed of the Catalina, took off about 7:00 a.m. and arrived over their target about two hours later. The pilot of Matthews's B-25 dove down a hill and rounded out about one hundred feet above the airfield. Crammed into the gun compartment on the left side of the bomber, Matthews strafed the airfield with his .50 caliber machine gun while the bombardier dropped bombs. After firing just a few rounds, the machine gun jammed, and Matthews moved to another gun on the right side of the aircraft. As he slid into position, he saw that the right engine was on fire.

Matthews shouted to the engineer in the turret, pressing him to retrieve the tail gunner so they could move into safer positions. The pilots were harder to alert: the intercom was out. A nine-foot-long open bomb bay gaped between the enlisted crew in the rear of the aircraft and the officers in the cockpit, an insurmountable chasm. Matthews grabbed spent casings off the floor and flung them at the pilots. He finally got their attention.

Matthews dashed back to the other two enlisted crew. Together they broke the windows in the fuselage and threw the waist guns overboard to prepare for a hasty evacuation after ditching. Then they sat in their ditching positions and waited for impact. The B-25 hit the ocean. It bounced once, then stayed put. Water poured through the broken windows. The fire from the engine spread onto the water on the right side of the fuselage. As the fire moved into the fuselage, the tail gunner and engineer went out the left window. Matthews splashed water on the fire and then released the life raft into the water. As he climbed through the window, he discovered that the life raft hadn't deployed from its hatch on the side of the fuselage. He tugged on the hatch, and the raft fell into the water. With a knife he carried on his leg, Matthews cut the rope securing the raft to the fuselage and towed the raft to the left wing tip, where the rest of the crew had gathered. All six crew members climbed into the raft. They pushed themselves about one hundred feet away from the burning wreckage before it sank. The flight engineer, with a bad gash in his leg, was the only one seriously injured. Crew members applied bandages to the engineer's wounds; he began to vomit, so the crew transferred him to a one-man dinghy that had floated out of the wreck. After tying the dinghy to the larger raft, the crew sat back to wait for rescue from the Catalina they knew was nearby. Two B-25s from their attack formation circled reassuringly above them, ready to provide firepower support.

Help was on the way. As Matthews and his crew had descended into the sea, Frank Rauschkolb and his Catalina crew had arrived near Zamboanga.

"Mayday! Mayday!" The Catalina crew heard frightened cries filling the airwaves. In addition to Matthews's bomber, two other B-25s had also been shot down. The single OA-10 would have to rescue the survivors from all three crashes.

The lead B-25 pilot of the remaining airborne bombers directed the Catalina crew to a B-25 that had ditched about a mile offshore from Zamboanga. Matthews and his crew would have to wait; they had made it to a safer position about two miles from shore. Four B-25s circled above the surviving five crew members from the other B-25. No one was sure what had happened, but an enlisted crewman had either been trapped in the cockpit or drowned shortly after getting out. Ten minutes after receiving directions from the lead B-25, the Catalina crew spotted two life rafts with survivors.

As the OA-10 neared the rafts, five Japanese barges rushed forward, firing mortars and machine guns. Shrapnel and explosions peppered the Catalina's tail and splashed into the surrounding water. The radio operator called the circling B-25s for help. The bombers strafed the barges, and the enemy guns fell silent.

Rauschkolb touched down, and the five survivors scrambled aboard through a door in the rear of the fuselage. Just then a mortar shell from a gun onshore crashed through the side of the Catalina. A fist-sized hole appeared at the waterline. Seawater poured into the hull.

One of the just-rescued B-25 pilots dashed to the cockpit and yelled, "Let's get the hell outta here!"

Helmantoler, the Catalina's copilot, shouted back, "There's two more crews out there in the water somewhere."

"Screw 'em. Let's get outta here!"

The frightened aviator didn't sway Rauschkolb. The lead bomber pilot still airborne saw that the first crew was safely aboard the Catalina. He radioed that the second downed B-25 was located just a few minutes away on a reef, about five hundred yards off the shore. Shore-based guns had fired furiously on the crew as they abandoned the bomber and paddled away in their raft. Somehow no one was hit.

Rauschkolb turned the Catalina toward the second set of survivors. But his aircraft was now perilously heavy, with five extra people on board, as well as the unexpected seawater and the extra fuel they carried for the long-range mission that day. Takeoff would be too risky, so Rauschkolb taxied on the water. Shells from shore guns splashed all around the Catalina, and the left engine quit. No amount of coaxing from the flight engineer, Tech. Sgt. Robert Jones, could restart the overheated engine. Abandoning his knobs and switches in the cockpit, Jones climbed on top of the wing. Wearing nothing but shoes and a pair of cutoff shorts, he ignored the artillery shells whizzing in the air and manually cranked the engine until it restarted.

After twenty minutes of taxiing through unrelenting gunfire, the Catalina made it to the raft with the second set of survivors. As they closed in for the pickup, a radio call announced that a Japanese plane had been spotted in the area. The Catalina's gunners ran to their positions, ready to fire at the approaching aircraft. At the last minute someone realized the interloper was a U.S. navy patrol aircraft.

Rauschkolb and his crew turned their attention back to the second set of downed airmen, who clambered aboard the Catalina and sat on any available space. The aircraft was starting to resemble a slumber party, with some men hunkered down in the tail section and gun blisters while others sprawled along the floor of the cargo area.

By now the crew of Ed Matthews's B-25 was starting to worry. The airmen had now been in the water for nearly an hour.

But Frank Rauschkolb wasn't done. About ten minutes after he picked up the second crew, someone announced the position of Matthews's crew, about twenty miles from the Catalina. Again, Rauschkolb decided to taxi to the rescue point. It took an agonizing hour. Two B-25s circled above them for protection the entire trip. The Catalina's navigator and radioman formed a bucket brigade to bail the seawater leaking into the cabin.

After nearly two hours in the water, the remaining survivors spotted two silver discs that appeared offshore and began moving toward them. They assumed that Japanese forces had spotted them and were coming to capture them. But as the discs grew larger, Matthews and the others realized they were the rotating propellers of the Catalina. Within a few minutes all six survivors were on board.

Now Rauschkolb had a new dilemma: with seventeen extra men, his aircraft was dangerously overweight for a takeoff. He bounced at full power across the wave tops for ten minutes. The Catalina failed to get airborne. Rauschkolb ordered all guns and ammunition tossed overboard. After ten more minutes of bouncing, the Catalina would still not lift off.

Rauschkolb got rid of the last thing he could: fuel. He asked Jones, the flight engineer who had climbed atop the wing to restart the engine, to dump as much fuel as he could while keeping enough to fly home. Jones, using only his intuition, dumped four hundred gallons overboard, leaving a hazy green oil slick on the dark blue sea. Fearing that even the smallest spark might ignite the water, no one moved as the precious liquid poured out of the plane.

When Jones proclaimed the OA-10 light enough for takeoff, they tried again. By now the seas had roughened, and Rauschkolb tore forward for another ten minutes, bouncing off increasingly higher waves. Finally, the aircraft catapulted into the air long enough to stay there. Decades later copilot Helmantoler remembered the cheers of the B-25 crew members as they rose from the water.

The two B-25s still aloft with the Catalina, satisfied that their teammates were safe, departed for Morotai. The Catalina's radio operator called the base with the good news that they carried seventeen survivors. As the OA-10 lumbered for four hours across the ocean, almost every colonel and general on the island heard the news and gathered at the airfield ramp. Rauschkolb landed the airplane on the runway at 4:15 p.m., eleven hours after departing. Taxiing to the ramp, where several ambulances and their welcoming party waited, the Catalina ran out of fuel.

Waiting for a tow vehicle, Helmantoler turned to Jones.

"You cut it a little close there, Sergeant."

Jones grinned and winked at his superior, basking in the glow of a job well done.

Ed Matthews climbed into an ambulance, where his squadron's flight surgeon handed him a fifth of whiskey. After a three-day stay in the hospital, each B-25 crew member was awarded a Purple Heart and sent for a week of R&R in southern New Guinea.

For his heroism that day, Frank Rauschkolb received the Distinguished Service Cross, an award only one step below the Medal of Honor. The other five Catalina airmen received the Silver Star, just one step below Rauschkolb's award. Two decades later 2nd Lt. Russell Johnson, the navigator-bombardier for the first B-25 crew rescued, would play the role of the Professor in the hit television show *Gilligan's Island*.

Rauschkolb's rescue would have been much less dramatic had it occurred in the European theater. There he could have taxied a few dozen miles at most to shore after picking up the survivors. But taxiing wasn't an option in the Pacific, where friendly territory was often hundreds of miles away. Rauschkolb had no choice but to attempt the risky takeoff. His rescue was one of many in which Catalina crews in the Pacific overcame the aircraft's shortcomings with their knowledge and ingenuity. In addition to the Catalina's takeoff and landing problems, the B-17s used for search and dropping life rafts had a limited range and often could not accompany Catalinas that followed bombers on a mission. Thus, there was no way to drop a large raft to a downed aircrew, and the OA-10 crew had no choice but to land to pick up survivors. B-29s, with longer ranges, only became available for life raft delivery toward the end of the war. Together the OA-10 and B-17 amassed an enviable rescue record. But it seemed the two aircraft mostly became models for how not to design search and rescue aircraft.[39]

That the AAF, rather than the navy, was doing rescue in the Pacific theater surprised many commanders. The navy PBY-5 Catalinas were better than the AAF's damage-prone OA-10s. It made sense that the navy would pick up the air-sea rescue mission in the Pacific, but the navy didn't want the mission. Navy rescue forces were dedicated to saving aviators who operated from carrier aircraft; navy leadership did not want to dilute those rescue forces by adding rescues for shore-based aircraft into the mix.[40]

However, navy aircraft did conduct rescue missions when they had aircraft available. PBY-5 Catalinas performed rescues when not patrolling for submarines, and seaplanes small enough to carry on cruisers and battleships, called "Kingfishers," also helped. A PBY-5 pilot, Lt. Nathan Gordon, earned a Medal of Honor for a rescue on February 15, 1944.[41]

The navy helped more with rescues in the last year of war in the Pacific theater. It developed dedicated rescue forces after the U.S. strategy of island hopping toward the Japanese mainland stretched the endurance limits of the land-based AAF amphibians. In 1944 the navy formed six rescue squadrons, numbered VH-1 through VH-6, to support the push to the Mariana Islands, Iwo Jima, and Okinawa, in turn.[42]

The first navy rescue squadrons were equipped with the PB2B-2, a version of the Catalina built by Boeing in Canada. Besides structural damage from water landings similar to the AAF experience, the PB2B-2 suffered from other problems. Since landing strips weren't available, the navy used tender ships to service their seaplane fleet. The tenders couldn't fit underneath the Catalina's wing. Instead, they maneuvered alongside, often colliding with the planes, bumps that were harder on the Catalina than the tender.[43] Also, the Catalina sat low in the water, and seawater washed over the top of the fuselage when the plane was moored, ruining electrical systems and radios. Often rescue crews jumped in and out of multiple aircraft before finding one that worked well enough to take off.[44]

Navy rescue squadrons later used PBM-3 and PBM-5 Mariner flying boats, which could only land in the water. The Mariners were much taller than the Catalinas and had more powerful engines. The Mariners could take off in very rough seas, especially when equipped with an innovation called "jet-assisted takeoff" (JATO), small rockets mounted to the aircraft that fired for an extra push at the top of a swell.[45]

Navy Catalina and Mariner crews quickly adapted to conditions in the Pacific. If the water was too rough for a landing, the crews used a trick learned in the European theater: land in calmer water and taxi up to the survivors.[46] The rugged Mariners could also sustain more damage than the Catalinas and still fly. On May 12, 1945, a Mariner from VH-3 had a hard landing in fourteen-foot seas that buckled the hull and damaged engine mounts, tail feathers, and one flap. Not a problem: the crew picked up thirteen survivors, fired their four JATO rockets, and launched off the top of a swell. The flying boat staggered into the air as the pilot pushed the Mariner's nose down to gain flying speed for an uneventful trip home, although the aircraft never flew again.[47]

In the last seven months of the war, the navy's dedicated rescue squadrons participated in more than one hundred rescues.[48] Despite the distances and rougher seas, aircrew who ditched in the Pacific had a better chance overall of surviving than those who ditched in the European theater. About one-half of Pacific crews were rescued; only about one-third of European crews were.[49]

The navy had more ships in the Pacific, along with submarines, to help with rescues. Also, beginning in 1945, weakened Japanese forces meant fewer attacks from shore guns and fighter aircraft during rescues.

But something was still needed for rescuing aircrew who crashed on land behind enemy lines. In the late stages of the war, a new aircraft was introduced that would revolutionize search and rescue: the helicopter. Leonardo da Vinci had first sketched the idea for an "aerial screw," a machine that could fly vertically, in the fifteenth century.[50] Although Leonardo never turned his idea into a flying machine, his concept inspired inventors four centuries later.

But engineers learned that helicopters were much harder to develop than airplanes. Within a decade of the Wright Brothers' first powered flight in 1903, inventors around the world turned out somewhat practical airplanes; in 1910 enough airplanes and pilots existed to hold the world's first air race at Reims, France. Inventors such as Russian Igor Sikorsky and Frenchman Louis Charles Breguet developed experimental helicopters as early as 1908, but the machines lacked the natural stability of a properly designed airplane, making the helicopter difficult to fly. Experimenters found it relatively easy to lift off the ground a few feet and hover, but translating that lift into a forward motion was much harder.[51] Inventors finally demonstrated a practical solution on May 4, 1924, when French aviator Étienne Oehmichen flew a helicopter around a one-kilometer course.[52]

As Europeans pushed helicopter technology forward, the U.S. Army rushed to catch up, signing a contract for an experimental machine in June 1921 with propeller expert George de Bothezat. His creation achieved an altitude of six feet during its first flight on December 18, 1922.[53]

The de Bothezat helicopter never achieved sustained forward flight, and it would take two more decades and a looming war to motivate additional army research. Sikorsky, who immigrated to the United States in the 1920s, developed the first operational U.S. military helicopter. A prototype flew in early 1942 and finished testing at Wright Field in Ohio a year later. Six months after that, the army ordered twenty-nine helicopters, dubbed the "YR-4B."[54]

The army sent the first helicopters to an air commando unit in Lalaghat, India. Before introducing the helicopter, the First Air Commando Group relied on small liaison aircraft, the L-1 and the L-5, to evacuate wounded soldiers and airmen. But those aircraft required a clear area several hundred feet long for landing and takeoff. Friendly forces trapped in jungles or on mountainsides had to be rescued by hiking to them, which could take days or even weeks. Many survivors died from injuries or were killed or captured by the Japanese. The helicopter was an almost miraculous solution.[55]

The first YR-4Bs arrived in Burma in January 1944 on cargo aircraft. Mechanics assembled the machines so the handful of newly trained helicopter pilots could start flying them. The new invention got off to an inauspicious start: the first helicopter crashed on its first flight, killing the pilot.

One month later, on the morning of April 21, 1944, an Air Commando L-1 liaison aircraft piloted by Tech. Sgt. Ed Hladovcak and carrying three British soldiers crashed into a rice paddy in Japanese-held territory in Burma, more than five hundred miles away from the YR-4Bs. The four men crawled into the jungle at the base of a mountain about a half-mile away and hunkered down in a clearing. They watched Japanese soldiers comb the wreckage and fan out to look for them. A few hours later an L-5 pilot spotted the downed crew and dropped them a note telling them to move up the mountain to stay away from the Japanese. The pilot also noticed a sandbar on a nearby river where he could land to pick up the crew, but he knew the four men would not be able to get to the sandbar on their own. They needed the helicopter.

Carter Harman, a second lieutenant who had been a journalist before World War II, received a call in Lalaghat telling him to fly one of the YR-4Bs to Taro, Burma (fig. 2). The commandos flew with only one pilot, so Harman stuffed extra fuel cans in the copilot's seat and brought a litter. He spent the next twenty-four hours traveling to Taro, stopping every hundred miles to refuel.

FIG. 2. Lt. Carter Harmon (*standing, left*) with his YR-4B Helicopter.
(Courtesy "This Day in Aviation," U.S. Air Force)

Upon arriving in Taro, Harman was told to proceed to a commando staging base called Aberdeen, another 125 miles away.

While Harman made steady progress toward the L-1 crash, the downed crew languished in the jungle clearing, scared witless by any sound that resembled gunfire. In the oppressive heat the British soldiers' wounds began to fester.

Harman took off from Aberdeen and flew to the sandbar, where a waiting L-5 led him to the four men. Harman knew he would have to make four trips, as the YR-4B held only one person besides him. He worried whether the helicopter's engine would be up to the task in the heat.

Harman managed to land the helicopter in the clearing where the men waited. Hladovcak, who had not been seriously injured, dashed over to the helicopter and shouted, "You look like an angel!" Indeed, the banana-shaped craft probably did resemble an angel, a majestic beast descending from the sky to a hover, with rotors replacing wings to beat the air into submission.[56]

Harman didn't feel like an angel, but there was no time for religious debate.[57] Hladovcak loaded the most seriously injured British soldier onto the helicopter, and Harman took off. After unloading the soldier at the sandbar, he picked up a second soldier. As he neared the sandbar again, the engine overheated. It clanked, gasped, and spewed vapor. Then it quit. Harman landed safely, but the engine wouldn't restart. They were stuck for the night, deep inside enemy territory.

Their luck held. The engine started the next morning, and Harman retrieved the last British soldier. As Harman neared Hladovcak for the final pickup, soldiers broke out of the trees and headed for the sergeant. But Harman got there first, and Hladovcak climbed aboard. The underpowered YR-4B clawed the thin mountain air in a hover above the soldiers, who held their fire. The aircraft momentarily lost power and sank toward the ground, but the engine recovered, and Harman flew away. They went back to Aberdeen and learned that the "attackers" weren't Japanese; they were friendly irregular soldiers who had been trying to reach the survivors to rescue them.

After the Air Commandos proved the utility of helicopters in combat, the Eighth ERS became the first regular military rescue unit to use the fledgling machine. When the war was almost over, the Eighth ERS was established in May 1945 to support the China-Burma-India theater. The unit used three helicopters to make forty-three rescues over land in the next four months.[58] Since the helicopter carried only enough fuel to fly about one hundred miles, C-47 cargo aircraft searched for survivors; pickup by helicopter followed. Even with their short service during the war, army planners noted how well the helicopters carried out rescue missions.[59]

Rescue forces had a huge impact on aircrews during World War II. They saved lives and returned experienced aviators to the cockpit, aviators who cost more than $200,000 each to train. Above all, rescue forces gave airmen confidence that someone was there to help if they got into trouble.[60]

Despite progress in search and rescue capabilities, the AAF never fully embraced the mission during World War II. In particular, training lagged throughout the war. The official Air-Sea Rescue and Emergency School at Keesler Field in Mississippi didn't open until the spring of 1944, only a few months before the D-Day invasion that eventually ended the war in Europe.[61] With little direction and poor equipment, instructors cobbled together enough of a curriculum to train four rescue squadrons for overseas duty during the next year. By early 1945 school personnel had figured out how to do their jobs. That meant it was time for the army to start shutting it down. The school was disbanded in 1946.[62]

Search and rescue capabilities slipped away after the war. Air power advocates believed the results of strategic bombing during World War II had validated the need for a separate air force. Congress agreed and passed the National Security Act of 1947 that established the United States Air Force and transferred all AAF and air corps personnel to the new organization.[63] A year later the Secretary of Defense, James Forrestal, published *Functions of the Armed Forces and the Joint Chiefs of Staff*, essentially stripping any significant air operations from the army. The air force received obvious missions such as air superiority and strategic air warfare but also not-so-obvious missions such as providing airlift for all the services, which included the transport of airborne army forces.[64]

Forrestal's document was silent on search and rescue responsibilities, but before the reorganization, AAF leadership had decided to continue the mission, albeit in a reduced manner. It still wasn't clear to the Joint Chiefs of Staff who ought to have the rescue mission overall, since the army, navy, and coast guard each had some capabilities. Some thought it made the most sense to give the mission to the coast guard since it had the most experience based on its record of sea rescues since 1915. AAF leaders argued that the coast guard would be inadequate for worldwide rescue capabilities, since its operations focused on U.S. coastal regions. The navy, which had fought the Joint Chiefs over establishing a joint rescue organization during the war, was the least interested; at the end of the war the navy deactivated its six dedicated rescue squadrons.[65]

There was even opposition within the AAF on how to handle the rescue mission. Army leaders proposed assigning rescue squadrons to the Air Transport Command, but Maj. Gen. Harold George, who led the command, fretted that he didn't have the equipment and resources to conduct rescues around the globe. George felt so strongly about his position that he even recommended that the navy take the mission, a suggestion that must have seemed blasphemous to other AAF officers.[66]

Someone finally cut through the arguing. In November 1945 Lt. Gen. Hoyt Vandenberg, who ran the Pentagon office that oversaw all AAF operations, directed the Air Transport Command to take the rescue mission, and in March 1946 the Air Rescue Service was established. Still, Air Transport Command moved at a glacial pace in developing worldwide rescue capabilities; for the next two years the Air Rescue Service had squadrons active only within the United States.[67]

The impetus to transform the Air Rescue Service into a worldwide capability came from Lt. Col. Richard Kight, a transport pilot with no background in rescue.[68] Kight took command of the Air Rescue Service in West Palm Beach, Florida, in December 1946. Over the next six years he slashed through Air Transport Command bureaucracy to expand his fledgling service into a global organization. Along the way he led the development of new rescue techniques and equipment, even doing much of the equipment testing himself. He also penned "The Code of an Air Rescue Man," which reads: "It is my duty, as a member of the Air Rescue Service, to save life and aid the injured. I will be prepared at all times to perform my assigned duties quickly and efficiently, placing these duties before personal desires and comforts. These things I do That Others May Live." "That others may live" continues as the motto of military rescue units to this day.[69]

Kight introduced several new rescue aircraft during his tenure, including the H-19 and H-21 helicopters and the SA-16 Albatross aircraft. The S designation stood for "search and rescue" and the

A for "amphibian." Even with the new equipment, the Air Rescue Service suffered from outdated equipment and shortages of funding, personnel and parts. Many overseas units had only one or two aircraft and a handful of people.[70]

As rescue services began to recover, military researchers worked to improve those services by designing new equipment and techniques that increased a pilot's chance of surviving a crash and being rescued. Ideas ranged from the practical, such as ejection seats for high-speed aircraft, to the fantastical, such as self-rescue systems. An aviator ejecting from an aircraft in combat would likely still require some sort of rescue by another aircraft, but a self-rescue system might eliminate the need for rescue forces altogether in many situations, reducing the number of personnel put at risk. The large lifeboats dropped to survivors were envisioned as a sort of self-rescue; many of the boats were outfitted with oars or small engines that an industrious and uninjured person or crew could use to get to shore, assuming the crew knew which direction to go and had enough stamina or fuel to get there. But the large lifeboats didn't really provide self-rescue since a search crew had to find the survivors to drop the boat.

True self-rescue has been a fantasy of combat aviators for decades. The helicopter held out hope that aviators could be rescued from behind enemy lines, but with the helicopter's limited range, they couldn't go down too far from friendly territory. As nuclear weapons became a favored deterrent strategy, planners realized that in the awful event of a nuclear war, aircrews shot down over the Soviet Union could be hundreds or thousands of miles inside enemy territory. Rescue by others would be nearly impossible, and self-rescue ideas abounded. Dozens of James Bond–like ideas have been proposed: boats, portable helicopters, balloons, jet packs.

One of those ideas in the early 1950s involved balloons and my father, Arnold Ebneter. He dropped out of the University of Minnesota in the fall of 1950, just a few months after the Korean War started. There were no student deferments in those days, and expecting to be drafted, he signed up to join the air force. As he waited to report to pilot training, he found a job as a balloon pilot with General Mills.

General Mills, usually associated with food products, branched into military hardware during World War II. After the war the company had a contract with the navy to develop balloons for classified missions. It was never entirely clear to my father exactly what the navy was doing with the balloons, but he was soon flying, and occasionally crashing, balloons during test missions at White Sands Proving Ground in New Mexico.

The balloons my father flew were not the majestic, colorful hot-air balloons depicted on glossy brochures that offer romantic sunrise and sunset rides in a suspended wicker basket. These balloons were made from clear plastic the thickness of a sandwich bag and inflated with helium. A utilitarian wooden seat dangled below the twenty-five-foot-tall balloon; the pilot was attached to the seat by a harness that included an emergency parachute.

Taking off and climbing in the balloons was easy; landing them was not. After the pilot had descended to about one hundred feet above the ground, he tossed a rope contraption overboard. The lowest twenty-five feet of the rope was a garden hose filled with ten pounds of sand. When the rope touched the earth, the part containing the sand dragged on the ground, reducing the weight of the balloon by ten pounds. For a few seconds the balloon stopped descending. In that tiny window the pilot used the rope to haul himself to about five feet above the ground. He then pulled a cord that ripped a hole in the top of the balloon, and the deflated rig dropped the rest of the way to the earth. My father thought he could do better than this unwieldy getup. Inspired by fanciful old-fashioned balloon paintings, he built a foot-high, two-pound anchor that resembled a giant treble fishhook. The first time he tried the anchor, it caught on a piece of sagebrush, and the wind turned the balloon into a pogo stick. My father banged onto the hard-packed caliche desert floor and shot thirty feet back into the air. It might have been a spectacular carnival ride, but after three bounces my father admitted defeat. He cut the anchor line, let the balloon climb back up, and then dropped his rope and made a regular landing.

In March 1952 the navy got the idea that the balloons might be useful for self-rescue. Years later my father realized the idea hadn't been thought out well. For one thing, how was someone supposed to carry the balloon? Perhaps in a large suitcase, but even if he could carry it, how was he supposed to find a source of helium to inflate it? Helium tanks are not exactly lying around on street corners in remote locations around the world.

The navy also imagined that the people who would ride these "escape balloons" might not have any flight experience. They told my father that the demonstration would be conducted by two people who had never been on an airplane before and then promptly put them on an airplane to Minneapolis.

The training did not get off to a good start. The trainees had linebacker physiques, and my father hadn't considered how to adjust the balloon's slings and harnesses to accommodate someone much larger than himself. After numerous tries, the two would-be balloonists finally fit, and ground training commenced. My father gave them a manual to read and explained how to drop ballast to allow the balloon to rise above the ground. Once they reached three thousand feet or so, they were to drift in whatever direction the wind took them and allow the balloon to gradually descend on its own as the helium escaped. My father also explained how to land the balloon with the rope and gave them a cover story to use in the likely event someone discovered them after they touched down: they were taking part in an atmospheric research program. What could go wrong?

On March 26 the trainees took off for an overnight flight to test the escape concept. The first balloonist performed his tasks as instructed and landed within three miles of his target, well within the navy's goal of eleven miles. Since no one from the program was around to meet him, he walked to a nearby farmhouse, whose occupants received him graciously, feeding him breakfast and letting him nap in a spare bedroom until the recovery crew from Minneapolis arrived.

Meanwhile, the second trainee was having a very bad day. Nothing in the training manual had explained how to read the altimeter, and in the first of a series of misjudgments, the student drifted along at only three hundred feet instead of the desired three thousand feet. When he began descending, he noticed nearby telephone lines, and instead of allowing the balloon to drift over them and then land, he tried to touch down before the obstacle. Given his lack of experience, he hit the ground too hard, too near the wires. He shot back into the air, right into the telephone lines, which completely entangled him.

Hanging upside down, he struggled to extricate himself from the telephonic spiderweb without killing himself or further damaging the wires. He managed to drop to the ground and pull most of the balloon free but not before a farmer in a nearby house observed the unusual activity. Instead of going to the farmhouse and using his cover story, the student walked away, abandoning the balloon and its equipment. The farmer called the Wausau County sheriff while the student hiked to nearby Stratford, Wisconsin.

Upon arriving in town, the student called the recovery crew in Minneapolis and, without mentioning his inauspicious arrival, asked them to pick him up. He checked into a nearby hotel and went to sleep. By the time he woke, the sheriff had tracked him down and very much wanted to talk about the strange scene that had been reported, but the student refused to talk.

The media went nuts.

"Mystery Man Drops from Sky Near Stratford" screamed the front page of one small-town Wisconsin newspaper. Dozens of stories about the incident splashed across newspapers throughout the Midwest.

While the hullaballoo from the Mystery Man caper died down, the navy decided it would be best for the balloon program to lay low for a while. With the program's cover blown, the navy gave up on balloons-as-rescue, and the incident altered the direction of my father's life. He had earlier turned down his pilot training slot and received a draft deferment to continue working on the balloon program, but he now found himself with nothing to do just as his draft deferment was about to expire. The air force again agreed to send him to pilot training, and my father accepted, even though it meant postponing his upcoming wedding to my mother, after the invitations had already been printed and mailed.

The air force's recommitment to the search and rescue mission in the late 1940s would have meant little if aircrew members couldn't get out of a crippled aircraft or survive a crash landing. The ever-increasing speeds of jet-powered aircraft led to significant problems. It was almost impossible for a person to climb out of a cockpit of an airplane going faster than 150 miles per hour: the windblast created a force that few aviators could overcome.[71] Some sort of assist was needed, and engineers found the solution: the ejection seat.

The idea for an automated way to get out of an airplane had been around for some time. The September 1, 1916, issue of *Aviation* magazine reported that Charles Broadwick of Los Angeles dropped pilot Terah Maroney, who was wearing a knapsack parachute, through a trap door in an airplane from fifteen hundred feet.[72] But an ejection seat wasn't demonstrated until January 1942, when German test pilot Helmut Schenk ejected from a Heinkel He-280 prototype. Schenk first jettisoned his canopy and then pulled a release lever; compressed air shot his seat clear of the aircraft, and he rode his parachute to the ground, unharmed.[73]

James Martin, a British engineer, began developing ejection seats in 1942, after his friend and business partner, Capt. Valentine Baker, was killed in the crash of a Martin-Baker MB3 prototype.[74] The basic concept of an ejection seat is quite simple: the aircraft seat is attached to a set of rails, similar to a small railroad track. When the pilot pulls a handle, an explosion pushes the pilot and seat up the rail and out of the aircraft. The earliest seats used compressed air or gunpowder charges, but rocket motors quickly took over.[75]

Before the pilot can leave the aircraft, the canopy has to go. Most canopies are automatically jettisoned using small explosive cartridges when the pilot pulls the ejection handle, although some early aircraft had a separate handle that got rid of the canopy. Some canopies are designed for the pilot to eject through; a cutting device at the top of the seat shatters the canopy a fraction of a second before the pilot shoots through the hole and into the air.

Once the seat, with the pilot in it, is out of the aircraft, a small parachute called a "drogue chute" pops from the top of the seat to slow it down and turn it right side up so the pilot-seat combination is stable before the main parachute deploys. If the pilot is low enough, below about ten thousand feet, the parachute deploys as soon as the seat is stable; if the pilot is at a high altitude, a pressure sensor keeps the parachute from deploying until a lower altitude. This delay gets the pilot down quickly; if the parachute deployed at twenty-five thousand feet, the pilot would have to drift down for twenty minutes or so. It's cold up there, and the pilot has a limited supply of oxygen in a small bailout bottle that goes with the seat, so it's best to get down as fast as possible.

Simple in concept, the ejection seat is difficult in practice. For one thing, the seat has to shoot high enough so the pilot doesn't hit the aircraft's tail or, for a propeller aircraft, the propeller. The seat also must function under the extreme motions and g-forces of an aircraft spinning wildly out of control. And if the seat performs perfectly, the pilot can still be injured by ejection forces or by the windblast as they exit the aircraft at speeds near or above supersonic.[76]

In August 1946 an army doctor named John Paul Stapp reported to the Biophysics Branch of the Aero Medical Laboratory at Wright Field near Dayton, Ohio, to study the problems associated with pilot escape technology.[77] Doctors at the laboratory had a tradition of volunteering as research subjects, such as high-altitude bailouts. Stapp soon joined in the tradition.[78] In early 1947 Stapp moved to Muroc Army Air Base, later Edwards Air Force Base, in the Mojave Desert, to conduct deceleration tests and try out different aircrew restraint systems. He used a rocket-propelled sled attached to a two thousand–foot–long track built on top of a dry lakebed.[79] The doctor was interested in determining how much force a human could withstand during ejections and crash landings. He also hoped to prove that it was possible for a pilot to survive a supersonic ejection.[80]

After several months of testing with dummies, Stapp strapped himself into the sled on December 11, 1947, for the first human run. The sled accelerated to 150 miles per hour and then braked to a halt in a matter of seconds; Stapp withstood the deceleration forces with no injuries. In follow-on tests during the next several years, Stapp's decelerations reached as high as forty-five times the force of gravity.[81] Although he was often injured during higher-speed tests, his research proved that humans could survive very large forces in accidents and ejections. The trick was to design crew restraints and ejection seats so that high forces were of very short duration, like a boxer's jab.[82]

In July 1951 Stapp arrived at Holloman Air Force Base in New Mexico to conduct additional research on deceleration, windblast, and pilot seating configurations using a longer sled track originally built to test missiles.[83] Sleds on the longer track could go much faster, and a better braking system created higher deceleration forces. The braking technique was a marvel of simplicity: a huge pool of water between the concrete walls that held the tracks and a scoop attached to the front of a sled. The scoop slammed into the water, creating an explosive wave on both sides of the track. The sled came to a screeching halt.

Human subjects are no longer allowed during sled tests, but ejection seat technology continues to evolve, and Stapp's research is still relevant to modern ejection seat designs. The Holloman High Speed Test Track is now ten miles long and still uses the water braking system for some tests. In the mid-1990s, when I was the commander of the 846th Test Squadron that runs the track, we always made a last-minute check of the "pool" before a sled run with water braking to be sure it hadn't attracted any thirsty local critters. Coyotes don't fare well in a collision with even a small sled going several hundred miles per hour.

When I worked at the track, we had two ejection seat research programs, one that developed the technology to allow safe ejections for smaller pilots and one that examined the technology used in a Russian ejection seat. During one sled run, the rockets fired, and the sled rocketed forward. The ejection seat and its attached dummy shot into the air. But the drogue chute didn't deploy. I watched in horror, along with a large crowd of researchers, as the seat flipped over in the air and plummeted the dummy headfirst back to the ground. This is why we test things without real people.

Several companies make modern ejection seats. Martin-Baker seats have become the standard for many military aircraft used throughout the world, particularly the U.S. Navy. Martin-Baker seats have saved the lives of more than seventy-five hundred aircrew members. Each person saved automatically becomes a member of the Martin-Baker Tie Club. Membership includes a small card attesting to the bailout and the aviator's membership number, somewhere between 1 and more than 7,500. Members may also purchase a tie decorated with red triangles that represent the DANGER: EJECTION SEAT logo stamped on aircraft with ejection seats.

During the five-year interlude between World War II and the Korean War, technologies related to escape, survival, search, and rescue leaped forward. Jets with ejection seats began to replace propeller-driven aircraft, helicopters grew larger and more capable, and the Air Rescue Service began using the sa-16 Albatross. The Air Rescue Service also began to train specialized rescue personnel called "pararescue jumpers" (PJs) who jumped to assist a downed airman or other injured person with medical aid, survival, and evacuation. The earliest PJs were doctors (dubbed "paradoctors") and medical corpsman trained in 1943 at the U.S. Forest Service Smoke Jumpers School in Missoula, Montana. The first use of parachutists to assist in rescuing survivors overseas occurred in August 1943 in the China-Burma-India theater. A doctor and two medical corpsmen jumped into the jungle to assist twenty survivors, including reporter Eric Sevareid, who had parachuted from a c-46 with engine problems. The three PJs stayed with the survivors for a month until they were all healthy enough to make a ten-day trek to safety.[84]

LEAVE NO MAN BEHIND

In May 1947 a successful paradoctor jump into the Nicaraguan jungle to reach survivors of a b-17 crash further reinforced the need for jumpers to assist with rescues. Later that year the first set of pjs began training at the Pararescue and Survival School at MacDill Field near Tampa, Florida. Within a few years the pj career field evolved from teaching medical professionals how to jump and survive to training young enlisted personnel on everything from how to pack a parachute and jump out of an airplane to emt-like medical skills and using a dog team.[85] By the time the Korean War began, dozens of pjs had been trained.[86]

The Korean War provided the first opportunity for csar crews to try out the new technologies and pjs. However, the rescue mission got off to a shaky start. When North Korean forces invaded South Korea on June 25, 1950, the only rescue capability in South Korea was a small air force unit in Seoul equipped with World War II leftovers—the h-5 helicopter, which was a follow-on to the Sikorsky yr-4b; sb-17s for dropping lifeboats; c-47s for searching; and l-5 liaison aircraft. The unit was undermanned, but that problem was solved by sending men on temporary duty from the Third Air Rescue Squadron in Japan and other units. Several new sb-29s and the amphibian sa-16s also soon arrived, but those aircraft brought headaches along with their improved capabilities. Maintenance troops had no experience on the new aircraft, and a nonexistent supply line meant that parts were hard to come by.[87]

The navy also operated helicopters during the Korean War, but those helicopters weren't designated for use in search and rescue. When not performing their assigned missions of sweeping for mines, observation, and spotting naval gunfire, navy helicopters picked up downed pilots who bailed out over both land and water.[88] But the navy mostly picked up its own pilots, who tended to go down in the sea fairly close to an aircraft carrier.[89]

Both air force and army helicopters were widely available in Korea, and at first the machines were used almost exclusively for evacuating soldiers wounded in battle to a "mash" unit for treatment. Roads were so poor in South Korea that it could take more than an hour to transport a casualty to a doctor by ambulance. A

helicopter could cover the distance in five minutes. Using helicopters, the mortality rate among wounded soldiers was halved,
from 4 percent in World War II to 2 percent in Korea.[90]

Moving soldiers was relatively safe since they were retrieved
from friendly territory. However, the air force still needed to develop
doctrine and techniques for using helicopters to rescue aviators
from behind enemy lines. When Capt. Robert Wayne bailed out
of a fighter aircraft over North Korea on September 4, 1950, only
two months into the war, the air force helicopter squadron commander was reluctant to order his pilots, untrained in combat
flying, to make the rescue. He told Capt. Paul Van Boven, an H-5
pilot, that it was his decision if he wanted to cross into enemy
territory; the commander would not order him to do so. Wayne's
wingman had stayed above him to guide the helicopter and provide fire support, and Van Boven had no qualms about taking the
mission. As the helicopter neared the scene, Wayne's wingman
strafed the area and killed an approaching North Korean soldier,
clearing the way for the H-5 to hover a few feet above the downed
pilot. The medic pulled him into the helicopter. Van Boven earned
a Silver Star and was credited with making the first search and
rescue behind enemy lines in Korea. The rescue proved again
one of the reasons for rescuing downed pilots: Wayne was a top-
notch pilot who had shot down two enemy aircraft on June 27,
the second day of aerial combat.[91]

Rescue pilots in Korea discovered that the skills they had learned
for peacetime operations didn't transfer well to combat flying. In
combat pilots often flew overloaded helicopters while being shot
at by small arms and antiaircraft artillery. Crews quickly learned
what to do when the shooting started. Climb. Jink right. Jink left.
Descend. Keep randomly climbing, descending, and jinking until
clear of the threat. To reduce weight, pilots minimized the fuel
they carried. They compensated for any remaining heavy weight
by taking off with forward motion in a nose-low attitude instead
of climbing straight up.[92] Crews also relearned many lessons
from World War II, such as the need for rescue planes to take off

before faster bombers and fighters so the entire package of aircraft arrived together at a rendezvous point.[93]

Even with improved tactics, the helicopters were vulnerable to ground fire. On October 1, 1950, the air force lost its first helicopter to enemy fire as an H-5 crew returned from an unsuccessful search mission. While flying about three hundred feet above a road, a buried antitank mine detonated. The blast knocked the H-5 into a hillside, but the crew was unharmed, and a jeep returned them to friendly territory. Nearly a year later, a helicopter hit by enemy fire made it back to friendly territory, but the crew's luck didn't hold long enough to land. A loosened rotor blade sliced off the tail cone, and the aircraft spun out of control into the ground, killing both the pilot and medical attendant.[94]

The H-5 was not a good rescue platform for Korea. The little helicopter couldn't operate in poor weather, high winds, or even at night. With no armament H-5 crews had to hope for support from fighter aircraft as they made pickups, support that at first was ad hoc at best. With better engines and other improved capabilities, the H-19 that began to replace the H-5 in 1951 could fly in all weather, but it still lacked armament to shoot at the enemy. Night rescues remained elusive: the rugged terrain made night flying hazardous, and it was almost impossible to find anyone on the ground at night. However, fighter support for rescues improved throughout the war and eventually included Rescue Combat Air Patrol (RESCAP) aircraft that were airborne anytime a combat mission took place. When an airman went down, the RESCAP aircraft flew to the site to shoot at North Korean soldiers trying to capture the airman; the RESCAP crews also guided in the rescue helicopter.[95]

The SA-16 Albatross, later called the "HU-16," made its debut during Korea (fig. 3). In addition to reversible-pitch propellers to shorten landings, the Albatross had JATO to shorten takeoffs. Designed specifically for search and rescue, the aircraft carried a complete medical kit and litters for injured aircrew. However, the SA-16 couldn't operate in seas much higher than five feet. Icing in cold weather, a frequent condition in Korea, caused another

Fig. 3. Korean War rescue aircraft; H-5G helicopter and SA-16 (later HU-16) Albatross. (Courtesy National Museum of the Air Force, U.S. Air Force)

problem. But overall the Albatross was a good platform, rescuing about one-third of airmen from hostile seas.[96]

During the Korean War, the Air Rescue Service rescued nearly one thousand U.S. and allied personnel from hostile territory.[97] In particular, the PJs proved their worth, routinely jumping from helicopters over land and the SA-16 over water to assist survivors.[98] Given the Air Rescue Service accomplishments, rescue forces expected their mission to continue after the war. But once again, U.S. civilian and military leadership focused on strategies that centered on nuclear weapons. Even worse, the air force no longer recognized CSAR as a wartime mission, considering it merely an extension of the air force's peacetime mission.[99] Rescue crews no longer trained for combat. Instead, they waited around at bases with flying missions in case they were needed to support a peacetime accident.

Around 11:30 a.m. on June 30, 1956, a TWA Super Constellation and a United DC-7, together carrying 128 people, collided over the

Grand Canyon at twenty-one thousand feet. The collision ripped the tail off the Constellation and severed much of the DC-7's left wing. Coats, pillows, silverware, luggage, U.S. mail, and stacks of one hundred dollar bills spilled from the back of the Constellation as it plunged in a near vertical dive and crashed about three hundred feet above the Colorado River onto a relatively flat area called Temple Butte. The United DC-7 staggered about one mile north before it slammed into rocks just below the top of a massive formation named Chuar Butte and slid into a rugged gulch. Both fuel-laden aircraft burst into flames, and two columns of black smoke rose over the ochre-and-mustard-colored terrain.[100]

No one reported the collision. After both aircraft missed a compulsory radio report, air traffic controllers and airline ground personnel spent twenty minutes trying to contact the pilots before declaring the airplanes missing. Fearing a collision, personnel from the Civil Aeronautics Administration (CAA) alerted officials at Nellis Air Force Base to help find the airplanes and any survivors, however unlikely that might be.[101] Capt. Byrd Ryland, from March Air Force Base in California, was appointed as commander of search and rescue operations, and he called for help from other nearby military bases.[102]

Helicopter pilot 1st Lt. Miles Burd, who had been at pilot training with my father years earlier, was mowing his lawn that afternoon when a phone call summoned him to nearby Luke Air Force Base, Arizona. Burd learned he was needed for a search and rescue operation in the Grand Canyon. Burd took off with another pilot and a flight surgeon in one H-19 and headed north, accompanied by a second H-19 flown by his best friend, 1st Lt. Daryl Strong.[103]

When the helicopter pilots weren't standing by for search and rescue of airmen who crashed on Luke's gunnery training range, they assisted local and federal authorities with car accidents, flash floods, lost hikers, and even tracking the car of a suspected felon.[104] All Luke helicopter pilots became experts at the best flights of all: dropping into the depths of the Grand Canyon.[105]

By the time the Luke helicopter crews touched down in the parking lot of a hotel near the Little Colorado River, they knew what they were looking for.[106] They also knew generally where to look. About an hour after the crash, Palen Hudgin, a sightseeing pilot and owner of Grand Canyon Airport, saw smoke and assumed it was from a wildfire. Just before sunset, after hearing a radio broadcast about the missing aircraft, he and his brother Henry flew to the smoke, where they tentatively identified the Constellation's tail. There was no telephone back at the airport. After landing the brothers drove to the Grand Canyon National Park headquarters to call TWA and report their finding.[107]

At dawn Burd and Strong took off in one H-19, and Capt. Jim Womack and 1st Lt. Phil Prince took off in the other.[108] By then both Palen Hudgin and an SA-16 Albatross crew from Hamilton Air Force Base in California had spotted what they assumed was the United wreckage, but the fixed-wing aircraft couldn't land for confirmation.[109] Burd and Strong flew back and forth at random over the canyon and were about to head to Grand Canyon Airport to refuel when Burd spotted a glint on Chuar Butte.[110] Burd moved closer to attempt a landing on what looked like a giant grease spot from twenty-five feet in the air. With nothing flat to set down on, he touched one wheel to the ground, and the flight surgeon leaned out and grabbed a piece of the wreckage.[111]

Burd and Strong joined Womack and Prince, who had maneuvered down to the charred TWA wreckage. They walked around the grim site, the air suffused with death and the stench of burned oil and fuel.[112] The flight surgeons conducted a futile search for survivors.[113]

Both helicopters flew to Grand Canyon Village, where at least twenty reporters peppered them with questions.

Burd told them, "We found the crash and we have a piece to verify it."

The reporters went crazy. So crazy, they even besieged the pilots when they went into the bathroom.[114]

Womack lamented to the reporters, "There's not a hell of a lot down there that anyone's going to get out."[115] Recovering remains from a civilian crash wasn't part of the air force mission, so the helicopter pilots were ordered back to Luke on Monday morning to support training missions. Sixty years later Burd reflected the air force's attitude at the time when he told me, "There's no use to stop one mission to do something that's futile."[116] It didn't seem to occur to air force leadership that there might be a humanitarian reason to participate.

The crash sites were inaccessible by road and too remote to reach on foot; helicopters were needed to recover the remains and wreckage. Although the air force lost interest, the army didn't. By a stroke of luck, the army had several H-21 helicopters, along with U-1 Otter light cargo aircraft, on temporary duty at Fort Huachuca near the Arizona-Mexico border. Normally based at Fort Riley, Kansas, and Fort Devens, Massachusetts, the aircraft and pilots were testing new navigation procedures in Arizona. At dinnertime on the evening of the collision, the unit commander, Maj. Jerome Feldt, learned of the accident and got in touch with Ryland, who jumped at the opportunity to use the army aircraft. By nine thirty that evening a colonel from Fort Huachuca had given Feldt's unit permission to join the search. The army aircraft arrived at the bare-bones Grand Canyon Airport midmorning on Sunday.[117]

It's not clear why the army chose to do the mission. Perhaps they had a desire to help out or saw it as a chance for good training in mountainous terrain. But given the ongoing air force and army rivalry over aviation missions at the time, it's also plausible that army leaders saw the recovery effort as a way to one-up the air force and put another quill in their quiver in the race to nab helicopter missions.

Regardless of army motivations, "Operation Granite Mountain" had begun.

Sunday evening Feldt decided to use the H-21s to search for signs of life, deliver personnel and equipment to the wreckage, and fly the dead to Grand Canyon Airport. Remains would be loaded onto Otters and transported to a makeshift morgue in Flagstaff. The Otters would also fly "bird dog" cover to watch out for other aircraft so the helicopter pilots could focus on flying and help relay messages when the helicopters were beyond radio coverage below the rim.[118]

Early on Monday, July 2, Capt. Walter Spriggs and Chief Warrant Officer Howard Proctor took off in an H-21 with about a half-
ton of equipment and supplies and five searchers, including two
paramedics and a coroner. With Feldt flying bird dog, the helicopter left three searchers on the southeastern rim of the canyon to reduce weight and dropped into the canyon to see what
they were up against. Although Spriggs and many of the army
pilots had flown in Korea's mountainous terrain, they had never
encountered anything as rugged as the Grand Canyon. However,
Spriggs and Proctor easily negotiated the landing on a small pin-
nacle about sixty yards from the main wreckage at the TWA site.
After off-loading, they returned to the rim to ferry the remaining searchers.[119]

The searchers confronted a horrific scene: charred bodies missing limbs, the body of a man lodged under a rock so tightly it was
almost impossible to remove, a penny embedded in a woman's
wedding ring. That first day the searchers filled five rubberized
bags containing human remains. A few articles were unscathed,
including a toy boat and 148 letters that somehow survived from
sixty-six pounds of U.S. Mail.[120]

Spriggs and Proctor next headed to the United site at Chuar
Butte, which jutted fourteen hundred feet above the river on a
nearly vertical slope.[121] The combination of terrain and high tem-
peratures created swirling winds and violent drafts that shot the
helicopter up and down like an elevator and thwarted two landing attempts.[122]

Army pilots made three more flights into the canyon that morning, hauling government and TWA officials along with more gear
and removing the crash bags.[123] By 10:00 a.m. sixty-knot winds
and severe turbulence shut down flying, a pattern that would
repeat over the next two days, as the H-21s shuttled in personnel
and supplies and carried out twenty-one more crash bags.[124] The
remains of the seventy TWA passengers were buried in a mass
grave in Flagstaff after a combined Protestant, Roman Catholic,
Jewish, and Mormon service that included five honor guard members from the army recovery team.[125]

The United crash site was much more difficult to reach, so the army shuttled in thirteen mountain climbers to complete the task. Five of the men were Colorado climbers that United had used previously to recover wreckage, and eight were Swiss climbers that Swissair had sent to the United States at its own expense as a goodwill gesture.[126] The Swiss climbers arrived with twelve hundred feet of steel cables and forty-seven bags of equipment containing everything from parachutes to cooking supplies.[127] Over the next four days the climbers removed all fifty-eight United victims using a "Tyrolean traverse" system of ropes and pulleys devised by the Swiss to hoist the bags up the cliff to the waiting helicopters.[128] The coroner was able to identify half of the bodies.[129]

On July 10, after seventy-five H-21 flights had carried fifty-eight passengers, six tons of equipment, and sixty-eight crash bags in and out of the canyon, one last helicopter dipped below the rim for a final search.[130] In its haste to return to Fort Huachuca, the army abandoned most equipment and supplies; a 1976 cleanup crew found C rations, ropes, a piton, and an empty can of Schlitz beer.[131]

Miles Burd and the other air force pilots and crew, along with twenty-four army officers and warrant officers, received medals at the White House.[132] United paid its climbers $150 per day and treated them to country club banquets and dude ranch horseback riding.[133]

The Fort Devens pilots also returned home with a mascot. With little to do after flying in the canyon each day, the pilots obtained a baby burro they named Duke. Pilot Wilbur Isenberg became Duke's caretaker, feeding him cigars, apples, and carrots. When the unit returned to Massachusetts, the baby burro made the cross-country trip in Isenberg's Buick convertible.[134]

In the aftermath of the collision, the U.S. government vastly improved airline safety. Congress passed legislation in 1957 that formed what became the Federal Aviation Administration (FAA) and the National Transportation Safety Board. The FAA updated the ancient air traffic control system in the United States. Working in concert, the two federal organizations transformed commercial aviation into the safest form of transportation in the world.[135]

American ingenuity and optimism dangled the promise of a bright future. War began receding into the distant past; many thought Korea an anomaly, unlikely to be repeated as nuclear weapons took a lead role in defense strategies. The Soviet Union had yet to launch the Sputnik satellite and few people had heard of Vietnam, a small country in Southeast Asia that shared a border with China. American technology dominated, churning out a plethora of mass-produced consumer goods such as televisions and washing machines, along with rockets and supersonic jet aircraft. My father flew one of those jets, the F-100, at Foster Air Force Base in Texas. Not to be outdone, the navy's answer to the F-100 was its own supersonic speedster, the F-8, which first flew in 1956 and captured the imagination of a teenage boy in a California farming town.

3

Willie

NINE-YEAR-OLD WILLIE CLUTCHED HIS BB GUN. HE AND HIS older brother, Don, had received the guns for Christmas. Standing in the backyard, they aimed at nothing in particular in the orange grove next door. Willie fired, relishing the popping noises the shots made. Then Don shot a sparrow perched on the backyard fence. The bird fell onto the other side of the yard.

"Go pick it up," the older brother ordered.

Willie dropped his gun and, shoulders slumped, walked around the fence. He knelt down and picked up the bird, cradling it in his hands. As he trudged back to give Don his prize, Willie felt the sparrow's life fading away, the last heartbeats and gasps for air. He handed the still-warm animal to his brother, feeling sick to his stomach. What had been a living creature a minute earlier was no more, its life silenced for no good reason. Willie knew then that he could never kill for sport. In later years he never joined his friends who hunted doves. He still had fun shooting the BB gun, but he only aimed at fence posts and tin cans. He carved his name on the gun's forestock with a wood-burning iron so his possession wouldn't be confused with Don's or other playmates'.

The sparrow was Willie's second encounter with death. One day, a few months earlier, Willie and Don walked along the farm road near their house. Something above them sounded like laughter. Startled, both boys snapped their heads up and spotted a man on a power line a few yards away. The lineman slumped over, and they realized he hadn't been laughing: he had been electrocuted.

The brothers sprinted home to tell their mother, Paralee, what had happened. She called for help, but the lineman was already dead. Willie had vague memories of relatives dying, but the lineman was the first time he saw someone die before his eyes. One minute someone was there, and the next minute they were gone. Willie felt a sadness in his heart he had never felt before. He felt the same sadness when his brother shot the sparrow.

In the late 1940s the aftermath of World War II still hung over the United States; more than 400,000 Americans had died during the fighting overseas. Willie had two uncles who had likely seen death during the war, but they never shared their experiences. Paul Lewis, one of Paralee's brothers, was a cook in the coast guard; another brother, Perman, was a gunner on the navy's SBD Dauntless dive-bomber. During visits to Oklahoma the uncles showered Willie and Don with affectionate teasing. Willie didn't know exactly what his uncles had done during the war, but just being in a war was enough: Paul and Perman were like gods, and he aspired to be like them.

Reminders of the war filled the skies of California. Playing together outside, Willie and his cousin Garland often heard B-36 bomber airplanes overhead as they descended into Castle Air Force Base, ninety miles southeast. The aircraft's six engines and aft-facing propellers produced a distinctive rumbling. The boys knew just when to look up to see the awesome machine lumbering above them. The B-36 was so big that the tires were nearly twice as tall as a man.

Like many young boys, Willie was fascinated by all things military. One of the houses he lived in growing up had a dirt backyard just large enough to fit the outline of an imaginary aircraft carrier that could handle bicycles. Using sticks, the brothers carved out a fifteen-foot-long carrier deck. Willie cut wings from cardboard boxes and mounted them on the handlebars of his bike: an instant navy airplane.

Borrowing techniques gleaned from watching movies about airplanes, Willie quickly mastered the art of carrier landings on the skinny flight deck. He first rode his bike parallel to the carrier and displaced a few feet away. As he passed one end of the flight deck, he steered the bike as fast as he could toward the line marking the end of the deck, then slammed on his brakes and skidded to a stop with a puff of dust. The goal was to stop just a few feet past the end of the deck. If he stopped short of the line, he would have crashed into the back of the aircraft carrier. If he stopped more than a few feet past the line, he would have to go around for another try: a "bolter," although he didn't know the term at the time. Willie always stopped at just the right moment, and he soon considered himself a fully qualified carrier pilot.

For Willie playing soldier and pilot and other games was all about fun, until he had an inkling that war could do terrible things. Willie and Don often stopped their bikes outside a house with a grape arbor surrounded by a fence. They leaned their handlebars against the fence and stood on their pedals to reach across and snag a few grapes. One day Don reached over the fence and jerked his arm back. He sat back down and pedaled away furiously, Willie chasing after him. When Willie caught up, Don panted: "There was a weird guy sitting in the yard. He just stared at me."

Back home the brothers told Paralee about the strange man. She explained that the man had fought on Iwo Jima during the war. They never saw their reclusive neighbor again.

Willie Dean Sharp was born on October 17, 1940, in Oklahoma to John and Paralee Sharp. The family resided in Blanchard, about thirty miles south of Oklahoma City, right in the middle of the state.

Both of Scottish descent, John and Paralee were born and raised in Oklahoma. John, the oldest of five children, was mechanically gifted. His parents forced him to drop out of school after sixth grade to work on the family farm. John joined a small band of other boys who had also left school. The band of boys latched onto bootleg alcohol as their primary source of entertainment, instead of going to dances and dating girls, like other teenage boys. The lack of socializing left John shy and ignorant about girls. He might never have met a woman to marry if not for the fact that he was friends with Paralee's brother Paul.

John and Paralee married in the early 1930s and settled in Blanchard, where John found work as a mechanic. Paralee was a schoolteacher. Willie's only sister, Juanita Paralee, was born in 1934 and lived for three days. She is buried in Blanchard.

When Willie was two, Oklahoma's poverty became so oppressive that John and Paralee decided to join two of his brothers in California. John found work as a farm laborer in a small town in California's fertile Central Valley. The family lived in a farm labor camp, in a tent with a wooden floor. A year later the family moved north, when John found a lucrative job more suited to his mechanical skills in Oakland, working for Douglas Aircraft Company as a machinist.

John's machinist job ended with the war in 1945, and the family moved again, this time south to Dinuba, an agricultural community about twenty miles south of Fresno. John opened a garage. Paralee kept the books for the garage and also found a job as bookkeeper and proofreader for the local newspaper, the *Dinuba Sentinel*.

Willie and Don helped out in their father's garage. At first Willie did only the smallest jobs, such as washing tools and sweeping floors. By the time he was about ten, he was allowed to hold droplights and search for the right tool to hand his father during a repair.

One day, as John worked on an engine with a wrench, Willie accidentally bumped his father's hand with the light and burned him.

John bonked Willie's forehead with the wrench.

"Goddammit! Watch what you're doing!"

Blood ran down Willie's forehead and dripped off his nose. He fought back tears of pain, his own and the pain he had caused his father. Tears would only make things worse.

Just then his Uncle Ben, Garland's father, walked into the shop and stared at Willie.

"What happened to you?"

"Oh, I just hit my head."

Willie knew his father would try to make it up to him. He always did. He never apologized, but he might praise Willie or make some other nice comment or even take him for some ice cream.

Once or twice each month Paralee got a letter from her sister in Oklahoma, a rambling multiday recitation of events that covered everything from what Willie's aunt had for dinner to a cut on someone's hand. The letters warranted the attention a Super Bowl might today, with the small Sharp family gathered in rapt attention as Paralee read aloud, reciting arcane details about the lives of their midwestern relatives.

Dinuba was close to the foothills of the Sierra Nevada and a three-hour drive from Yosemite National Park, but other than camping by the side of Route 66 during summertime trips back to Oklahoma, Willie's childhood was bereft of hiking, camping, or hunting. A year of living nearly outdoors in a tent at the labor camp had apparently robbed John and Paralee of any desire for the wilderness. Willie and Don became small-town kids, especially after they moved into a house in downtown Dinuba only a few blocks from John's garage.

Moving into town had another benefit as far as Willie was concerned: easy access to the State Theater. In the late 1940s and early 1950s, television wasn't yet widely available, so Saturdays meant movies at the theater and newsreels that occasionally mentioned a war going on in a distant place called Korea. No one in Willie's family was involved in Korea—his parents' generation was too old and their offspring too young—but some of Willie's classmates had a brother or sister overseas. For Willie and his friends the best part about the theater was the occasional giveaway of surplus World War II equipment such as canteens and web belts, stuff any self-respecting American ten-year-old could use for playing soldier.

On Sundays the family went to a charismatic church, where congregation members spoke in tongues. Willie dutifully went to Sunday school, but he never believed a word of it. A whale that swallowed a man? How could that be? And why did Jesus feel the need to walk on water? Was he showing off? Willie never found a personal relationship with any sort of god. As he grew older, he realized that even if he had believed in a god, he couldn't have been friends with the Christian God because why would that god let so many bad things happen?

In seventh grade Willie picked up the name he would use for the rest of his life. His family always called him by his middle name, Dean. He had no idea why—it's just what they did. Since his family called him Dean, his friends did too. When he entered seventh grade, he had a homeroom for the first time, and every morning the homeroom teacher called roll, reading names from a list.

"Willie Sharp," the teacher called.

"Here," Willie said, then added, "It's Dean."

"Oh, okay."

This exchange continued for several weeks until Willie gave up. His family still called him Dean, but he became Willie to everyone else.

On Memorial Day in 1956, fifteen-year-old Willie perused the *Fresno Bee*. When he turned to page 4 of the front section, a picture captured his soul: a brand new navy airplane called the "Crusader." Willie fell instantly in love with the sleek fighter jet. It was the fastest, baddest airplane he had ever seen. Slung low to the ground with a high wing that poked above the fuselage, the Crusader looked ready to go to war, even though the jet was still undergoing flight tests at Edwards Air Force Base, located 170 miles southeast of Dinuba. The caption under the photo read: "Versatile—The United States Navy's new F8U1 Crusader not only will operate at supersonic speeds but also at low speeds required for aircraft carrier operations. The short landing gear makes the plane accessible for maintenance and servicing" (fig. 4).

Willie stared at the picture for several minutes, fantasizing what it might be like to fly the Crusader. He figured a ride in the jet must be more exciting than skidding to a stop on his bicycle during his play carrier days, but he couldn't fathom what it must be like to fly faster than the speed of sound. And he certainly couldn't imagine that he would ever fly such an amazing machine. Willie loved all things mechanical, but flying airplanes seemed like something that other people did, special people, not the son of a mechanic.

Fɪɢ. 4. Photo of the ꜰ-8 (originally xꜰ8ᴜ-ɪ), similar to the one that Willie saw in the *Fresno Bee* in 1956. (Courtesy Vought Heritage Foundation)

But Dinuba, like many small towns, had an outsized knack for producing future aviation stars. Two brothers, Richard and Burt Rutan, also attended Dinuba High School. Richard was a year ahead of Willie in school and would go on to fly ꜰ-ɪ00 fighters for the air force on some of Vietnam's most dangerous missions, called "Misty ꜰᴀᴄ." Younger brother Burt became an aeronautical engineer and brilliant aircraft designer, churning out dozens of unconventional-looking aircraft built with composite materials. In addition to selling plans for his homebuilt aircraft designs, Burt created the Beechcraft Starship business aircraft and in 2004 won the xᴘʀɪᴢᴇ for the first privately designed rocket to achieve spaceflight. In 1986 Richard, along with Jeana Yeager, piloted a Burt design, *Voyager*, on the world's first non-refueled around-the-world flight.

But in the late 1950s Willie and the Rutans were just small-town kids with high hopes for the future, a future that seemed very fuzzy to Willie. He knew there was a world beyond Dinuba, and he suspected access to that world had something to do with going to college. He didn't study very hard in high school, but he got good grades and was always on the honor roll.

One of Willie's older cousins had taught him to swim in an irrigation canal, and he developed into a strong swimmer but never joined his high school swim team. Instead, he was a high jumper on the track team and occasionally ran in relay races. He was good enough to set a new Dinuba High School record for the high jump, but his feat didn't last very long before one of his neighbors set yet another record. To round out his extracurricular activities, he played snare drum in the marching band.

Willie got his first motorcycle when he was thirteen, purchased with money he saved from a newspaper route and odd jobs like mowing lawns. He couldn't legally ride the motorcycle, but no one in Dinuba seemed to care, not even the police. The police station was next door to John's shop, and the cops were used to seeing Willie drive his father's truck around town, picking up and delivering parts and supplies. Adding a motorcycle to the mix wasn't a big deal, as long as Willie didn't do anything stupid.

After Willie was old enough to get his driver's license, he gave up the paper route and began working at the local Safeway. One day a customer asked him if he would install a fence on his farm. Willie agreed and drove to the farm. While taking a break from digging, he wandered into a barn and spotted a 1937 Ford covered with a tarp. The twenty-year-old car seemed to be in good condition, but the battery was dead. The car belonged to the farmer's former son-in-law and was a painful memory. Willie saw an opportunity in the farmer's distress. He asked if he could have the car as payment for installing the fence.

The farmer seemed happy to be rid of the car. When Willie finished the fence, he drove back to Dinuba for gas and a battery for the Ford. In town Willie spotted Garland's younger brother, Ray, who needed no convincing to help. They soon had the Ford running. It was time for a road test.

Willie took the wheel. After all, it was his car, and at one year older than Ray, he was also the more experienced driver. Willie floored the gas pedal and reached about sixty miles per hour. It was a warm day, and the boys barreled down the farm road with the windows rolled down, reveling in the hot, noisy air that filled the sedan. After a few minutes Willie pulled over, and Ray got into the driver's seat. He sped back toward the farm, driving faster and faster, until a tractor leaving a field pulled out in front of them.

Ray swerved too hard. The Ford rolled upside down, and the door on Willie's side popped open. As the car started to roll upright, Willie flew out the passenger side and landed on his ass in the soft dirt of a ditch. Stunned, he watched in horror as the Ford finished righting itself and rolled to a stop about fifty yards away. He was sure Ray was dead.

Willie staggered to his feet and sprinted to the smashed Ford.

Ray sat upright in the driver's seat as if nothing had happened. He had clutched the steering wheel through the entire ordeal. Willie helped his cousin out of the car, and they stared at the wreck. There didn't seem to be a single spot that hadn't been crushed or dented.

The cousins trudged back to the farm and drove to town to borrow John's pickup truck and a chain to tow the Ford. Willie retrieved the battery, but he was in the hole for the money he didn't get from the farmer and the gas he'd bought. At least the junkyard owner, a longtime family friend from Oklahoma who perhaps remembered some of his own youthful escapades, took the wreck for free.

Willie graduated from high school in 1958. Thinking that he might become a teacher, he decided to major in English and enrolled in Reedley Junior College, a few miles from Dinuba. After getting his associate in arts degree in 1960, he wanted to get away from the endless dust of the Central Valley. He was accepted at the University of California in Santa Barbara. The beach sounded romantic, and he had a friend who was going there. Living by the ocean, he expanded his repertoire of water sports, learning to surf, snorkel, and scuba dive. When he wasn't in the water or at school, he worked as a busboy at a Farmer John's Pancake House.

One summer in college Willie worked for a crop duster named Bud Kliewer, who flew an old Stearman biplane. Willie still knew nothing about airplanes, but the crop duster needed him as a flagger on the ground. Each morning Kliewer gave Willie a set of aeronautical charts marked with the fields they would be dusting that day. Each location was numbered in order, and the chart depicted highways and major roads that Willie was familiar with. After figuring out where the first location was, he hopped on his motorcycle and drove to the field carrying a rolled-up flag in a tube on the bike. On arriving, he stood at one edge of the field with the flag raised while Kliewer flew toward him about twenty feet above the ground, released his chemicals over the field, and pulled up and turned around. During the turn Willie walked a specific number of paces and stuck the flag in the air again. The pilot–ground crew dance continued for dozens of passes until the field was complete. Then Willie rolled up the flag, stuck it in his tube, and rode over to the next field. Around noon Kliewer dropped a cardboard note as he flew over Willie to let him know where and when to meet after lunch. Even though the pilot was traveling at about one hundred miles per hour, Willie never had to walk more than a few feet to pick up the note.

As Willie neared graduation in Santa Barbara, his father died. John had been having heart problems, so his death wasn't unexpected, but Paralee needed help selling the shop and tying up John's estate. Willie moved back to Reedley and transferred to Fresno State to finish his degree and help run the family business, until his mother sold it six months later.

Now in his early twenties, Willie resembled an older, dark-haired version of Eddie Haskell on the hit TV show *Leave It to Beaver*. The lanky blue-eyed surfer had been through many girlfriends, but nothing had yet stuck. One day at lunch with a friend, he noticed a tall brunette in an orange sweater walking toward him on the sidewalk. As she neared, the sun lit up her face and made her eyes sparkle. When her eyes met Willie's, something he'd never felt before hit him, like a cartoon shock, and left his heart thumping wildly.

"Do you know who that is?" Willie asked his friend.

"No, but I know who she hangs around with."

Willie chased down the mutual acquaintance and learned that the girl with what he called the "crazy green spider eyes" was named Nina Bishop and, more important, wasn't seeing anyone steadily. Willie asked her out. She was two years younger and an art major.

In late 1962, as Willie finished his last semester of college in Fresno, he started to think more seriously about what to do after he graduated. U.S. forces were building up in Southeast Asia, mostly advising and training forces in South Vietnam, a former French colony that had become a pawn in the Cold War. The situation looked like it might be heading for real war, and Willie knew two people who had been drafted. He was pretty sure he didn't want to be in the army. Running around a jungle carrying a rifle didn't appeal to him. His family tradition was in the sea services anyway, so he began to think about joining the navy. Nina approved of his idea. With a college degree he could attend Officer Candidate School (ocs). Other than what he had seen in the movies, Willie had no idea what navy officers did, but he envisioned himself standing on the deck of a ship wearing ensign shoulder boards.

Don had recently returned from a two-year navy stint as an enlisted corpsman, and he was interested in being an officer as well. The brothers visited a recruiter together on campus at Fresno State. The recruiter had an irresistible deal for them: if they would fill out a stack of paperwork and take initial screening tests, they could go to a nearby airport and get a short hop in a propeller-driven training aircraft, the t-34. Both brothers jumped at the chance. It was Willie's first time in an airplane, and he thrilled at the sight of the ground dropping away as the pilot climbed out after takeoff. Sitting in the back seat of the little trainer, the engine's vibrations coursed through his body, connecting him to the airplane and making him feel safe. Both Willie and Don passed their initial screening, and the recruiter arranged a commercial flight to Oakland so they could visit nearby Alameda Naval Air Station for additional tests, physical exams, and interviews.

At Alameda a naval aviator named Dusty Rhodes interviewed

Willie. The aviator suggested that Willie consider Aviation Officer Candidate School.

"I don't know how to fly," said Willie.

"We don't need you to know how. We like to train you ourselves anyway."

Willie could hardly believe what he had just heard. It might be possible to fly that beautiful fighter airplane he had fallen in love with almost a decade ago—an airplane he had never actually seen, except in a picture. But he was sure the Crusader was what he would fly if he were accepted. He changed his application to Aviation Officer Candidate School.

As Willie and Donald killed time between events in Alameda, Willie started talking to another recruit.

"Are you here to interview for ocs, too?" Willie asked.

"No, aviation cadets. I haven't finished college yet. And you?" The other recruit had a noticeable German accent. Without a bachelor's degree, he would have to complete flight school before he could be commissioned as an ensign.

Willie acknowledged that he was eligible for regular flight school since he had graduated from college.

"I'm Willie Sharp."

The other recruit shook Willie's extended hand. "Dieter Dengler."

With his accent and name, Willie assumed that Dieter was from Germany, but he didn't pry. Instead, he asked the other recruit what he wanted to fly after he finished flight school—because, of course, they would all finish flight school.

"The Spad."

Willie thought he must have heard wrong. "A Spad? You mean that ancient propeller airplane?"

"Yes, the Spad." Dieter spoke with a determination that Willie didn't question, even if he couldn't understand why anyone would choose a slow, Korean War era airplane when one could aim for the most modern supersonic hotdogging jet in the navy's inventory, the Crusader.

After tests and interviews and more waiting, the navy notified Willie he had been accepted for ocs and flight training. Nina and

Paralee were thrilled, and Willie felt that his life was starting to fall into place. Joining the navy had just been a concept until that point, but now even the F-8 seemed like it might be within reach. The only downside was that Don had been rejected. Willie felt sorry for Don, but he also felt a bit euphoric as he sensed a repositioning in his relationship with his older brother. Willie moved toward his own life and dreams, dreams now out of reach for Don.

Willie graduated from Fresno State in January 1963. He and Nina married on March 3 in the reception hall of a small church near Bakersfield and the Kern River, where Nina had grown up. After a quick honeymoon in Las Vegas, Willie flew to Pensacola, Florida, to begin "preflight" training, the pre-commissioning school he had to pass before becoming an ensign and moving on to pilot training. Officer candidates couldn't have their wives with them during training, so Nina stayed in Fresno to finish the school year.

Preflight was a whirlwind of marching, inspections, naval history, traditions, and how to be a naval officer. Most material was taught by marine sergeants. One day, as Willie neared graduation, he spotted the name Dengler stenciled on the back of one of the drab uniforms worn by a group of newly arrived candidates. Willie ran over.

"Hi, Dieter!"

Dieter Dengler smiled at Willie, happy to see a friendly face.

With the packed training schedule, there wasn't much time to talk. Willie wished Dieter well and moved on. He wondered if Dieter still only wanted to fly Spads.

One day Willie got a message to report to the personnel office. A clerk explained that there was something wrong with his enlistment records. Someone had entered his first name as William instead of Willie, and the mistake had rippled through his records. The error wasn't caught until a routine review. Willie assumed the navy would correct the mistake, but the clerk had another idea: he thought it would be easier if Willie changed his legal name. With only a few months in the navy, Willie was already familiar with military bureaucracy, and he figured the clerk was probably right.

FIG. 5. Willie receiving his commission on July 5, 1963.
(Courtesy Willie Sharp)

All he had to do was fill out a piece of paper and get it notarized, something he could do without leaving the base. Within an hour he became William Dean Sharp. But everyone except his family still called him Willie. A relative told him later that his rash decision broke his mother's heart, but she never mentioned it to him.

Willie was commissioned an ensign, the lowest officer rank in the navy, on July 5, 1963 (fig. 5). Nina arrived in Pensacola at the peak of summer heat and humidity. The air was so saturated she could almost see the moisture. Everything felt damp; mildew seemed to form everywhere.

Nina hated the humidity as much as Willie loved pilot training. After two weeks of ground school, he took his first training flight in a T-34. Once again, he found the thrum of the engine reassuring. However, he now sat in the front seat as a student pilot instead of the back as a passenger. His instructor sat in the rear seat.

Willie paid close attention to what his instructors told him; his bravado masked a lack of confidence in his ability to fly. But the recruiter had been right: Willie's lack of experience meant he had no bad habits to break. Unlike some students with civilian flying experience, Willie took easily to the T-34, although the airplane's crisp flight controls made it easy for even beginners to point the aircraft's nose in the right direction. The only complicated part about flying the airplane was the three distinct engine controls that had to constantly be repositioned depending on the phase of flight: a throttle to change the power setting, a propeller control to set the propeller rpm, and a mixture control for the fuel. A student could easily wreck an engine if he moved the controls in the wrong sequence or in the wrong direction, but Willie soon mastered the engine. Within a few flights he learned the basics of flying: climbs, descents, turns, and combinations of those, along with flying slowly and at cruise speeds. Takeoffs and landings were a little harder, but his confidence grew with every flight, and within a few weeks he was flying well enough to solo—to fly the airplane all by himself for the first time.

On August 26 Willie taxied to the end of the runway for his first solo flight. As he pulled onto the runway, he experienced the same mixture of satisfaction and terror most pilots feel on their first solo: I finally got rid of the instructor! I can do this! But can I really get this thing back on the ground without killing myself?

Willie's first solo consisted of just a few takeoffs and landings—he would take off and fly a rectangular path about the runway, called a traffic pattern, to line up for a landing. After landing, he would taxi back and take off again for another trip around the pattern. His instructor waited on the ramp next to the runway and observed Willie's every move. The budding pilot talked aloud as he flew around the pattern, as if the instructor still occupied the back seat, calling out airspeeds and altitudes, along with reminders such as "gear down." Talking aloud helped him remember everything to do. With each landing his confidence soared.

Willie and Nina celebrated the solo flight with dinner and margaritas. Nina had already learned what was involved in marrying a future naval aviator. She quizzed Willie for hours on arcane material such as Morse code and the meaning of semaphores—hand signals and flags used to communicate on the chaotic flight deck of an aircraft carrier.

After soloing, Willie continued his T-34 training, learning basic aerobatic maneuvers such as loops and rolls and how to recover from a spin. During a spin the airplane rotates about the vertical axis as it descends toward the ground. Pilots must know how to recognize a spin and recover from it in case they accidentally get into one.

Willie loved doing spins in the T-34. He first pulled the throttle to idle, then raised the nose to slow the airplane until the wing stalled. As the nose of the airplane dropped due to the loss of lift, he stomped on one of the rudder pedals, and the T-34 happily entered the spin. After four or five revolutions of plunging toward the earth, Willie stomped on the opposite rudder pedal to slow the rotation and then pushed the stick forward to break the stall. As the airplane straightened out, he added power and pulled the nose up to recover from the dive. At first his instructor just asked him to recover, but as Willie became more skilled, he had to make the T-34 stop spinning on a particular heading; that meant he had to pick something on the ground and push the stick forward at just the right moment. Going from controlled flight to uncontrolled flight and recovering back to controlled flight was another confidence builder. With every spin Willie became more the master of his airplane, preparing him for more challenging aircraft and maneuvers.

Willie performed well enough in T-34 training that the navy selected him to fly jets instead of multi-engine propeller aircraft. He and Nina moved to Meridian Naval Air Station in Mississippi. The couple rented one side of a duplex and moved in with their meager possessions, including a cat and many tins of canned food. Deposits, along with first and last month rent payments, left them dead broke, with no paycheck forthcoming for two more weeks. They lived on the canned food, but it ran low the last few days before the paycheck arrived. Willie supplemented his diet with the milk his training squadron had for coffee. After getting paid, Willie and Nina had a steak dinner at a restaurant across the street from their apartment. When it was time for the check, they learned that the restaurant owner was also their landlord and he had paid the bill.

Willie's second phase of pilot training was in the T-2A Buckeye, the navy's primary jet trainer. Willie's instructor again sat in the back seat while Willie sat in front. The first thing Willie noticed about the jet was that the reassuring vibration of the propellers was missing. Instead, the jet engine whined. But Willie quickly came to appreciate the T-2A's other qualities: the airplane had air conditioning, was much quieter, and accelerated much faster than the T-34. The T-34's multiple engine controls were gone, replaced by a single throttle that took care of everything. His jet training included navigation, formation flying, air-to-air combat techniques, and tons of field carrier landing practice—simulated carrier landings on a small runway marked out on a larger runway.

Landing is the hardest maneuver to learn for most pilots. Take-offs are relatively easy to master: taxi onto the center of the runway, push the throttle forward, and let go of the brakes. As the airplane starts to move, keep the nose on the centerline, usually using the rudder pedals. At a certain speed, pull back on the yoke or stick to move the nose of the airplane toward the sky. When the airplane is moving fast enough, the wing lifts the machine into the air. If the airplane has retractable landing gear, the pilot usually raises it once the airplane is definitely climbing—"positive rate of climb," in pilot parlance. If the airplane uses flaps to build more lift during the takeoff, the pilot also retracts the flaps during the climb.

There are many variations on takeoff that account for winds from different directions, runway conditions, the type and weight of the aircraft, and other factors, but most pilots learn the basic takeoff within a few tries.

Landing is much harder. Setting up the landing isn't too difficult—set the throttle to a predetermined position, lower the gear and flaps if needed, move the nose of the airplane to the right attitude to achieve the desired approach speed, and line the nose up on the centerline of the runway. At this point the airplane is about five hundred to one thousand feet in the air and one to five miles from the runway. For an air force–style landing, the pilot aims the nose at the beginning of the runway. If everything is perfect, all the pilot has to do is keep the nose of the airplane pointed at the spot on the runway. But things are rarely perfect—a small gust bumps the nose out of position or makes the airplane speed up a few knots. Or the throttle isn't perfectly set, and the aircraft sinks a little faster than expected. Or both of those things happen at once. The pilot moves the stick and throttle to get the airplane back where they want it, and then something else happens. The approach often becomes a continuous series of small corrections as the airplane descends toward the runway following an imaginary line in the sky called a "glideslope." If the pilot can't see the runway due to weather, an electronic beam on the ground provides a glideslope indication to a cockpit instrument.

The pilot can't keep the nose pointed at the runway until touchdown or the nosewheel will hit first. The airplane is also going too fast to land; if the pilot tries to touch down, the airplane will bounce. So the last part of the approach is a "flare," in which the pilot gradually pulls up the nose to bleed off speed and touch down on the main landing gear. The flare works well on a regular runway because it makes for a soft touchdown for passengers and puts less stress on the landing gear. But the flare is also somewhat unpredictable—it is impossible for even a highly skilled pilot to reliably touch down at the exact same spot on every landing. It's a finesse maneuver that requires a great deal of skill. Most pilots require dozens of landings before they get it right. Willie learned to make flared landings in the T-34 trainer, but after that he learned a different technique more suited to carrier landings.

Navy pilots increase the predictability of their landings by flying the approach with the nose raised during the descent. Instead of flaring the airplane at touchdown, the pilot simply flies the airplane onto the runway or carrier deck in what many call a "controlled crash." The landing is more precise, but the touchdown is harder than a flared landing. To take extra pounding, navy landing gears are much beefier than air force landing gears.

Landing on the deck of a carrier heaving up and down and side to side by ten feet in rough seas is probably the most difficult maneuver in aviation, harder than formation flying, dogfighting, and aerial refueling. These maneuvers are usually flown at higher speeds and altitudes, where there is some margin for error. Near perfection is required for every carrier landing. Touching down even a few feet short can be disastrous. Hit the back of the boat, and you will likely kill everyone on the airplane and endanger people working on the flight deck.

Multiple problems have to be solved during a carrier landing. First, the pilot has to maintain a glideslope that intersects the desired touchdown point. But since the airplane is flown in a nose-up attitude, the pilot can't point the nose at the flight deck. The pilot also cannot see the tailhook. And the required glideslope depends on the distance between the cockpit and the tailhook—generally, the longer the airplane, the steeper the glideslope. Add in a moving flight deck, and the pilot needs some help: "the meatball." The meatball is a system of lights that carrier pilots follow for every landing. When the aircraft is on the correct glideslope, a bright yellow light—the meatball—is centered between two horizontal rows of green lights. If the pilot gets too high, the meatball moves above the green lights; if the pilot gets too low, the meatball changes to red and moves below the green lights. If the pilot keeps the meatball centered, the tailhook should snag the third of four wires strung across the carrier deck. In addition to the meatball, another pilot on the ground, called a landing signal officer (LSO), helps carrier pilots stay on the right path.

Even with experienced aviators and multiple safeguards in place, a carrier landing can be a dicey proposition: an airplane can come down just as the carrier goes up. That happened to a colleague of mine, who ruined an F-4 in the 1980s. The hard landing punched both main landing gear struts through the wings. But it's easy to get rid of carrier airplanes damaged beyond repair: unceremoniously shove them over the side of the ship.

Willie and his classmates treated their training runway as if it were a real carrier. For each approach the students aligned their aircraft with the runway centerline and picked up the meatball. One of their instructors stood on the ground next to the runway and acted as LSO. The LSO talked to the pilots, giving them feedback about their position and instructions on how to fix any problems, such as "Getting a little low, add power." For the practice landings there were no wires on the runway; the goal was to follow the meatball and the LSO instructions. As soon as a pilot touched down, he added power to go around for another approach and landing. This also simulated a bolter approach in which a pilot missed all four of the wires on the carrier—the added power made sure the aircraft got safely airborne again for another try.

Catching the third wire on the deck with one's tailhook is the best carrier landing. Four cables lie across the deck twenty feet apart, numbered one through four beginning at the stern, or aft end, of the boat. Landing between the number two and number three wires means the pilot has landed in the exact center of the box made by the four cables, and the tailhook should grab the third wire and pull the aircraft to a stop. Landing a few feet short, the pilot should catch the number one or number two wire, and landing a few feet long, the pilot should catch the number four wire. Those landings are acceptable, and weather conditions may cause even the best carrier pilot to miss the number three wire or have a bolter. A pilot who cannot nail number three consistently will be at the bottom of the carrier pilot food chain. It doesn't matter how good a carrier pilot is at the rest of their job; if they can't land well, they may not be a carrier pilot for long.

Willie quickly mastered the art of flying the meatball, which entailed constant minor and sometimes major changes in power along with moving the nose of the T-2A up and down or side to side to keep the jet in the precise position for a perfect simulated landing. The practice landings were relatively easy since the ground doesn't heave like a flight deck in high seas might.

Ironically, calm winds on the carrier make it harder to land. Carrier aircraft are designed to land with about a thirty-knot "wind over deck" for a less stressful touchdown. The natural wind over the deck is usually less than thirty knots, so the carrier steams into the wind to make up the difference. The landing deck on modern carriers is angled away from the rest of the ship. As the ship steams faster, the crosswind increases across the deck, and a pilot has to make constant small corrections back to the centerline to compensate. Older carriers like the ones that Willie operated off of spewed black clouds of smoke that billowed over the ramp at the rear of the deck. The more power needed to reach thirty knots wind over deck, the more smoke the ship belched. The smoke sometimes interfered with visibility and created up and down drafts that caused an approaching aircraft to rise or sink close to touchdown.

After dozens of practice landings on the motionless runway, Willie and four other students were ready to make a real carrier landing. On May 5, 1964, the five students and their instructor, each in his own jet, flew across the Gulf of Mexico to the training carrier, the uss *Lexington*. Enlisted men wearing color-coded shirts crawled about the carrier to launch and recover aircraft. Green Shirts hooked airplanes up to catapults and handled the landing cables. Yellow Shirts guided the planes on the deck. Purple Shirts, also called "grapes," refueled airplanes. White Shirts did safety and first aid. Red Shirts handled ordnance and put out fires. There would be no ordnance today, but everyone hoped to avoid someone in a white or red shirt.

While the students orbited above, the instructor landed, parked his airplane, and walked over to the LSO stand on the port side of the carrier. When facing the incoming pilots, the jets would be to the left of the instructor, now acting as LSO.

Willie and the others started making practice landings; on the first two circuits they kept their tailhook up so they wouldn't catch the wire. They simply touched down and immediately added power to take off again. On the third circuit Willie's instructor told him to put his tailhook down.

Oh wow, this is it, Willie thought. He grabbed a small yellow handle on the right side of his instrument panel and pushed it down to lower the hook. As he flew away from the carrier, he mentally prepared for the wire to grab the hook instead of his jet becoming airborne again. He turned back toward the carrier and made a radio call that ended with "Buckeye" and the amount of fuel he had. The cable operators used the type of aircraft and fuel number to adjust the tension of the cables to account for the total weight of his airplane. In a real-world landing the amount of fuel was also an indication of how important it was to get someone onto the carrier: if a pilot was low on fuel, he had priority for landing. Other pilots might be sent around for another try.

Willie followed the ball down the glideslope, listening intently for corrections from the LSO. He slammed onto the flight deck between the number two and three wires and added full power, but this time the arresting wire yanked him to a stop. He decelerated more quickly than he had expected, but his whole body lit up.

"I did it!"

There was no time to savor the moment. He had about thirty seconds to get out of the way for the next student. A Green Shirt signaled him to raise the Buckeye's tailhook; the cable dropped away and slid back into place on the flight deck. A Yellow Shirt guided him to the catapult, where he began a carefully choreographed dance with the Yellow and Green Shirts that would conclude with his aircraft zooming into the sky. A blast deflector lowered, and Willie taxied his nosewheel along the catapult track and over a mechanism called a "shuttle." The shuttle was attached to a giant steam-powered catapult below the flight deck. As a Yellow Shirt waved Willie forward, a Green Shirt rolled underneath the Buckeye and hooked its tail to a wire using a "holdback fitting" about the size of a two-pound dumbbell. Willie kept taxiing slowly until the jet stopped, held in place by the holdback fitting. At that point a Green Shirt hooked the shuttle to the Buckeye with a cable called a "bridle," and the shuttle moved slowly forward until the bridle was tight between the aircraft and the shuttle. The Yellow Shirt then passed control to another Yellow Shirt called the "shooter," who gave Willie the signal to run up his engine: two fingers circling above his head. Willie rested his feet on the floor of the cockpit and ran up his engine to full power, scanning his instruments and checking his flight controls. In the meantime the catapult machinery below the flight deck cranked up the steam pressure required to launch the T-2A. When Willie was satisfied his airplane was ready, he saluted the shooter. The shooter saluted back and dropped to tap the flight deck with the fingers of one hand while the other arm pointed forward. Everyone was ready. The catapult controller in a catwalk next to the flight deck pushed a button on a control panel, and BOOM! The holdback fitting broke as designed and released the catapult. The piston pulled the Buckeye down the track and flung the little jet into the air.

As soon as Willie saw water below, he raised the gear. The acceleration was breathtaking—he was at flying speed in just a few seconds. He felt much more of a thrill than he had expected. Mostly, he was pleased that everything had gone well. After several more landings and catapult shots that day, Willie was deemed carrier qualified. The carrier flight was the last time he flew the T-2A; it was time to move to more sophisticated airplanes and learn how to be a fighter pilot. He was on his way to the top of naval aviation's food chain.

The last phase of Willie's pilot training was in Kingsville, Texas, first flying TF-9J fighter trainers and then the supersonic F-11. He learned the basics of fighter pilot tradecraft: dogfighting, firing a gun, launching rockets and missiles, and even dropping a few bombs.

On August 2, 1964, as Willie neared the end of pilot training, North Vietnamese boats in the Gulf of Tonkin attacked the USS *Maddox* as the U.S. destroyer conducted reconnaissance. Two nights later a second incident was reported. Although the circumstances of the second attack were murky, President Johnson ordered reprisal attacks on North Vietnamese naval facilities. The attacks were carried out by sixty-seven naval aircraft launched from two carriers, the *Constellation* and the *Ticonderoga*.[1] Even though the North Vietnamese shot down two American aircraft, killing one pilot and taking the other prisoner, the incident electrified Willie and his classmates: they might soon be flying in combat.

FIG. 6. Nina pinning on Willie's wings on September 18, 1964.
(Courtesy Willie Sharp)

Many of their instructors were jealous; except for a handful who had flown in Korea, most of them had not seen combat. Their younger charges might beat them to it.

A few weeks before graduation, each pilot in Willie's class filled out a form listing the aircraft he wanted to fly and whether he pre-ferred the West Coast or the East Coast, although the navy made no guarantees that a pilot would get what he wanted. Willie wrote the F-8 at the top of his list and asked for a West Coast location. A few weeks later his dream came true: an F-8 at Miramar Naval Air Station in San Diego.

On September 18, 1964, Willie became a naval aviator. During the graduation ceremony Nina pinned gold pilot wings above the left breast pocket of his white dress uniform (fig. 6). A few days later the couple headed to California for the last step in Willie's long fighter pilot apprenticeship. Thrilled to return to their roots, Nina was especially glad to leave behind the suffocating humid-ity of the southeastern United States.

The conflict that Willie and his classmates were about to enter had been building for decades. French colonizers left Vietnam in 1954, after being defeated by Ho Chi Minh's Viet Minh forces at Dien Bien Phu.[2] In July 1954 the country was divided into two pieces at the seventeenth parallel after peace talks in Geneva.[3]

The earliest U.S. forces in Vietnam were ground units that arrived in the mid-1950s. These units focused on training South Vietnamese soldiers so they could protect their country from external aggression, in particular North Vietnam.[4] The peace didn't last long: in September 1959 the Viet Cong began their insurgency with the goal to reunite the two countries under the communist regime in Hanoi.[5]

In November 1961 U.S. Air Force crews began training South Vietnamese air force pilots in counterinsurgency operations.[6] The operation was called "Farm Gate." Despite the publicly stated goal of training, U.S. crews were soon flying combat missions against the Viet Cong.[7] Since bringing in advanced airplanes would signal that the United States was much more involved in Vietnam than the government admitted, the air force initially kept up the charade by flying only older propeller-driven aircraft, such as T-28 trainers and B-26 bombers. Most senior military leaders didn't think they were fooling anyone.[8]

The air force was also reluctant to bring search and rescue (SAR) aircraft to Vietnam; the presence of those aircraft would also indicate the United States was involved in combat. But a year after arriving in Vietnam, the air force had already lost six aircraft to Viet Cong machine guns and small arms.[9] Acknowledging the need for rescue services, the air force had established a SAR center at Tan Son Nhut Air Base near Saigon in late 1961. However, the handful of assigned rescue coordinators had no aircraft to task for SAR missions.[10] Instead, the coordinators relied on army helicopters and the CIA contractor, Air America, which was flying men and supplies into Southeast Asia.[11] The army and Air America crews had no training for combat search and rescue (CSAR).

Even if the air force had been willing to send SAR aircraft to Vietnam, Air Rescue Service crews had lost the expertise gained during Korea. By 1961 rescue personnel had been slashed by more than 75 percent, from 7,900 to 1,600.[12] Current rescue units had no combat training, and their equipment was woefully inadequate for South Vietnam's jungles and mountainous terrain. Most of the Air Rescue Service helicopters were limited to firefighting support and picking up pilots who bailed out near a base.[13]

The navy also got involved in the early war. In the fall of 1961 carrier aircraft flew reconnaissance and other support missions, including taking photographs for making maps of both North and South Vietnam. In August 1962 five EA-1F aircraft arrived at Tan Son Nhut to help the South Vietnamese detect incoming enemy aircraft. The EA-1F carried a radar and other equipment that could detect enemy aircraft from much farther distances than a typical fighter aircraft could.[14]

In June 1963, as the chaos in South Vietnam grew, air force major Alan Saunders arrived at Tan Son Nhut to work at the SAR center.[15] The unit now had an official name: Detachment 3, Pacific Air Rescue Center, acknowledging that CSAR in Vietnam was now a real thing.[16] Saunders knew from his experience in Burma during World War II that finding downed aircraft in jungles could be difficult, if not impossible. When an airplane hit the jungle canopy, the trees opened up, the machine dropped in, and the trees closed back over with not so much as a dent in the foliage. Even if the aircraft ignited a fire, there was usually no burn mark. Fuel splashed and spread out across dozens of trees, and the canopy was so high that the fire wouldn't make it to the top of the trees.[17]

By the time Saunders arrived, scores of people had been lost to aircraft crashes in Southeast Asia, yet there were still no formal rescue forces available. The major knew that several of his predecessors had failed in their attempts to get the air force to listen, but he also noted that none of those requests had been made through formal channels.

Saunders likened the lack of formal request to a problem with getting supplies. You can gripe all day to the supply officer about how much you need a desk, and the supply officer might even sympathize with you, but he's not going to do anything about it until you fill out the right form and submit it through the right channels. Saunders needed to do the same thing to get some rescue forces. He asked his commander if he could conduct a study to justify the use of professional SAR forces in Vietnam.[18]

Saunders and his small staff of rescue controllers dug up statistics on loss rates and casualties and examined their operating environment—the threat, terrain, and weather. They wrote a report in September and sent it up through their chain of command to Maj. General "Buck" Anthis, a pilot with combat experience in both World War II and Korea who was responsible for all air force operations in South Vietnam. Saunders's report spent more than two months winding its way through a long list of staff offices before reaching Anthis's desk.[19]

As his report crawled toward Anthis, Saunders fumed over what he viewed as army ineptness that cost lives. In November an army helicopter crashed into the ocean at night off the South Vietnamese central coast. All four crew members survived and jumped into the ocean. Swimming about in their floatation gear, the crew expected to be rescued. A pilot in a cargo aircraft nearby dropped two flares and said he could see the beaches as if it were daytime, but the army's higher-echelon commander was reluctant to send helicopters for the rescue: his pilots weren't trained to fly at night, which is what had caused the first accident. The downed helicopter's copilot swam to shore with a broken arm and hid overnight in bushes. The other three crew members drowned. Saunders lamented the lack of trained rescue forces that would include men who knew how to fly at night and hover over people in the water to pick them up, and pararescue personnel who were scuba qualified and could jump into the ocean to help. Air force rescue crews did this sort of thing all the time as they practiced recovering space vehicles and astronauts. Saunders knew it was important to support the space program, but weren't the lives of soldiers and airmen important too?[20]

As the casualties mounted, Saunders decided to take more control of the staffing process. The army was already using air force requests for army helicopters to assist with SAR missions as justification for bringing more army helicopters to Southeast Asia. Given their desire for more helicopters, army leaders wouldn't relish any ideas the air force might have to get their own CSAR forces. Fearing the army might block his request for air force search and rescue forces if it caught wind of the staff package, Saunders recommended that General Anthis send the package strictly through air force channels to the higher-level command, the United States Pacific Command. Saunders knew this might slow down the package for a while, as Pacific Command would surely send it to the army to get its concurrence, but then the army staff would have to explain to their superiors why they insisted on not using specially trained and equipped air force personnel.

Anthis agreed with Saunders's strategy, and it wasn't long before Saunders got a phone call from an army officer asking him to help answer a few Pacific Command questions, exactly the response Saunders had hoped for. The army officer said he would send a Pacific Command message with the questions to Saunders, but the major never received it. Early in 1964, he called back and reached an army colonel, two ranks superior to Saunders. Saunders explained patiently that he had never gotten a copy of the message regarding the rescue capabilities.

"The message never went out," said the colonel.

"Why?"

"Because I don't approve of it."

"Why?"

"Because the army can do it."

"Sir, they're not trained to do it."

Given the recent army aircrew deaths in the water, Saunders might have thought his last point was obvious, but the colonel retorted, "We'll train them."

"But they're not equipped to do it."

"We'll equip them."

Saunders tried one last plea. "But it isn't their mission."

"We'll make it their mission."[21]

Saunders gave up, but he had a backup plan. General Anthis asked another general to help put pressure on the army to concede the search and rescue mission to its rightful owner, the air force. About three weeks later the army sent a message: "Okay, we'll go along with it."[22]

Saunders asked the Air Rescue Service to move units to Southeast Asia. Saunders wanted four units with H-43 helicopters, but planners instead chose only two units with C-3 helicopters, which Saunders considered too big and unsuitable for operating in Vietnam's jungles and rugged terrain. And more than two units were needed to cover the vast north-south distances in Vietnam and multiple types of terrain, including beaches, jungles, and mountains. Helicopters making rescues in the delta area didn't need a long cable and winch like helicopters in the jungle needed for pulling people up through dense foliage that grew as high as 250 feet. But Air Rescue Service planners had never been to Vietnam, and they fell back on what they knew how to do, trying to accomplish the mission efficiently.[23]

During his tenure, with the jungle swallowing up aircraft, Saunders was proud that they had only been unable to find 2 out of about 250 aircraft his unit searched for.[24] When searchers couldn't find people and didn't have information that they had been captured, Saunders's unit listed the mission as suspended. In those cases aircraft often dropped leaflets offering rewards. Rewards were for turning in equipment, not people, since the Geneva Conventions didn't allow ransoms. Saunders figured it was okay to say, "We'll give you thirty-five thousand dong for the parachute if the man is with it, or we'll give you seventeen thousand dong if he isn't with it." That way whoever found the parachute would have an incentive to keep the person alive if he wasn't already dead. The leaflets rarely worked; Saunders was aware of only one instance when a leaflet drop resulted in someone coming forward, and that information turned out to be useless. A Viet Cong operative sent a message through an intermediary that he held a captured B-26 pilot. The intermediary told Saunders the operative wanted him to provide the pilot's name, rank, and serial number to confirm the Viet Cong had the pilot. That was backward from the way it was supposed to work. Saunders told the operative: "No. You ask them to tell us what his name, rank, and serial number is, and we'll tell them if they've got him." He never heard anything back.[25]

Not long after Saunders arrived in Vietnam, a twenty-six-year-old pilot, Capt. Richard L. "Dick" Whitesides, departed the United States for Bien Hoa Air Base, South Vietnam. The California native had graduated from the United States Military Academy at West Point in 1959, where he played squash and tennis, in addition to being a prolific weight lifter.[26] Upon graduation he was commissioned a second lieutenant in the air force, a common practice before the fledgling Air Force Academy was running full steam. After pilot training in Texas and Nevada, he became a helicopter pilot and was stationed at Hamilton Air Force Base in Marin County, California. Both he and his high school sweetheart, Judith, now his wife, were thrilled to be back in their native state, close to relatives in their hometown, Stockton. A son, John, was born.

Whitesides didn't fly helicopters in Vietnam. Instead, he checked out in a small single-engine airplane called the o-1, which was used for training South Vietnamese air force pilots. Like his predecessors, Whitesides was officially an instructor pilot, but he also flew missions to support combat operations, such as flying as an observation or reconnaissance aircraft to spot targets.[27]

On November 24, 1963, Whitesides directed strikes against heavily fortified Viet Cong positions. Again and again, he flew his defenseless o-1 toward the action to spot targets. Once he found a target, he fired a small rocket that landed nearby and belched a column of smoke into the air. Other aircraft, armed with bombs or other munitions, moved toward the smoke to destroy the target. At some point Whitesides's o-1 was damaged and partially disabled. He remained in the fight and continued to point out targets, including the location of many large Viet Cong guns. For his actions Whitesides became the first Vietnam War recipient of the Air Force Cross, a medal second only to the Medal of Honor.

The mission on November 24 wasn't unusual. Since arriving a few months earlier, Whitesides had flown in dozens of similar battles. The combat was so intense that he told Judith he didn't expect to survive his tour in Southeast Asia.

Whitesides celebrated his twenty-seventh birthday in January 1964. Two months later, on March 26, he took off from Khe Sanh at two fifteen in the afternoon for a two-hour visual reconnaissance mission. Khe Sanh lay just south of the Demilitarized Zone between North and South Vietnam and just east of the border with Laos. The observer in Whitesides's back seat was Capt. Floyd J. Thompson, an army Special Forces officer.

No one was terribly concerned when Whitesides and Thompson failed to return at 4:15 p.m.; any number of issues could cause a minor delay, and the o-1 had enough fuel to fly for more than another hour. Five o'clock passed, with still no sign of the o-1. Ground personnel began a communications search—calling aircraft in the air and nearby bases. Had anyone heard from or seen the overdue aircraft? Sometimes an airplane had to make an emergency landing at a remote facility, on a road or in a field, and it might take some time for a crew to get back in touch. The communications search turned up nothing. At five forty, when the o-1 would have run out of fuel had it still been flying, Alan Saunders and his crew began to coordinate a full-scale search and rescue operation. Weather and approaching darkness delayed the search until the next day.

For the next sixteen days Saunders coordinated about a dozen flights each day searching for the o-1 in and around mountainous terrain covered with dense jungle and teeming with Viet Cong. More than two hundred South Vietnamese soldiers and U.S. Special Forces personnel joined the search on the ground. The ground search turned up several villagers who claimed they had seen a small aircraft flying just above treetop level, spewing smoke, about six miles from Khe Sanh. The villagers said the airplane appeared to turn back toward Khe Sanh. More searching and the offer of a reward turned up nothing. Whitesides and Thompson, along with their plane, had been swallowed up by the jungle.

On April 11 the search was suspended. The same day 200,000 leaflets were dropped offering a reward for information regarding the status of the missing crew or aircraft. Whitesides's superiors held out hope; his commander, Col. Benjamin Preston, noted in a report that "Captain Whitesides was an excellent pilot and it is possible that he could have survived and been captured."

Six weeks later, on May 21, a Viet Cong defector reported that he had seen Viet Cong forces shoot down an o-1 in late March. There were two Americans in the airplane. The defector claimed one was killed in the crash and the other was wounded and captured by the Viet Cong. The report renewed a flurry of searching. Two weeks later the jungle still refused to surrender the o-1.

On June 2 the United States gave up and dropped an additional 100,000 reward leaflets in villages near the suspected crash site.

Back in California, Judith Whitesides waited along with son, John, now a toddler.

On November 4 Radio Hanoi broadcast a statement purported to be from Capt. Floyd James Thompson, who "was captured by the patriotic guerrillas in Quang Tri Province when his [aircraft], manned by Richard Whitesides, was shot down on 26 March." The statement did not mention the fate of Whitesides. With Thompson apparently a prisoner of war (POW), any chance that Whitesides had survived now appeared remote.

On March 27, 1965, one year and one day after the o-1's disappearance and with no further word from either Whitesides or the North Vietnamese, the air force declared "a presumptive finding of death" for Capt. Richard L. Whitesides "due to hostile action while participating in Viet Nam operations."

Floyd Thompson became the first POW of the Vietnam War. Richard Whitesides joined a growing list of personnel deemed missing in action (MIA). Judith and John Whitesides joined the ranks of those left to wonder.

Throughout the summer of 1964 Alan Saunders continued to advocate for the H-43B helicopters he considered suitable for Vietnam.[28] The helicopters could fly search and rescue missions but were also used for a mission called "crash rescue." During a crash rescue the H-43B pulled aircrew and passengers from aircraft wreckage that was often burning. Most of the accidents occurred on a runway or near a base. When an aircraft crashed, an H-43B was airborne in less than ninety seconds. The helicopter carried a spherical fire extinguisher about three feet in diameter, hoses, and other rescue equipment in a one thousand–pound "fire suppression kit." The fire suppression kit, nicknamed "Sputnik," was slung beneath the helicopter. At the crash site the H-43B crew dropped off the Sputnik, along with one or more firefighters, who started laying a path of foam to the burning wreckage. The H-43B pilots then hovered at ten feet, where a huge volume of air from the helicopter's counter-rotating rotors pushed the foam along the path to create a safe corridor. The air from the rotors also moved the fire away from the open path and the wreckage. Firefighters then used the extinguisher to further control the fire while rescuers pulled survivors to safety.[29]

The H-43B rescued many aircrew members from burning aircraft, but the helicopter was designed for crashes that occurred on or near air force bases, not for combat search and rescue. Saunders asked that any H-43s sent to Vietnam be modified for combat. Among his recommendations were upgraded engines, self-sealing fuel tanks, shatterproof glass, armor plating around the crew seats and fuel lines, and gun mounts on the doors. Stateside powers pushed back on the gun mounts, insisting that the H-43 wasn't a weapons platform. Saunders knew that; he planned to use the guns for defense only, shooting back at Viet Cong who fired on the helicopter. If the enemy didn't get return fire after shooting at a helicopter, they wouldn't try to hide, they would just waltz out of the jungle and shoot down any helicopter that flew over.[30]

In June 1964 two H-43BS from Okinawa arrived at Nakhon Phanom (NKP) Royal Thai Air Force Base (RTAFB) near the Thai-Laos border.[31] Two Albatross aircraft also arrived at Korat RTAFB near Bangkok, followed by two more HU-16s at Da Nang Air Base on South Vietnam's east coast.[32] But Kaman, the company that built the H-43B, told the air force it would take another three months to modify helicopters still in the United States to the configuration that Saunders wanted. It would be at least September before the newer aircraft, called the H-43F, showed up in Southeast Asia. More than a year had passed since Saunders's original request.

The bureaucracy and delay would be a good M *A *S *H * episode if not for the people dying needlessly in the jungles and forests of Vietnam.[33]

But Saunders's efforts weren't for naught. When the shooting war escalated that August, the procedures and people he put into place paved the way for the first air force SAR helicopters to deploy to South Vietnam.

On Sunday, August 2, the day of the incident in the Gulf of Tonkin, Capt. John Christianson and his family arrived back at Minot Air Force Base, North Dakota, after visiting family. Christianson flew H-43B helicopters for rescue missions at the base. As one of the top graduates in his pilot training class, the young pilot's instructors had expected him to request a fighter airplane, but an H-43 flying around one day had captured his heart. Most pilots also avoided remote, frigid Minot if they could, but the Oregon native happily accepted the assignment to fly helicopters for rescue missions.[34]

That Monday morning Christianson discovered that his small rescue unit, officially named Detachment 2, Central Air Rescue Center, was on deployment alert, gearing up to go somewhere. The unit had been put on alert before, but it had always been a paperwork exercise. This looked like the real thing. No one knew where they were going, but with newspaper headlines and television news anchors blaring reports of the Gulf of Tonkin incident, it wasn't too hard to figure out. Most people on the base, including Christianson, had never heard of Vietnam.

On Thursday, August 6, Detachment 2 got the official order to deploy. The unit owned only two helicopters, and they both needed major maintenance. Someone borrowed two fresher helicopters from nearby Grand Forks Air Force Base. Maintenance personnel at Minot disassembled the two loaner H-43Bs and loaded them onto a C-124 cargo aircraft as Christianson and his squadron mates rushed home to notify their families and get their personal affairs in order. They then rushed about the base, collecting equipment for the deployment. Base Supply issued the unit .38

pistols and M-1 carbines. The base fire department gave them four firemen to use the two fire suppression kits they took along.

The next day, August 7, twenty men from Detachment 2 boarded a C-130 and flew to Travis Air Force Base in California to spend the night. About two in the morning Christianson awoke to a banging on the door and someone shouting: "Hey, guys, get your tail ends down here. We got a bus waiting for you!"

Twenty bleary-eyed airmen stumbled onto the bus and climbed back onto the C-130. The aircraft took off and headed west. The rising sun backlit the Golden Gate Bridge. Christianson thought of Tony Bennett's hit "I Left My Heart in San Francisco." The song burned into his memory at the sight of the bridge. Eight hours later the C-130 landed at Hickam Air Force Base in Hawaii, where the Pacific Air Rescue Command commander told them they were going to Vietnam. He didn't know much else.

After Hawaii the C-130 flew to Wake Island for refueling and on to Clark Air Base in the Philippines, where a couple of command post airmen boarded. Then it was on to Da Nang, where the base commander greeted them with "Who the hell are you, and what are you doing here?"

It was an inauspicious beginning to an ill-defined mission with ill-suited equipment. But Saunders finally had H-43s in Vietnam, even if they weren't the modified versions he preferred (fig. 7).

There wasn't much action at first for the H-43s in Southeast Asia. The helicopters were assigned to missions over land, and many of the downed aircrews made it to the waters of the Gulf of Tonkin, where the Albatrosses or navy helicopters picked them up. The city of Da Nang was safe, so Christianson and other bored pilots roamed the streets, buying knock-off Rolex watches and eating sweet and sour pork at the Grand Hotel.

In November a unit equipped with the H-43F models that Saunders coveted arrived from the United States to replace Christianson's unit. Rather than return to the States, Christianson, along with another pilot, Jim Sovell, went to NKP in Thailand to replace two pilots.[35]

About the same time the H-43Fs arrived in Da Nang, F-100

FIG. 7. HH-43B helicopter at Danang, 1964, with air force pilots Jim Sovell
(*left*) and John Christianson. (Courtesy John Christianson)

pilots from the 613th Tactical Fighter Squadron did too. They
were part of the 401st Tactical Fighter Wing at England Air Force
Base near Alexandria, Louisiana. My father, a captain and F-100
pilot at the time, belonged to another squadron in the 401st. I was
seven and had never heard the word *Vietnam*. My father was often
overseas, traveling with his squadron to places where F-100s sat
on alert status, loaded with bombs and ready to take off, in case
World War III kicked off. I knew nothing about any of this—I just
knew that my father was gone a lot and brought home presents,
like a fez from Morocco. During one of his deployments, he got
to know another captain named William Martin, who deployed
to Da Nang that November with the 413th.

On November 18, 1964, right after Christianson and Sovell
arrived at NKP, Martin took off from Da Nang with a second F-100
to escort a reconnaissance mission in Laos. As Martin attacked
a gun emplacement on the ground, antiaircraft artillery hit his

fighter. He ejected near the border with North Vietnam, and his wingman radioed for help. An Air America aircraft responded first, but an HU-16 soon arrived, followed shortly by two navy Spads. The Spad pilots took out the gun emplacements with their 20 mm cannons and spotted what they thought was the F-100 wreckage. With the enemy guns now gone, the HU-16 called NKP and asked for helicopters to fly to the wreckage and pick up Martin.[36]

Two H-43s launched from NKP carrying the two copilots that Christianson and Sovell were replacing. The helicopters flew ten miles until they reached the Mekong River that divided Thailand from Laos. But they couldn't cross the river: under the Byzantine rules of engagement in Southeast Asia, the crews needed permission from the U.S. ambassador in Vientiane, Laos, to cross the border. As someone scrambled to call the embassy, the H-43s ran low on fuel and returned to NKP.

While the helicopters were being refueled, a small cargo aircraft landed; it was headed for Okinawa, and the crew offered a ride to anyone who wanted to go. The two copilots who had been turned back from the Laotian border jumped at the opportunity.

Christianson and Sovell were happy for some action. The copilots ran to grab their bags for the return flight home as the two replacement pilots launched in the H-43s. This time someone had worked some magic: the helicopters flew straight across the river into Laos. They were soon joined by the waiting Spads and HU-16, which escorted them to where they thought Martin and his F-100 had landed. But an extensive search turned up empty-handed; it seemed the jungle had swallowed another aircraft. As darkness fell, the would-be rescuers returned to their home bases and regrouped.[37]

Overnight the SAR center coordinated thirty-one aircraft that could be used to search the next morning: thirteen air force F-105 fighters, eight F-100s, six navy Spads, two air force H-43s, and two Air America helicopters. At that point it was the largest number of aircraft assembled for an SAR mission in Vietnam.

By midmorning an HU-16 and four F-105s had found Martin's parachute and F-100 on a prominent formation on the limestone karst. As the F-105s attacked a nearby gun emplacement, the HU-16 brought in the two Air America helicopters, escorted by four T-28s. The copilot of one of the helicopters was lowered to the parachute on a hoist, but Martin was dead; he had apparently succumbed to injuries sustained while landing on the jagged limestone terrain.[38]

Two weeks after Martin's shoot-down, Willie flew his first flight in the F-8. He had no idea who Capt. William Martin was nor that he had been shot down. Exactly one year after Martin's shoot-down, Willie would be thankful for the actions of another person he had never heard of, Maj. Alan Saunders. The unsuccessful rescue forces mourned Martin's death, but at least the rescue forces could return his body to his family. The large assembly of aircraft that found and recovered Martin proved CSAR in Southeast Asia had come a long way in only one year. CSAR was still immature, but for the capability that existed, much credit was owed to the pleadings of Saunders.

4

The Crusader

TO WIN IN COMBAT, EVERY WARRIOR NEEDS TO BELIEVE IN three things: themselves and their training; their commanders and their orders; and the performance of their weapons systems.[1] Willie's pilot training had instilled in him the belief that he could fly, a belief that sometimes bordered on cockiness. He had come to believe and trust his commanders; he might not always understand why a superior officer asked him to do something, but he understood that orders and rules were necessary to accomplish a mission while keeping him as safe as possible as he screamed through the air at hundreds of miles per hour or slammed onto a carrier deck.

Willie was about to enter the last part of his apprenticeship, learning to believe in his equipment and how to extract the best possible performance from it. Flying the F-8 Crusader, he wasn't an ordinary pilot. He was a knight of the sky, a fighter who specialized in shooting down other aircraft, a mission called "air superiority," or air-to-air combat.

Attack pilots fly aircraft that resemble fighters, but they mostly drop bombs, a mission called air-to-ground. The air force makes little distinction between pilots who fly fighter planes such as the F-16 and those who fly attack aircraft such as the A-10; they are all called fighter pilots, and they are all treated the same. But in the navy the distinction is huge, something I learned decades ago, when I inadvertently asked a navy F-14 pilot if he flew the A-4.

The F-8 Willie was about to fly wasn't the prettiest jet around.

The fighter looked like a giant hot dog with a tail that stuck straight up in the air. Airborne, its single engine howled as if in pain. It could be hard to fly and was especially unforgiving during carrier landings. But most pilots who flew the Crusader fell in love with the sometimes unwieldy craft. Some even called it "my mistress." Willie's lust had started at fifteen when he spotted that first grainy photo of an F-8 in the *Fresno Bee*, when he had fantasized about being a pilot. He was finally about to meet his fantasy.

Beloved by the pilots who flew it and the mechanics who kept it flying, the F-8 has largely been forgotten by history. When a magazine editor asked me to write an article about the airplane, I had only a hazy idea of what an F-8 looked like. After an internet search revealed the Crusader's admirable combat record in Vietnam and the nickname "Last of the Gunfighters," I figured I was just uninformed. After all, I was a flight test engineer in the air force, not a fighter pilot. So I conducted an unscientific poll of three air force fighter pilot friends to see what they knew about the F-8. The results weren't very encouraging:

"Is that a navy plane?" Yes.

"I think it flew mostly air-to-ground." No.

"I don't think it had a very distinguished career." No.

None remembered the nickname Crusader.

The single-engine, single-seat F-8 was the navy's answer to the air force's sleek supersonic air superiority stud, the F-100. Airborne, the two aircraft performed similarly; they were about the same size and used the same engine. But the navy had to slow its speedster enough to land on the deck of an aircraft carrier, a problem the air force didn't have. Even with long runways, the F-100 could be a handful; the original aircraft touched down on the runway at speeds above 180 miles per hour. After many locked brakes and blown tires, the F-100's manufacturer, North American Aviation, added flaps to later models.

North American proposed a carrier version of the F-100 for the navy's F-8 competition, but Vought Aircraft prevailed in the battle of blue prints and engineering calculations. Vought's design proposed an effective, if somewhat inelegant, solution to the carrier landing: a "variable incidence wing" hinged at the rear that adjusted the angle of the wing relative to the fuselage, giving the aircraft more lift when needed for the critical phases of takeoff and landing.

In March 1955 the F-8 prototype was disassembled at the Vought plant on an airfield in Dallas, loaded onto a C-124 cargo aircraft, and flown to Edwards Air Force Base. The air force had been flying the supersonic F-100 for nearly two years by then, and test pilot Jon Konrad made sure the navy caught up quickly: he pushed the F-8 past Mach 1 during its first flight on March 25.[2]

The Crusader's main job was to stomp Soviet MiGs. To do the job, the F-8 had four 20 mm cannons, two heat-seeking Sidewinder missiles, and thirty-two rockets. Sen. John Glenn, who flew the F-8 as a marine test pilot, became an immediate fan.[3] When I interviewed him in 2015, he lamented having to fly the F-86 in Korea instead of the F-8. The four cannons would have easily outgunned the MiG-15, and although the F-8 had about the same turning capability as the MiG, Glenn believed the Crusader would have the upper hand in controlling an air battle because it could go higher and faster.

The F-8 wasn't flawless; Glenn ran into problems with the cannons during the development program. The guns were mounted to the engine duct, two on each side. Firing the guns individually worked fine, but when he tried firing all four together in a two-second burst, the duct flexed and bullets sprayed forward randomly, like a beginner who hasn't learned how to hold a pistol steady. There was no way a pilot could count on hitting anything. Later aircraft had a beefed-up duct, but the initial solution was to send what Glenn called a cross-eyed airplane to the fleet. To make up for the flexing, engineers adjusted the boresight that aimed each gun so it looked to the opposite side of the airplane: the guns mounted on the left looked right, and vice versa. After firing the gun a few more times, engineers averaged out the errors to make final boresight adjustments.[4]

In the spirit of inter-service rivalry, the Crusader began snatching records held by the F-100 and garnering prizes such as the

Collier Trophy, a prestigious award presented each year by the National Aeronautic Association. It went to the F-100's designer, James Kindelberger, in 1953. In 1956 the entire Vought and navy design and development teams took home the award for the F-8's innovative design and for the fact that it became the first operational aircraft to fly faster than one thousand miles per hour.[5]

The same year the F-8 also set a speed record of 1,015 miles per hour over a closed course at China Lake, smashing the F-100 record of 822 miles per hour from the previous year. The air force was impressed enough to give the F-8 an air force award for speed, the Thompson Trophy. The triumph was short-lived: the following year the air force grabbed the record and trophy back, flying 1,207 miles per hour in an F-101, a slightly newer fighter than the F-100. When the trophy was retired in 1961, the F-8 was the only navy airplane to win.[6]

In 1957 Glenn flew an F-8 nonstop West Coast–to–East Coast using afterburner power for the entire trip, except when he pulled back the throttle to slow down three times for in-flight refueling. He crossed the country in three hours and twenty-three minutes. Glenn convinced his superiors that the flight would be an excellent way to demonstrate the ruggedness of the F-8's engine, but a hidden benefit was that the project stole the transcontinental speed record from the air force.[7] The gloating didn't last long: an air force F-101 snagged the record again a few months later.

The Crusader entered the U.S. Navy and Marine Corps fleets in the late 1950s. Pilots couldn't wait to fly the F-8, although emotions during their first flights in the jet ranged from sheer exhilaration to sheer terror. There were no simulators in those days. And there was no second seat for an instructor. A new pilot just strapped into the jet and hoped he got it right. Pilots who had never flown an airplane with an afterburner before had to be extra careful: instead of rumbling many thousands of feet down the runway before becoming airborne, the F-8 leaped into the air like a jackrabbit.[8] Once airborne, things didn't slow down. Pilots had to push the nose down and raise the landing gear before they sped past 220 knots, or they risked damage to the gear. They also had to bring the variable incidence wing back down so it was flush with the fuselage.

If takeoffs were exciting and busy, landings were another thing altogether. After many landing accidents, especially by inexperienced pilots, the aircraft gained a reputation as an "ensign killer."[9] Even with the variable incidence wing, the F-8 flew much faster during approaches to land than other carrier aircraft. The higher touchdown speed wrecked a lot of the lightweight landing gear installed on early F-8s. To make matters worse, the port strut held the reservoir for hydraulic fluid. If a pilot damaged the landing gear during a bolter, the hydraulic fluid drained out as he flew around for another try at landing. The aircraft reverted to a backup hydraulic system to keep the flight controls working, but if the backup system failed, it was time to eject.

The landing gear was crucial, and so was the tailhook. On early aircraft both broke regularly. While landing in 1957 on the USS *Hancock*, John Miottel broke the tailhook off his jet when he touched down. With no hook to grab a wire, he was quickly airborne again. But he couldn't land on the carrier without a tailhook. His superiors decided he should fly his disabled F-8 into a barricade on the flight deck designed to stop an airplane in an emergency like Miottel's. The barricade resembled a twenty-foot-tall tennis net—except this net had to stop twenty tons of metal traveling at 150 miles per hour (fig. 8). Miottel flew a normal approach, slammed onto the deck, and headed into the barricade. Everything seemed fine, until the barricade tore off the F-8's left landing gear. The Crusader pivoted on its left wingtip and veered off the port side of the carrier. Ejecting at that point would have been deadly, but Miottel kept his wits about him; as he plunged toward the ocean, he jettisoned his canopy and yanked a handle that released him from the ejection seat. He survived, and in addition to a good "war story," he made up a joke: "The old aviator's maxim that 'Any landing you can walk away from is a good landing' was amended to incorporate the words 'or swim.'"[10]

Other pilots also had tailhook problems with the F-8. In 1960, during a night landing on the USS *Saratoga* during a Mediterra-

FIG. 8. Unlike John Miottel's unsuccessful recovery, this F-8E was
stopped by the barrier "net" on the USS *Ticonderoga* in 1967.
(Courtesy Wikimedia Commons, U.S. Navy photo)

nean cruise, Bob Shumaker couldn't get his tailhook to come
down. Operations personnel on the carrier told him to fly to Italy
for a landing, but he didn't have enough fuel.

"Find the tanker then," radioed a voice from the *Saratoga*.

With his heart beating a little faster, Shumaker found the tanker
in the inky sky. As he pulled up to get more fuel, someone on the
tanker called and said, "I'm flipping every switch in here, but I
can't get the hose to come out."

Shumaker returned to the carrier for his last hope at landing:
the net barricade that had tried to grab Miottel's jet a few years
earlier. But the Green Shirts couldn't get the net to come up.

Shumaker was down to his last option: his Martin-Baker ejection seat. He climbed to three thousand feet and pulled the ejection handle. At that altitude and flying straight ahead, the ejection
should have been as routine as ejections can be. But after he sep-
arated from the seat, his parachute didn't open. Shumaker exe-

cuted his well-rehearsed emergency procedure: he yanked the D-ring to manually deploy the chute. Nothing happened. With the water racing toward him, he pulled harder. The chute finally opened. A nearby destroyer picked him up and returned him to the carrier via a highline, an inglorious end to his flight.[11]

The Crusader had other ways to kill pilots. The fighter's swept-back wings made the aircraft faster, but they also made it easier to lose control of the airplane and harder to recover. Shumaker had almost bailed out of an F-8 years earlier, when he pushed a Crusader too far during his training. He had climbed to fifty-five thousand feet to avoid clouds. He tried to turn around, but in the thin air, the flight controls no longer worked well. The airplane spun out of control and entered the clouds he had been so desperate to avoid. Regaining control of a spinning sweptwing aircraft is a difficult maneuver even for test pilots who can see the ground, but after losing about twenty-five thousand feet in altitude, Shumaker managed to move the flight controls in the right way to get out of the spin.[12]

The F-8 could also kill unwary mechanics. When a pilot started the engine on the flight deck, the intake was down so low that no one could walk anywhere near the front of the jet. More than once, someone got sucked into the intake. If they were lucky, someone nearby would race over to grab the guy's ankles and signal the pilot to shut down.[13] Maintenance personnel had to crawl down the twenty-foot-long engine duct on occasion, and sometimes, as a joke, someone would whistle through the tailpipe, scaring the man inside half to death as he scrambled out of what he thought was an engine start.

Once airborne, the Crusader was a joy, although intercepting airborne targets like MiGs required a lot of art. The F-8's first-generation radar could only see a target from about eight miles, so a controller on the ground or a ship called out the direction and distance of a target to the Crusader pilot, who then had to figure out how to fly close enough to the target to pick it up on his plane's radar. F-8 pilots spent a lot of time training in various intercept techniques.[14]

The jet was ready for war by the time Willie arrived at Miramar in October 1964; most of the bugs had been worked out. A reconnaissance version, the RF-8, was also available. The new F-8E model that Willie trained in could carry four thousand pounds of external weapons such as bombs, giving the aircraft an air-to-ground mission in addition to air superiority. Short-statured Red Shirts weren't enamored with bombs on a high-wing aircraft, though. It might take ten guys standing on tiptoe struggling to load a five hundred–pound bomb.[15]

Willie was anxious to try out the F-8. But before he and the other trainees could get anywhere near the jet, they had to sit through forty hours of ground training on its systems and pass a survival course. The survival training included how to get out of a disabled jet, how to stay alive afterward, and how to avoid the enemy while doing so. Pilots initiated an ejection from the F-8 by yanking on one or both looped handles attached to the seat above the pilot's head. The loops also pulled a canvas "face curtain" from the top of the seat down and over the pilot's helmet and visor for additional protection. If the pilot couldn't reach above his head, a second handle was attached to the seat between the pilot's legs. However, the face curtain made the upper handles the preferred ejection method.

The Martin-Baker MK-F5 ejection seat could be a lifesaver, but it was no panacea, Willie learned. For the seat to work properly, the airplane had to be at least fifty feet above the ground and flying at least 120 knots. Ejection seats in the early 1960s had relatively narrow windows of survivability, and many pilots were killed or seriously injured during ejections. High-speed ejections were, and still are, a problem, although the MK-F5's designers came up with a way to reduce flail injuries caused by the windblast: canvas garters above and below the pilot's knees that clipped into the seat and pulled his legs in during an ejection. Aviators called the garters "pilot spurs" because the metal fittings jangled as they walked.

Willie practiced an ejection in a ground trainer. He followed the instructor's directions to flatten his body into the proper position—head pressed back against the seat, arms and legs tucked in. He pulled the handles and got a kick in the butt that shot him about thirty feet up a set of rails. He felt as if he'd been rear-ended in a car. This "ejection" didn't involve a parachute; the seat stopped at the top of the rails before gently lowering him to the ground.

Willie's practice ejection mirrored my own initial training in many ways. I, too, strapped into a generic ejection seat and, as instructed, sat up as straight as I could and pushed my head firmly against the back of the seat. I then yanked on two ejection handles on the outside of my legs and shot about fifteen feet into the air on a set of rails. Even with what I thought was good posture and a jolt that seemed no worse than a hard landing in an airplane, my head snapped forward. Nothing bad happened—my neck wasn't even sore afterward—but it made me realize that ejections could be dangerous, though less dangerous than staying with a crippled airplane.

During "hanging harness" training, an instructor suspended me about three feet above the ground in the harness that would normally attach me to an ejection seat. I had to pretend I had just ejected. The instructor barked scenarios at me that I had to respond to either verbally or with actions:

"You've got a partially collapsed chute."

"Look for the line that wound over the top and pull it loose."

"You're landing in trees."

Visor down for more protection. Release the survival kit so it doesn't tangle me up in a tree. Put my hands up over my neck for extra protection.

"Landing on flat ground. Get ready to land."

I put my hands on the chest fittings that attached my harness to the parachute so I could get rid of it quickly in case of high winds. Don't want to survive the landing only to have the chute drag me across the desert or ocean at thirty miles per hour. Put my legs together, knees slightly bent, for the landing.

The instructor released me from the ropes holding me in the air. As I hit the ground, I fell on the side of my right calf and then my hip—a "parachute landing fall," designed to absorb the shock of the ground impact to protect my back.

The training was a lot of fun. We trained in groups and learned from our mistakes, laughing at our miserable parachute landing falls. The instructors made it look so easy. It was, after dozens of practice landings and a few bruises.

There was so much to remember, so many decisions to make. Would I remember it all? Would I make the right decisions?

Aircrew members who survived ejections reassured me that I would. In addition to being some of the best stories at the bar in the officer's club, ejection tales made for impromptu teaching moments. Some aviators related stories in excruciating detail, especially when fueled by a few shots of whiskey. Others recited "just the facts, ma'am" renditions. Most readily admitted mistakes they had made, and those of us listening learned from their experiences. Every story added at least one more piece of information that I filed away, hoping I might recall it someday if needed.

I even learned a bit about what a real ejection might feel like. A coworker who ejected from the back seat of an F-100 told me he was so sore the next few days that he could barely walk. As he recounted his tale, I remembered when a driver rear-ended my car on a freeway at about forty miles per hour. For several days afterward my body ached so badly that I couldn't pick up a ten-pound gym bag. That's what an ejection could do.

My survival training included two days of hiking and camping in mountainous terrain, where we learned the essentials of navigating by compass and how to signal for help. During another day of water survival training on a lake, I was attached by my harness to a speedboat and dragged through the water at about thirty miles per hour to simulate a splash-down in windy conditions. I felt like I had swallowed a gallon of water before I finally managed to unlatch my harness to get rid of the "parachute." Then I climbed into a giant yellow raft, which proved much more difficult than it looked, especially for those, like me, with little upper body strength.

Willie's survival training was similar to mine, but it focused on combat: how to evade enemy capture and, if captured, how to resist interrogation and torture and try to escape. The pilots knew this was serious stuff: the North Vietnamese had already shot down two dozen U.S. aircraft in a few months and had taken a navy pilot prisoner, Lt. (Junior Grade) Everett Alvarez.[16] The trainees were about to get a taste of his fate.

On the first day of survival school, the instructors loaded the pilots on a bus and dropped them on a hilltop. They had to pick their way through the terrain to the bottom of the hill without being "captured" by the instructors. Most of them failed. Willie wasn't captured, but he still wound up on a bus to the next stop, a fake POW camp complete with huts, guard towers, barbed wire fences, and guards speaking in foreign accents. The instructors tormented pilots with a starvation diet and interrogations. Willie got slapped in the face a few times.

The trainees were encouraged to escape, just as they would if they were real POWs. Each time the instructors shuffled the students to different enclosures, they looked for new escape opportunities. At one point Willie found himself with two others in a six-foot dome with a kind of doggy door at the bottom. When the "captors" came, Willie braced himself with his arms and legs between the walls and above the doggy door so that the instructors didn't notice him. They left with the other two "POWs." Apparently forgetting there were supposed to be three trainees, they neglected to lock the door. Willie escaped, but under the training rules of engagement, he had to turn himself in. Before he went back to "prison," he was praised and given a ham sandwich.

After survival school Willie began his official training on the F-8. He learned about a mind-numbing litany of systems—engine, electrical, fuel, hydraulic, pneumatic, variable incidence wing, and flight controls—along with emergency procedures, flight characteristics, and operating limitations such as the Crusader's maximum speed and altitude.

As in his previous training, exams were unending, checking Willie's knowledge of the F-8's operating limits, aircraft systems, and both normal and emergency procedures. Much of the information, especially operating limits and some emergency procedures, had to be memorized. Other information could be obtained at a more leisurely pace from a checklist or the F-8's flight manual.

Each step in becoming an F-8 pilot built on knowledge and experience gained in the previous step. After the book training, it was off to a procedures trainer, a mockup of the F-8 cockpit. Willie pretended to start his engine, taxi, takeoff, and land, pushing buttons and calling out imaginary instrument readings such as oil pressure and airspeed. He also practiced emergency procedures: what to do if the hydraulic system failed or the engine quit or he had an electrical problem.

From there Willie sat in an F-8 cockpit blindfolded with an instructor standing next to him on a ladder. Willie had to identify every critical item by feel and location: throttle, wing lock and unlock mechanism, and tailhook and gear handles. He had to find everything even if he couldn't see it, in case he had to land in a smoke-filled cockpit.

On December 3, 1965, Willie started an F-8's engine and taxied to the runway. His instructor was in another F-8 to watch over him and give advice. It was the first time Willie had taken off alone in an airplane he had not flown before. He pushed the throttle to the "military" power setting—the most thrust the engine produced without the afterburner—and scanned his instruments to make sure everything looked good. He released the brakes and shot down the runway like a cannonball. His instructor followed in wingtip formation a few feet to one side and behind him. The Crusader jumped into the air and wanted to climb when it should have still been accelerating. Willie pushed his control stick forward and rolled in some nose-down trim to keep the nose from coming up, but it still wasn't enough. He kept pushing the nose down and rolling in more trim until he realized he needed to get the gear up before he went much faster. He moved the gear handle up and looked back into the cockpit to move the wing lever. When the cockpit instruments indicated gear up, wing down, and both safely locked in place, he looked outside again.

Once Willie was comfortable in his new airplane, he learned to fly combat missions. Part of that involved searching for enemy aircraft and positioning himself to shoot the enemy down. Willie had to be behind a target to fire the F-8's gun to best effect or launch an AIM-9D heat-seeking missile designed to fly into the other aircraft's red-hot engine tailpipe and explode.

Learning how to maneuver to the rear of an enemy, while keeping the other aircraft from doing the same thing to him, was crucial. Early on he learned an important lesson. An instructor walked him to the back of his jet and pointed at the gigantic rudder and vertical fin that poked almost fifteen feet into the air.

"That rudder is your best weapon in a dogfight."

The instructor showed Willie how to adjust his rudder pedals so he could fully deflect the rudder and wring from it every last ounce of performance. A quarter-inch of movement or less, an almost imperceptible movement, might save his life someday.

Willie learned to use the rudder to his advantage—if he pushed on the rudder pedals with his feet just right, he could point the Crusader's nose anywhere he wanted it to go, even at slow speeds, when most airplanes are sluggish. It's a maxim of air combat that the pilot who can still point the nose when the airplane is about to fall out of the sky has the advantage. Willie soon discovered what John Glenn had learned nearly a decade earlier: as long as he didn't lose control of the aircraft, the F-8 had a real advantage over just about every other fighter out there.

Throughout his two years of flying training, Willie, like most aviators, also learned to avoid the flight surgeon, those specialists who monitor aviators, give them annual physicals, treat them for minor ailments, and follow up after treatments by other doctors. The physiology of the flight environment demands that aviators be in top physical condition. High altitudes make breathing difficult, high g-forces can cause a pilot to black out, and dehydration, long flights, and aircraft with only one pilot on board push human limits in an unforgiving environment. Even a cold can keep an aviator from flying. Taking anything stronger than an aspirin tablet before flight is at best frowned upon and at worst against regulations.

A small minority of aviators run to the flight surgeon for every scratch or sniffle, but most won't set a foot in the flight doc's office unless they have an appointment for a routine physical or they are about to die. All professional aviators are only one failed physical or one seemingly minor problem away from having their careers ruined. Avoidance of the flight surgeon can reach epic proportions, as I learned early in my air force career.

In the mid-1980s I lived in the Bachelor Officers' Quarters at Edwards Air Force. One Sunday evening I developed indigestion a few hours before bedtime. I'd had indigestion two or three times previously in my life; each time I had been dehydrated, and the problem cleared up after a few glasses of water. This evening, though, water didn't do the trick, and by midnight I was in agony, so much pain that I worried it might be appendicitis. I debated driving a couple of miles to the emergency room on base, but flight surgeon avoidance syndrome kicked in. If I went to the ER and there was nothing wrong with me other than indigestion, I would still be expected to visit the flight surgeon in the morning. At a minimum it would be a hassle, and worst case, the flight doc might decide to ground me for additional observation or further tests. I couldn't risk that. On the other hand, if my appendix burst in the middle of the night, I might die. But even the thought of dying wasn't enough to propel me to the ER.

After tossing and turning for another hour as I debated the pros and cons of the ER, I recalled an old Alka-Seltzer commercial—plop, plop, fizz, fizz, oh what a relief it is. Might that work? But where to get Alka-Seltzer? Everything at Edwards had been closed for hours. The nearest town, Rosamond, was twenty miles away. If the town's mini-market wasn't open, I'd have to drive another fifteen miles to Lancaster. What if I got sicker and had to pull off the road? There were no cell phones in those days; it might be hours before someone found me.

Then I remembered that the base's billeting office—the military term for a hotel reception desk—was open twenty-four hours a day. They sold small items like toothpaste, candy, and yes, over-the-counter meds. Ten minutes later I dissolved the precious tablets in water and drank it; the pain disappeared within minutes.

After that experience I always kept Alka-Seltzer in my medicine cabinet.

In the early morning of February 7, 1965, Viet Cong sappers attacked two American bases in South Vietnam, killing eight Americans.[17] Pres. Lyndon B. Johnson ordered a retaliatory attack, Flaming Dart I, against targets in North Vietnam. Twenty aircraft from the USS *Coral Sea* and twenty-nine aircraft from the USS *Hancock* attacked barracks and port facilities at Dong Hoi, just north of the demilitarized zone. One A-4 from the *Coral Sea* was shot down during the attack. The pilot ejected but was either killed during the ejection or died shortly afterward.[18] On February 11 Flaming Dart II took place, and Bob Shumaker, now a lieutenant commander flying off the *Coral Sea*, got the call for his first ever combat mission to attack barracks at Chanh Hoa near Dong Hoi. Flying low because of weather, Shumaker had just rolled in on his target when antiaircraft artillery smashed into the tail of his F-8D. The Crusader flipped upside down. Shumaker barely had time to pull the ejection handle. His parachute opened about thirty-five feet above the ground, and he broke his back in the subsequent hard landing.[19] He hid in some nearby bushes, but North Vietnamese soldiers captured him an hour later.[20]

Two days later President Johnson authorized airstrikes on North Vietnam, kicking off a three-year bombing campaign called Operation Rolling Thunder.[21] U.S. military leadership had originally envisioned unlimited airstrikes that would devastate the North Vietnamese. But Johnson and Sec. of Defense Robert McNamara liked the idea of using air power in a more controlled fashion.[22] Worried about potential Chinese or Soviet intervention, the political leadership preferred warfare that would send a message to Hanoi but could be scaled back if needed.[23] Air power also was attractive because it would require far fewer military personnel than an invading army.[24]

The original intent of Rolling Thunder was one of strategic persuasion, but it quickly became obvious that the North Vietnamese weren't being persuaded. By the summer of 1965 the campaign had turned away from bombing a handful of industrial targets such as power plants and factories and toward attacking roads, railroads, and bridges the North Vietnamese used to move supplies south for Viet Cong forces.[25] It would not be the last shift in U.S. strategy.

Each week U.S. commanders in Vietnam recommended target sets. These recommendations were passed in turn through the commander in chief, Pacific Command, in Honolulu to the Joint Chiefs of Staff at the Pentagon. Next they went to the State Department for approval. The State Department sent the list back to the Joint Chiefs, who handed it off to the White House. Johnson and his advisors reviewed the list during a Tuesday luncheon and approved the final targets.[26] This torturous process continued for the next three years as Rolling Thunder's focus changed from interdiction to oil storage facilities and to industrial facilities, with pauses in between intended to give Hanoi time to consider entering into negotiations.[27] Unfortunately, Ho Chi Minh never seemed to hear the message U.S. leaders were trying to send.

In the United States protests against the building conflict in Southeast Asia began a few weeks after the United States dropped its first bombs on targets in North Vietnam. On March 24 two hundred faculty members at the University of Michigan led a twelve-hour "teach-in" with seventeen hundred attendees. Young Republicans picketed the protesters. The building where the teach-in was held and a dormitory hosting other protest activities were briefly evacuated for bomb threats. Students voiced concerns over their perceptions of U.S. meddling in the self-determination of the Vietnamese people. The protest received little attention at first; the New York Times buried the story on page 9.[28]

On May 15 twenty-nine demonstrators sat down on Fifth Avenue in New York to block an Armed Forces Day parade. The incident made the front page. Police arrested the protesters, who were sponsored by a pacifist group called the "New York Workshop in Nonviolence." One bystander called the protesters "commies," and another advocated beating and kicking their brains in.[29] Less than a week later, police in Chicago arrested forty demonstrators who tied up downtown traffic for nine minutes. Clark Kissinger, from the Students for a Democratic Society, gave a short speech, while nearby construction workers yelled, "Why don't you get a job?"[30]

U.S. military aircrews tried to ignore politics and the protests swirling about them. They had a job to do, even if they had no idea why politicians in Washington picked the targets they did and restricted their ability to do things, such as not allowing attacks around Hanoi and Haiphong Harbor early in the campaign.[31]

With the kickoff of Rolling Thunder, air force aircraft poured into Southeast Asia, along with additional navy ships and aircraft carriers. The USS *Bon Homme Richard*, a San Diego–based carrier, originally scheduled for a Mediterranean cruise in 1965, was shifted to the South China Sea.[32]

My father and other F-100 pilots from the 615th Tactical Fighter Squadron (TFS) at England Air Force Base arrived at Da Nang in March to relieve the 613th TFS pilots already there. In addition to Bill Martin's loss the previous November, Maj. Robert Ronca had been shot down and killed on February 19, 1965. In Ronca's honor pilots back at England had performed a "missing man" flyover: four F-100s flew low over the base, and one of them pulled up and away from the rest of the formation. My father had experienced the loss of many squadron mates during his twelve years in the air force, but Ronca's flyover was the first time he saw the missing man formation. Before the war was over, he would see many more.

On June 12, just two weeks before the 615th pilots were scheduled to rotate back to the United States, two F-100 pilots took off for a close air support mission to help army troops in a battle with Viet Cong forces in the southern part of South Vietnam. As Capt. Lawrence Holland fired rockets at enemy gun positions and buildings, he was hit by ground fire. He ejected and landed in trees. An army helicopter landed in a nearby clearing to pick him up. Several crew members headed on foot into the jungle to find Holland. As they approached, they heard gunshots and saw Viet Cong dragging the pilot's body into a ditch. He was never heard from or seen again.[33]

Holland's wingman witnessed the scene from the air. Distraught at the loss of his flight lead and low on fuel, he chose to land at nearby Bien Hoa Air Base. When he called back to the squadron at Da Nang, the squadron commander decided the wingman needed a few days off before he flew again. My father was dispatched the next day with another pilot in a two-seat F-100F to bring the wingman and his airplane home to Da Nang.

By the time of Holland's shoot-down in mid-1965, the budding CSAR capabilities brought in by Alan Saunders in 1964 had started to mature. Albatrosses operating from Da Nang Air Base had a brief heyday in 1965 rescuing pilots who bailed out over the Gulf of Tonkin. Rescues in the Gulf sometimes had to deal with hostile fire from shore or automatic rifle fire from fishing boats, but aviators who ejected over water were far more likely to survive than those who ejected over North Vietnam. It was much easier to find and identify a man floating in the open water than one swallowed up by a jungle crawling with North Vietnamese or Viet Cong. Less time looking for someone meant more time to pick them up.[34]

Rescue coordinators adopted tactics similar to those used in Korea. HU-16s flew daily from sunrise to sunset. The early shift departed Da Nang just before sunrise and orbited in a racetrack pattern about twenty miles off the coast of North Vietnam until noon; a later shift orbited from noon until sunset. At first, to avoid radar detection and surface-to-air missiles, the HU-16 pilots orbited only fifty feet above the water. The aircraft was so low that when pilots turned around at the endpoint of each loop, they had to briefly climb so they wouldn't hit the water with their wingtip. Then someone pointed out that flying so low left a huge wake in the water, making the Albatross position obvious. After that pilots orbited at a more leisurely altitude of two thousand feet and only descended for a rescue.[35]

The HU-16's navigator helped maintain the aircraft's position using a radio navigation aid, the TACAN, carried aboard a navy destroyer in the Gulf. But the technique wasn't foolproof. One day, as an Albatross orbited above a broken cloud deck, one of the pilots, Capt. David Wendt, looked down between some holes in the clouds and glimpsed land.

Land! They must be over North Vietnam!

The pilots turned east, pushed the throttles to max power, and beat feet back to the Gulf as fast as they could at an agonizingly slow 150 miles per hour. It turned out the destroyer they were using as a navigation aid was in the wrong place.[36]

As the Albatross flew its pattern, armed aircraft orbited near them in a Rescue Combat Air Patrol (RESCAP). They couldn't pick anyone up but could use their guns to ward off hostile boats or land forces that might converge on the downed aircrew. RESCAP aircraft were any available aircraft that could attack ground targets; one day they might be Spads and another day the U.S. military's latest fighter aircraft, the F-4.[37] The older Spads were best for RESCAP. A low-and-slow-flying Spad pilot could spot ground targets more easily than a pilot in the faster jets. The Spad, officially called an A-1 Skyraider, usually carried more ammunition than a jet, could loiter for what seemed like forever, and, with its armor-plated underbelly, could take a huge amount of punishment from small arms fire. These traits made the Spad perfect at keeping lightly armed hostile forces at bay until an Albatross or rescue helicopter arrived.

If an aircraft went down, the pilot's wingman broadcast his position over the radio. The Albatross and RESCAP aircraft headed toward the location. The speedier RESCAP aircraft usually arrived over the downed aircrew first. They fired warning shots across the bow of any threatening sampans or junks and shot the boat if it kept approaching.[38]

Navy helicopters were sometimes available if a carrier was nearby, but the faster and better-positioned Albatross usually beat any helos to the scene.[39] However, if survivors weren't in immediate danger and a helicopter was available, Albatross crews usually waited for the helo to make the pickup. The helicopter was the preferred pickup aircraft for several reasons. The HU-16 was much sturdier than the World War II Catalina, but water landings still weren't risk free. Also, the HU-16 couldn't land on the carrier, so they returned navy pilots to Da Nang; the navy then had to send an aircraft to retrieve its pilot. In addition, the Albatross acted as an airborne command and control aircraft for rescue missions, keeping track of everyone and directing other aircraft to maximize effectiveness. If an HU-16 crew left the action to make a pickup, either another Albatross had to launch from Da Nang or the mission kept going without a command and control aircraft. In addition to relaying messages, the Albatross crew might also drop a smoke light, a flare that belched out smoke, to help the helicopter find the downed pilot. In some cases the Albatross crew dropped the smoke light some distance away from the pilot and circled about the smoke to deceive anyone watching from shore or an approaching boat. Despite the preference for helicopters, an Albatross crew wouldn't hesitate to rescue survivors in danger. Even when a helicopter made the pickup, the Albatross crew remained on station until the pilot was safe.[40]

In 1965, however, few helos were available for overwater rescues near North Vietnam. Air force helicopters at Da Nang operated exclusively over land, and navy helicopters stayed near their carriers, often too far from a downed pilot to be of much use. During 1965 air force Albatross crews rescued thirty-five U.S. aircrew members and one South Vietnamese pilot from the Gulf. Almost half were navy aircrew, including five F-8 pilots.[41]

Willie and Nina's first child, a girl, was born on April 1, 1965. Willie had little time to bond with his new baby. He had been assigned to fighter squadron VF-191 and would soon be joining the USS *Bon Homme Richard*, the carrier that had been diverted from the Mediterranean to the Gulf of Tonkin because of the widening war. Before he could report, he had to finish his training, including carrier qualification in the F-8. But there were no carriers left in San Diego to train on. The only available carriers were on the other side of the country.

A few days after Nina gave birth, Willie and the other F-8 trainees flew their aircraft to Cecil Field near Jacksonville, Florida. For the first week they practiced day and night approaches on a runway. Willie had yet to land an aircraft on a carrier at night; the F-8 would be his first. For that matter he hadn't landed any aircraft on any carrier since his last T-2 flight almost a year earlier.

As he had in pilot training, Willie talked to himself all the way around the traffic pattern and down final approach during any landing. In the F-8 he developed a procedure that worked almost every time. As he rolled out on final, he made small adjustments to track the centerline of the runway.

"Line up," he said, to remind himself to stay on the centerline.

"Airspeed." A reminder to check his airspeed and a light called a "donut" that indicated the F-8's angle of attack—the difference between the angle the nose was pointed upward and the angle the aircraft was descending. If he was a little fast, he pulled back slightly on the control stick to slow the airplane; if he was a little slow, he pushed forward slightly.

"Glideslope." The last reminder was to make sure he was still on the ball, not too high, not too low. Too high, he pulled back on the throttle a bit to reduce power; too low, he added power.

"Line up, airspeed, glideslope."

"Line up, airspeed, glideslope."

Listen for advice from the landing signal officer. At night the F-8's nose gear had lights the LSO used to help see where the aircraft was.

"Line up, airspeed, glideslope."

Then a slam onto the runway and back up for another try.

After almost two weeks of practice, the pilots flew to the USS *Forrestal* in the Atlantic Ocean for actual carrier landings. Willie made eight daytime landings on April 22 and four days later made his first night carrier landing. Landing at night was a lot scarier than landing during the day. At night he could see only two things: the meatball and the centerline and edge lights on the flight deck. But Willie trusted the ball completely. He was rewarded with the now familiar smash onto the flight deck followed by a screeching halt. With a little more practice, Willie found that night landings were in some ways easier than day landings: since he couldn't see much, there were fewer distractions. But he never lost his fear of crashing into the rear of the boat. Night carrier landings would always be the scariest thing he ever did.

Willie was back in Miramar by early May, eager to join his squadron but torn about leaving Nina and their new baby. At least Nina's mother was able to come to San Diego to help. Willie tried to get to know his daughter in two weeks as he packed his bags for an overseas flight to the Philippines, where he would meet up with his carrier. His bags included a gift from Nina: a pistol.

Willie and his fellow pilots had been issued .38 revolvers and had fired them during target practice. Loaded with tracer rounds, the weapon was good as a signaling device, but his new squadron operations officer considered it useless for defense. The officer had held a pre-deployment meeting with the VF-191 squadron wives, including Nina. Knowing their husbands would soon be headed to Vietnam, most of the discussion was about daily aggravations: what to do if a baby got sick or a paycheck didn't show up. He also recommended the wives buy their husbands a small-caliber automatic weapon for better protection if they got shot down. Growing up, Nina had wielded a shotgun plenty of times. She headed to the nearest gun store, where she selected a .22-caliber Ruger automatic pistol with a long barrel. When Willie got home that evening, Nina handed him the gun. The long barrel of the pistol touched the bottom of the left pocket of his survival vest, with the handle aligned exactly with the zipper. In an emergency the Ruger would be easy to grab. The gun was a perfect fit.

5

Bonnie Dick

WILLIE CAUGHT THE THREE WIRE ON HIS FIRST LANDING ON the uss *Bon Homme Richard*. His squadron commander was watching, and Willie knew he would be pleased.

Within a few seconds Willie realized that catching the wire was just the beginning of recovering on an operating carrier. His previous landings had all been on clean decks with little else going on. Landing on the *Bon Homme Richard* was like dropping into a riot in a construction zone. Bright lights glared, and men dashed about wielding lethal-looking tools. In thirty seconds another aircraft would be trying to slam onto the carrier. Willie needed to move away from the landing area and get past the "foul deck line," an alternating red and white line that distinguished the landing area from the rest of the carrier. If he didn't get out of the way, the landing signal officer would call, "Foul deck!" and wave off the next airplane. That airplane then had to go around and rejoin the conga line of other aircraft waiting to get aboard. A waste of gas and time, not to mention the hazard involved in going around.

A Yellow Shirt signaled Willie with a thumbs up into the downward palm of his other hand: raise the tailhook. As the tailhook came up, the cable dropped off and the Yellow Shirt ran a gloved hand along the wire to look for broken strands. Sometimes a cable snagged and refused to come loose from the tailhook; if that happened, another Yellow Shirt darted over to pound the cable loose with a sledgehammer-like tool. Cables can only take a certain number of traps before they have to be replaced, so personnel logged each trap, adding extra landings if the pilot caught the cable off-center or if the airplane weighed more than the cable had been set for. Fortunately, Willie's first real trap didn't have any problems.

After dropping the cable, Willie turned right, crossed the foul deck line, and taxied over to the relative sanctuary of the island, a gargantuan tower of "offices" in the middle of the carrier where staff and leadership watched over operations. Willie was lucky to fly the F-8: the little A-4 Skyhawks, sometimes called "Scooters," didn't have nosewheel steering to turn the aircraft on the ground. After an A-4 pilot dropped his cable, yet another crewman ran over and attached a tiller bar to the nosewheel to guide the Skyhawk out of the way.

As he passed the island, Willie signaled to the maintenance chief, who waited like an expectant father, that his F-8 was fine. Yet another Yellow Shirt signaled him to move to the front part of the carrier, away from the angled deck. Willie kept following the Yellow Shirt, who moved him closer and closer to the carrier's edge. He knew that at some point the Yellow Shirt would signal him to make a U-turn so his engine pointed toward the ocean and the nose of the airplane pointed over the flight deck. Willie inched ahead and glanced down. All he saw was water. For a few seconds of terror, he thought the F-8 was about to plummet over the side of the carrier. He had forgotten that the Crusader's cockpit sat several feet forward of the aircraft's nose gear. Just as Willie was certain he was going overboard, the Yellow Shirt signaled the U-turn. After that Willie trusted the Yellow Shirts fully. He never looked down again when taxiing on the flight deck.

By the mid-1960s the USS *Bon Homme Richard*—or *Bonnie Dick*, as many called it—was past middle age by aircraft carrier standards of the time. Named after a Revolutionary War frigate once under the command of Capt. John Paul Jones, the carrier was launched on April 29, 1944, by Catherine McCain, the grandmother of future senator McCain and wife of Vice Adm. John S. McCain Sr. The carrier arrived in the Pacific theater in June 1945 and participated in air strikes against Japan before the surrender in August. The *Bon Homme Richard* was converted to a troop transport and spent two months returning servicemen to the United States. Decommissioned in January 1947, the carrier came back into service during Korea.[1]

In May 1953 the *Bonnie Dick* once again went out of commission, this time to modify it for jet aircraft. The *Bonnie Dick* was one of several Essex-class carriers retrofitted to extend their service. This retrofit was more than just an update, though; it was the equivalent of adding a second story to an existing ranch house.

The carrier's straight flight deck was replaced with an angled deck.[2] On modern carriers the portion of the deck that runs true to the rest of the ship is used for launches, and the angled portion is used for recoveries. Carriers built during World War II and earlier had a single axial, or straight, deck used for both launching and recovery. The axial deck had already proved problematic even for slower aircraft. If a pilot's tailhook missed the wires during a landing, he crashed into a giant netted barrier strung across the flight deck; there was no room to add power and try again. But if the barrier didn't snare the aircraft, the plane slid forward until it stopped on its own or collided with aircraft, equipment, or people.[3]

With axial decks barely working for World War II era fighters, the navy worried that they wouldn't work at all when jet aircraft arrived. The axial deck was still feasible for early, slow jets but would be more dangerous for newer sweptwing fighters such as the F-8 that were already on the drawing boards. Higher approach speeds meant a reduced margin for error on final approach, which was bad enough. Worse, the barriers would be useless for stopping faster and heavier jets after a missed trap.[4]

In the early 1950s the Royal and U.S. Navies experimented with the idea of an angled deck. With a separate deck for recoveries, an aircraft that boltered could simply add power and fly around for another approach. There would be no danger to personnel and aircraft operating forward of the recovery area. After much experimentation the U.S. Navy decided on a cant angle of 10.5 degrees for the new deck.[5] The *Bonnie Dick* completed its modification at the end of October, 1955.[6]

Fig. 9. The USS *Bon Homme Richard* underway in 1965.
(Courtesy Naval History and Heritage Command, U.S. Navy)

On Saturday, April 3, 1965, sailors aboard the *Bonnie Dick* cast off its mooring lines, and the carrier departed Navy North Island (fig. 9). Willie, still finishing his training, was not on board. After leaving the harbor, the carrier turned southeastward and began flight operations. For the next six days personnel practiced aircraft launches and recoveries and checked out the carrier's systems, standard operating procedure before a ship departed on a cruise that would last for many months. Getting used to being at sea again after a months-long hiatus took time, and minor injuries were common. On the first day one sailor required stitches after bonking his head on a piece of angle iron, another sailor sprained his right ankle, and yet another injured a finger while mounting a gun. All were treated and returned to duty.[7]

The *Bonnie Dick* arrived back in San Diego on April 8 to begin final preparations for Vietnam. On April 21, at about 11:00 a.m., the carrier headed for Subic Bay, the navy's large port in the Philippines, with a planned stop in Pearl Harbor.[8]

FIG. 10. VF-191 Satan's Kittens aboard the USS *Bon Homme Richard*. Willie is in the front row, *second from right*. (Courtesy Willie Sharp)

Still in San Diego, Willie was anxious to catch up to his new squadron, VF-191, nicknamed "Satan's Kittens," sometimes called "Hell Cats," a nod to the official nickname and the Grumman F-6F Hellcats the squadron flew during World War II (fig. 10). Operating from the USS *Lexington*, Willie's predecessors destroyed six hundred aircraft in the Pacific theater, including sixty-one in a single day.[9] The squadron patch depicted a black cat standing upright and carrying three lightning bolts in its front paws. Technicians who maintained the squadron's life-support equipment— helmets, oxygen masks, G suits, and more—adorned the pilots' helmets with orange tape they cut into a shape that was supposed to be a cat. Instead, it resembled an inebriated jack-o'-lantern. VF-191 was one of two F-8 squadrons on the *Bonnie Dick*; the other was VF-194, nicknamed "Red Lightning." Each squadron started the cruise with eighteen pilots and twelve airplanes.

The second week of May, Willie flew to Travis Air Force Base in Northern California, where he expected to board a Pan Am jet airliner to Clark Air Base in the Philippines. As he waited in the passenger terminal, he heard his name paged: he had become a courier of classified materials. Willie had no idea why he was chosen from the hundreds of military personnel waiting for their flights; perhaps it was the top secret clearance he had received to fly the F-8. As an ensign, it wasn't his job to ask questions. He was issued a .45 automatic pistol and handed a bill of lading for several boxes of materials. After that he boarded a Slick Airways charter flight in a Canadair CL-44, a four-engine propeller-driven airplane about the size of a regional aircraft. Instead of flying nonstop in relative luxury, Willie hopscotched across the Pacific Ocean, sleeping in bunk beds on the plane, stopping once in Alaska and twice in Japan before landing at Clark.

The trip was two days of constant flying, landing, refueling, and taking off again. The pilots took pity on the newly minted naval aviator and let him fly for a bit. At every stop Willie had to unload some of the classified material and fill out paperwork. It was always raining, and when he reboarded the plane, he couldn't change clothes: his luggage had remained on the Pan Am flight. When he finally caught up to his bags at Clark, he found them stored outside. The humidity had mildewed all his clothing, but his shaving kit was fine. He caught a ride to the Bachelor Officers' Quarters at Naval Air Station Cubi Point, which was next to Subic Bay. After a shower and shave, he sent his clothes to the cleaners and settled back for three days to wait for the *Bonnie Dick* to arrive.

While he waited, Willie met up with two squadron mates who had also missed the carrier's departure. The trio constructed huge signs, one saying "VF-191 Rules" and the other "VF-194 Sux." Anything to get a leg up on the rival squadron. On Tuesday, May 18, they checked out a small motorboat from a nearby navy recreation facility and greeted the *Bonnie Dick* as it pulled into port that afternoon.[10] The three pilots furiously waved their signs at anyone paying attention on the flight deck.

A few days later Willie and several other pilots attended a twenty-four-hour-long jungle survival school. The instructor was a Filipino civilian armed only with a machete and a vast knowledge of

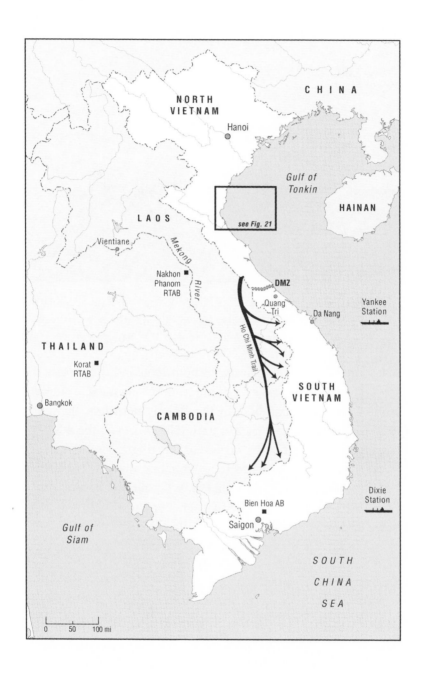

FIG. 11. Map of Southeast Asia in 1965. (Courtesy Erin Greb Cartography)

Fig. 12. An F-8E lands on the USS *Oriskany* in September 1966, similar to Willie's landings on the USS *Bon Homme Richard*. (Courtesy National Archives and Records Administration, U.S. Navy photo)

how to use indigenous plants for both food and nefarious purposes. He demonstrated everything from setting traps to cooking rice in a section of bamboo. By the end of the course, the pilots joked that it would be easier to train Filipinos to fly the F-8 than to teach U.S. pilots how to survive in the jungle.

As the carrier approached the port, pilots already aboard flew the *Bonnie Dick*'s aircraft to Cubi Point. The aircraft needed freshwater baths after spending weeks being splashed with corrosive seawater. Some also required specialized maintenance that carrier personnel couldn't perform. Willie flew two flights from Cubi Point, getting a refresher on his air-to-air combat tactics and making field carrier landing approaches.

After several days of onloading fuel and ammunition, the *Bonnie Dick* departed Subic Bay on Sunday, May 23, about 9:00 a.m., this time with Willie on board. At 11:30 a.m. aircraft operations began as the carrier steamed toward the Gulf of Tonkin (fig. 11).[11] Pilots made refresher launches and recoveries throughout the day and into the night. Willie made his first trap (fig. 12).

Willie made two more catapult launches and one more recovery that day. He then took an F-8 that needed a wash to Cubi Point and returned to the carrier in a different F-8. By now it was dark, and bad weather had moved in. The lights that outlined the carrier seemed to be moving everywhere. Terrified of hitting the back of the ramp, Willie flew too high and with too much power; he missed every wire on his first try. A bolter. Then a second bolter. The air boss directing aircraft activity from the Primary Flight Control (Pri Fly) room in the island radioed Willie to fly back to Cubi Point. It felt like running home with his tail between his legs. The next day he landed back on the carrier with no problems.

Another pilot hadn't been as fortunate. Just before midnight on the first day out of port, an RF-8 pilot made a hard landing, collapsing the nose gear and fracturing his first lumbar vertebra.[12] The RF-8 wasn't seriously damaged, but the pilot's cruise was over. He was replaced by another pilot, Pete Crosby, who soon became the first combat casualty of the cruise.

On May 26 Willie flew his first combat mission, a relatively simple "road recce," a reconnaissance mission to find and shoot enemy vehicles. Tucked in on the wing of a more experienced pilot, the younger pilot followed the leader about five thousand feet above a road just north of the demilitarized zone (DMZ) at the seventeenth parallel. Willie spotted two trucks and aimed his 20 mm cannons at the targets. He squeezed the trigger on his control stick, and the guns responded with "Brrt!" Vibrations coursed briefly through his body, reminding him of the reassuring thrum from his T-34 training days. Both trucks exploded, scattering shrapnel across the road.

"Take that, you fuckers!" Willie screamed as he pulled his jet away from the ground and yanked into a hard turn east toward the Gulf of Tonkin.

No one shot at Willie on his first mission, but he was soon flying regularly into enemy rounds fired from the ground. Every fifth round or so was a tracer containing a bit of explosive that lit up the shell's path. The tracers allowed the person firing the gun to adjust his aim.

On one early mission Willie became mesmerized by the blue

FIG. 13. Willie with Feedbag 108. (Courtesy Willie Sharp)

streaks of tracer rounds. The streaks looked enticing, like a slalom course to a skier at the top of a hill. For a few seconds Willie was sure he could fly through the slalom course in the sky. Then a sobering reality hit. For every tracer he saw, five rounds came at him that he couldn't. The streaks were more like a slalom course peppered with invisible boulders. Somehow he flew through the barrage unscathed.

"You little shits! You missed me!"

Most of the F-8s on the *Bonnie Dick* were only a few years old and had been upgraded with better radar, improved engines and a new missile called the "Bullpup" that a pilot could guide to the ground with a joystick by watching the missile's smoke trail. All carrier aircraft had foot-high numbers painted on the nose. The number was combined with a squadron's call sign to become the unique identifier for that aircraft, whether for talking on the radio or filling out paperwork. Satan's Kittens used the call sign "Feedbag," followed by a number.

Other than different numbers on the nose, the F-8s looked identical. But Willie had learned that no two airplanes, even if they looked the same, flew exactly the same. Although airplanes roll down an assembly line, aircraft are largely pieced together with human hands instead of through automation. This human touch results in airplanes that may fly somewhat differently from each other. Hundreds of hours of combat and maneuvering by inexperienced or overly aggressive pilots can also take a toll.

Some of the Crusaders on the *Bonnie Dick* were sweet and docile. Others had been flown hard and seemed ready to bite at the smallest mistake—an abrupt control stick movement during a hard turn that was inconsequential in one jet might cause small spasms in another. Some airplanes always seemed to have something broken—a piece of equipment not necessarily needed to fly, such as the autopilot, but still annoying. Others were even worse, broken so often they earned reputations as "hangar queens." Within a few weeks Willie decided his favorite steed was Feedbag 108; it was a joy to fly and never seemed to have anything wrong with it (fig. 13).

Willie knew he shouldn't become too attached to Feedbag 108. Pilots are cautioned against heroics to save their expensive aircraft during an emergency; that's what the ejection seat is for. Willie's superiors often told him, "Don't bust your ass, and don't bend an airplane." In other words, don't break an airplane, but if you do, don't kill yourself in the process. An air force mantra is more specific: "We can get another airplane; we can't get another you."

In 1965 a foot high NM was painted on the tails of all *Bonnie Dick* aircraft; the NM was the code for Carrier Air Wing 19, the collection of aircraft and squadrons assigned to the carrier. The Carrier Air Wing commander, commonly called "CAG," was John Tierney. To Willie and the other young pilots, Tierney was like a god. The Delaware native was a graduate of the U.S. Naval Academy, and he had flown A-1s and FJ-3 Fury jets before attending the Naval Test Pilot School.[13] He was as close as a mere mortal could get to John Glenn.

As the boss, Tierney flew both A-4s and F-8s (fig. 14). His official airplane was numbered "00" and had a distinctive red nose.

FIG. 14. A Satan's Kittens F-8E prepares for a catapult launch while an A-4C rises on the elevator. (Courtesy Wikimedia Commons, U.S. Navy photo)

Regardless of what airplane he flew, his call sign was "Rocket 88," an apparent reference to the Oldsmobile Rocket 88 and an Ike Turner hit song from the 1950s.

Each carrier squadron flew one type of aircraft. Besides the two F-8 fighter squadrons, the *Bonnie Dick* carried three attack squadrons: VA-192 and VA-195, with fourteen A-4C Skyhawks each; and VA-196, with twelve A-1 Spads. Like other carriers, the *Bonnie Dick* also had a menagerie of support aircraft: the RF-8A reconnaissance version of the F-8, UH-2 Seasprite helicopters, and electronic warfare aircraft that helped detect and jam enemy radars. One of the electronic warfare aircraft was the EA-1F, a four-seat version of the Spad, affectionately referred to as a "Queer Spad."[14] A navy commander who reported to Tierney led each squadron; a squadron commander was also called a "skipper." The squadron commander's deputy was officially an "executive officer," usually abbreviated as XO.

The *Bonnie Dick* operated in an area in the South China Sea dubbed "Yankee Station," southeast of Da Nang (in 1966 Yankee Station was moved north of the DMZ).[15] The carrier was accompanied by guided missile frigates and destroyers that rotated in and out of the formation on different days.[16] The frigates and destroyers often operated closer to the North Vietnamese coastline to protect the carriers. The smaller ships carried powerful radars, sonar, surface-to-air missiles (SAMS), and torpedoes so they could detect and destroy both air and submarine threats.[17] A destroyer or frigate also always remained near each carrier to act as a "plane guard," ready to help pull someone out of the water during a launch or recovery accident.

Five days after Willie's first combat sortie, the *Bonnie Dick* had its first combat loss. Aircraft from the *Midway* and *Bonnie Dick* attacked the Dong Phong Thanh Bridge in North Vietnam. Lt. Cdr. Pete Crosby, who had just replaced the RF-8 pilot injured in the hard landing, flew over the bridge to take pictures of the results. He was only a few hundred feet above the ground, skimming underneath a deck of clouds, when enemy ground fire hit his aircraft. Crosby was too low to attempt an ejection. His wingman saw the RF-8 roll onto its back and crash into a hillside. Crosby left behind a wife, three sons, and a daughter.[18] The Dong Phong Thanh Bridge would be a capable nemesis throughout the war; the bridge was unsuccessfully attacked so many times that pilots grimly joked the span must be reinforced with wing spars and ejection seats culled from all the downed aircraft. Crosby's death was Willie's first experience losing a fellow pilot; he was surprised at the mixture of relief and guilt he felt. Relief that it hadn't been him. Guilt that his squadron hadn't protected the pilot.

Loss is an inevitable part of combat, but fortunately, most *Bonnie Dick* missions didn't end with the death of an aviator. A typical combat mission started about ninety minutes before launch. The pilots first stopped at Air Intelligence, a room in the island where an officer briefed them on their targets, the expected threat, and the weather. Standing in front of a map that took up an entire wall, the aviators absorbed target locations, along with known "hot flak" sites where they could expect to encounter antiaircraft artillery. One intel officer briefed the pilots so often that he earned the nickname "Hot Flak." Within a few months the briefing would also include the location of a new threat, surface-to-air missiles.

The Air Intel room had a cartoon someone had clipped from a newspaper and taped to the wall. Boiling oil poured onto the center of three men as they climbed ladders against the walls of a castle under assault. A man on one of the other ladders said: "Don't worry about him. He knew about the boiling oil when he signed up!" The line became an epitaph for anyone killed, a bit of dark humor for testosterone-fueled pilots with no time to grieve before their next combat mission. Besides, no one thought it would happen to him.

After the Air Intel briefing, the pilots zigzagged their way through a maze of hallways and down several ladders—steep metal staircases—into the bowels of the carrier and to the squadron Ready Room. The two-car garage–sized room had theater-style chairs, a blackboard, and a podium for the mission briefer to use if he wanted. Pegs along the wall held the pilots' flight gear: G suits, harnesses, pilot spurs, survival equipment, and helmets. During the briefing the flight lead discussed the procedures he wanted to use; for example, rejoining on the left wing versus the right wing, what speeds and altitudes to fly, and where to join up after launch. Every flight leader had his own preferences, and it was Willie's job to do what the lead wanted.

After donning flight gear, the pilots' next stop was the Flight Deck Control Room in the island. Before leaving the Ready Room, some pilots said a short prayer. Others carried a good luck charm in a flight suit pocket. Willie began a ritual: he tapped the Ready Room bulkhead twice as he walked out. "A onesie and a twosie," he said to himself. On the way back in after a mission, he tapped once and mentally noted "and a threesie" to convince himself the mission had been as easy as one-two-three.

In the Flight Deck Control Room a diagram of the flight deck was laid out on a small table. Small cardboard silhouettes showed where each airplane was parked. Controllers moved the silhouettes manually to keep track of the never-ending action, resulting in the nickname "Ouija Board." The Quija Board's snapshot belied the chaos outside on the flight deck. As aircraft moved from the hangars below deck in elevators up to the flight deck, maintenance personnel lined airplanes along the edge of the carrier in whatever space was available. An aircraft was never in the same spot it had been the day before, or even earlier the same day, since aircraft were recovered somewhat randomly. The Ouija Board kept pilots from wandering about the flight deck in search of an airplane.

After learning where their assigned airplanes were parked, the pilots usually gathered on the flight deck around the island as they waited for their aircraft to be ready. Each aircraft had a young enlisted "plane captain" assigned to it. The plane captain performed routine maintenance tasks, like checking oil and hydraulic fluid levels and cleaning the canopy. A pilot couldn't walk out to his assigned airplane until the plane captain deemed it ready to fly. The readying of aircraft sometimes dragged on, and if the pilots had to wait more than a few minutes at the island, adrenalin and anxiety often fueled macho displays of affection: inserting a long piece of toilet paper into someone's harness so it dragged behind him or wetting a finger and sticking it in someone's ear.

Following his catapult shot, or cat shot for short, each pilot climbed to a rendezvous point, usually about thirty miles from the carrier, at an altitude of around twenty thousand feet. Once there, a pilot circled or joined with the other airplanes. It might take ten minutes or more to get everyone off the carrier and rejoined, so those who took off early had time to relax. Once everyone joined up, the pilots followed the flight leader toward either North or South Vietnam, depending on the mission.

On many missions Willie flew, A-4s bombed targets while he and other F-8 pilots provided defense against AAA or North Vietnamese MiGs. Like all fighter pilots, Willie yearned to shoot down an enemy aircraft, an "air-to-air kill," in pilot talk. Get five air-to-air kills, and you would be an ace, the best of all fighter pilots. But to kill a MiG, you had to see one first, and by the fall of 1965, not a single enemy jet had deigned Willie with its presence.

Willie's least favorite mission was dropping bombs. The Crusader was supposed to be a dogfighter, an airplane that killed other airplanes, not an airplane that killed things on the ground. He didn't mind road recce missions, in which he launched his rockets or fired his guns, but dropping bombs that just fell from the airplane seemed beneath the dignity of a fighter pilot. Sometimes, when the weather over North Vietnam was too poor for air strikes, F-8s were assigned to carry bombs to Laos. There the pilots circled about, waiting for a forward air controller (FAC) to direct them to a target. The FACS were air force pilots who flew slow airplanes a few hundred feet above the ground. But the F-8s couldn't circle all day waiting for a target to show up; when the pilots reached the "Charlie Time" for their recovery cycle back on the carrier, they had to leave, even if they hadn't dropped their bombs.

During missions the pilots also sometimes carried cameras given to them by Air Intel. The pilots snapped photos of ground targets and anything else they thought might be useful for analysts to use in planning future missions, along with unusual occurrences such as ejections (fig. 15).

Regardless of the mission, the pilots flew back to the carrier, where the landing was often the most frightening part of the flight. Anything that happened over Vietnam was over and gone and couldn't hurt a pilot anymore. But a bad landing could still kill him. Sometimes Willie scared himself so much landing in bad weather or at night that he couldn't get his legs to stop shaking until he climbed down from the Crusader.

A-1 pilots landed last because they carried the most fuel. The Spads could fly for hours, while the fighters carried at most about two hours of fuel. A fighter's range could be extended with aerial refueling, but it was easiest just to keep the Spads airborne longer; the A-1 pilots circled to the left and behind the carrier as they waited their turn.

After landing, the pilots returned to Air Intel, where they turned in their cameras and reported anything unusual, such as an unexpected AAA site, to pass along to the next wave of pilots. Sometimes the carrier leadership decided to cancel the next mission because a spot had become too dangerous.

FIG. 15. F-8 ejections were common but rarely photographed. In this photo Lieutenant Terhune from the USS *Coral Sea* ejects from his F-8 after his engine flames out over the South China Sea on August 11, 1965; he was rescued unharmed. (Courtesy National Archives and Records Administration, U.S. Navy photo)

The carrier had a rhythm. Half the planes on the carrier launched for their missions. While they flew, maintenance crews brought the second half up to the flight deck. Those airplanes launched. After the second wave was airborne, the first half returned. They were reloaded and relaunched. Then the second half returned. Repeat again and again for twelve hours.

The *Bonnie Dick* rotated schedules with the other carriers at Yankee Station. Typically, a carrier operated midnight to noon for two weeks, then 8:00 a.m. to 8:00 p.m. for two weeks, and then noon to midnight for two weeks. Many days Willie flew two missions, sometimes three. A typical day started with breakfast, followed by a nap, reading a book from the ship's library, adding to a letter he sent to Nina every few days, and watching other airplanes take off and land for a while. Sometimes there were movies in the Ready Room, but the movies were old, nothing first-run. Still, bored pilots would watch anything, and Willie was always on the lookout for pretty girls in the films.

Willie's roommate on the *Bonnie Dick* was Lee Van Boven, call sign "Bullets." For reasons known only to him, he often wore a bandolier when he posed for photos. Willie earned two call signs during his first cruise, both plays on his last name: "Super Blue," a reference to a brand of razor blades; and "Not So." Usually he was called Super Blue; if he heard Not So, he figured he was in trouble.

Almost everyone on the carrier smoked; ashtrays and ash cans abounded in staterooms and around the ship. The Officers' Store sold cigarettes and candy for a fraction of the price in a regular U.S. store. Willie preferred menthol. Alcohol was technically verboten, but many seasoned aviators kept well-stocked liquor cabinets.

The medicine cabinet in Willie and Lee's stateroom was perfectly sized to hold a reel-to-reel tape recorder. The roommates decorated their walls with *Playboy* centerfolds and listened to tapes, a mix of 1950s ballads, surfing music, and Beatles songs. Willie loved Bobby Vinton's "Blue Velvet," but his favorite was Roy Orbison's "In Dreams." It always made him cry. Sometimes he couldn't listen to it at all.

The only drawback to Willie's stateroom was the location, one deck below the catapult. Every full-power jet engine run-up made the room as noisy as a freeway. Vibrations that accompanied each launch popped open the door to the medicine cabinet. The roommates eventually scrounged a bungee cord to keep the door closed.

The catapult was noisy, but it wasn't the noisiest part of the ship. When I made an overnight trip to the *Carl Vinson* in 1987, I was assigned a room under the aft deck. Just as I nodded off, I was jolted awake by a loud whomp followed by a whoosh and a screech—an F-18 touching down, the pilot moving his throttle to full power, and the cable stretching to complete the trap. About ten seconds later the cable went bam, bam, bam, bam, as it clattered back into position for the next landing. Whomp, whoosh, screech, bam, bam, bam, bam, for the next ten minutes, then a bit of respite until the next set of airplanes arrived. I didn't get much sleep that night.

But people in noisy situations get used to the constant assault on their ears. After living in a high-rise apartment building next to a busy highway for many years, I hardly noticed the din, and it rarely disturbed my sleep. A friend of mine who flew F-14s off the *Constellation* in the early 1980s told me that in addition to being desensitized to the noise, his ears picked up anything out of the ordinary: the almost inaudible beeping on his wristwatch alarm clock woke him up every day.

On July 3 the *Bonnie Dick* began steaming back toward Subic Bay to replenish supplies and provide some R&R for the sailors and pilots. That afternoon the pilots and others held a memorial service on the flight deck for Pete Crosby. After a brief speech, the U.S. flag—"colors," in military parlance—were lowered to half-mast. Four pilots, dressed in short-sleeved white dress uniforms, solemnly marched to the edge of the flight deck carrying a wreath resting on a board. As a bugler played taps, the pilots saluted the wreath and slid it over the side, where it splashed into the water.[19] The stirring ceremony provided closure for some who otherwise had no time to mourn. But Willie felt that sliding a wreath into the water seemed trivial, like the cavalier way the pilots acted whenever someone died. He laughed along as other pilots joked, "He knew about the boiling oil when he signed up," but he never got used to the attitude.

Two days later, early in the morning, the *Bonnie Dick* moored in Subic Bay. Men spilled off the carrier, with officers banding together separately from enlisted sailors in search of alcohol, narcotics, women, and other vices; by 9:15 a.m. one sailor had already landed in the brig for being drunk and disorderly.[20]

Willie and the other aviators made daily excursions to the Cubi Point Officers' Club. Subic Bay also had an officers' club, but the aviators considered Subic the club for the other officers on the ship, the guys who didn't fly. The non-flyers wore black shoes, and the aviators, when not wearing flight suits, wore brown shoes. Black shoes went to Subic. Brown shoes went to Cubi, where they could see the runway from the club. One night Willie tried to buy fifty Stingers at the ten-cent-each happy hour price. He thrust a five-dollar bill across the bar, but the bartender suggested two at a time instead. Willie couldn't even finish a dollar's worth. Another night the pilots bought bottles of champagne and tried to ricochet the corks off the ceiling to hit other tables. Other times drunken aviators tossed napkins across the club at each other, catching musicians in the cross fire. The brown shoes occasionally raided the black shoe club, whose occupants usually didn't appreciate the rowdiness.

Cubi had a pecking order based on a pilot's steed. Brash fighter pilots like Willie were at the top of the aviation food chain, followed closely by attack pilots, with cargo and reconnaissance drivers taking up the rear. Helicopter pilots garnered the most respect of all: not only did they fly lightly or unarmed aircraft low, slow, and close to the enemy; they could pluck your ass off the ground or out of the water when you were no longer one with your airplane.

Helicopter pilots never had to buy a drink at the bar.

After hunkering down for a few extra days to avoid Typhoon Freda, the *Bonnie Dick* once again headed for Yankee Station on July 17.[21] Willie was back in the thick of combat two days later. On July 29 Satan's Kittens lost their first pilot, Lt. (Junior Grade) Edward "Dean" Brown, during a mission over South Vietnam. He was twenty-five years old, just a few months older than Willie.[22] Willie's life followed the same pattern for the next five months: four to five weeks of combat flying; loss and memorial services; two weeks or so of port calls in Subic Bay, Japan, or Hong Kong.

A basketball court was set up in the hangars, and some officers played, but Willie never joined in. Every so often, he attended a uso show. The entertainers performed on an improvised platform created by bringing one of the elevators in the hangar up a few feet. During Willie's first cruise the *Bonnie Dick* didn't rate any A-list entertainers, and he considered the shows lame. But he looked forward to monthly Steak Days, when the flight deck was cleared for a cookout. After stuffing themselves, everyone lounged about for a few hours. Then it was back to the grind of combat, interrupted by occasional entertainment from someone doing something stupid, like the pilot in Willie's sister squadron who accidentally fired his gun in the Ready Room.

The pilot was showing off his quick draw skills, yanking his revolver repeatedly out of his holster and shoving it back in. It went off. The other pilots dove for cover as the bullet ricocheted off the metal walls before slamming into a seat back. John Tierney was furious. To avoid another accident, he ordered all *Bonnie Dick* pilots to unload the first two chambers of their service revolvers. Tierney must have figured that since the revolver was really only useful as a signaling device, the two empty rounds wouldn't matter.

The enemy's first surface-to-air missile kill changed everything. On July 24, 1965, the North Vietnamese shot down a U.S. air force F-4 with an SA-2 surface-to-air missile (fig. 16).[23] Before that day all U.S. aircraft losses were from antiaircraft artillery, small arms fire, or accidents. At the low altitudes pilots used to attack targets with bombs or rockets, AAA could reach their aircraft. But AAA had a fairly limited range; above five thousand feet a pilot was safe from the rounds. Pilots flying to and from targets used the sanctuary of the higher altitude to avoid AAA. They only became vulnerable when they dropped lower to deliver their weapons. But a SAM could kill anything above fifteen hundred feet. If a pilot flew below fifteen hundred feet to avoid the SAMs, he could be killed by AAA. If he flew above five thousand feet to avoid the AAA, he could be killed by SAMs. Between fifteen hundred and five thousand feet was a kill box in which both could get him. The sanctuary was gone.

Pilots had known for months that the North Vietnamese were installing the SAMs. At several locations in North Vietnam, they could see a half-dozen rings being carved into the earth, the distinctive signature of a Russian SAM system. But they weren't allowed to touch the sites with their bombs or rockets until the loss of the air force F-4.[24]

A few days after the first SAM loss, fifty-five air force aircraft

FIG. 16. SA-2 surface-to-air missile site in North Vietnam; photo taken by Willie during a mission. (Courtesy Willie Sharp)

returned to destroy the site that had launched the missile. During the raid the North Vietnamese shot down four jets with AAA; the other fifty-one aircraft didn't kill any SAMs. On August 9 twelve aircraft showed up at a site that had been active the previous day but found that the enemy had moved on.[25]

Three days later the air force and navy finally got the go-ahead to make an all-out assault on the SAMs. Operation Iron Hand had begun.[26] A few days later the *Bonnie Dick* pulled into a port in Japan, and technicians descended on the A-4s and F-8s to install equipment to help defeat the SAMs. Several men from a lab at Massachusetts Institute of Technology (MIT) met with Willie and the other VF-191 pilots in the Ready Room to teach them about the SA-2 and the new missile warning system in the F-8. Willie was impressed with MIT's wealth of knowledge on the SA-2— performance, guidance, different modes of operation. The more you know about an enemy system, the more likely that you can defeat it. The missile warning system installed in the f-8 was a stopgap measure, part of a project called "Shoehorn" that literally shoehorned antimissile technology in every nook and cranny on tactical aircraft in the mid-1960s. The system in the f-8 wasn't much, just an amber light in the cockpit and a tone to the pilot that a radar was tracking him or a missile had just been launched. The system didn't provide any information about where the missile was or how to defeat it, but when the tone sounded, the pilot could start maneuvering and look toward the ground: the sooner he spotted a missile coming at him, the more likely he could out-maneuver it.

Willie found the information about the sams and the rudimentary warning system comforting; at least he had a chance to survive now. The Iron Hand search-and-destroy mission quickly became his favorite. For a typical mission an f-8 accompanied an a-4 to a sam site. For early Iron Hand missions, the a-4 dropped 250-pound bombs called "Snake-eyes," trying to destroy the missiles or the radar van that controlled the sam launches. Then a new missile, called "Shrike," was introduced. The missile took advantage of the radars: the electronic beams essentially called out, "Look over here, guys!" The Shrike tracked the radar beam coming from the van. It had a small warhead and could take out the radar van but not much else. After the a-4 launched, Willie followed the Shrike's smoke trail down. After shooting two Zuni rockets, he yanked his nose up to nearly vertical to get away from the ground as fast as possible. As he pulled away, the Zunis burst a few feet above the ground, scattering shrapnel everywhere and taking out missiles, guns, and anything else nearby.

One day that fall, enemy sams filled the sky. Willie had never seen the North Vietnamese fire so many at once. Missiles whizzed around him as he sent rockets toward the launch site.

"Diddle-diddle! Diddle-diddle! Diddle-diddle!" warned a high-pitched tone and flashing amber light: a missile was in the air. When the enemy fired one or two missiles, the tone was helpful, but with a half-dozen sams fired close together, the warning was just a bunch of noise.

As long as Willie could see the SAMs, he could avoid them. But it is the one you don't see that gets you. Just when Willie thought he had made it through the salvo, an out-of-control missile tumbled toward him. It looked like a telephone pole doing cartwheels. He yanked his F-8 to the right as hard as he could, but the missile clipped the leading edge of his left wing, jolting the aircraft.

Willie radioed his flight lead that he'd been hit. He couldn't see the damage, and as far as he could tell, the F-8 wasn't seriously wounded. There was no fire, his cockpit instruments looked normal, and the flight controls seemed to be working fine. When he pulled up on the wing of his flight lead, the other pilot reported that the missile had ripped a football-sized chunk of metal out of the wing. It was the combat equivalent of a skinned knee. Willie made a normal approach and landing back on the *Bonnie Dick*.

Willie was lucky that day. Many aircraft and pilots survived hits from AAA, but a direct hit from a SAM's four hundred–pound warhead traveling at four times the speed of sound was almost always lethal.[27] On the other hand, the thirty-five-foot-tall missiles were easier to spot and outmaneuver than the smaller AAA shells. AAA batteries could scoot easily to new locations and were almost impossible to detect until they fired. The fixed SAM sites were easier to see from the air, and the enemy had to haul the SAMs and supporting equipment into the sites and set them up, a process that took several hours. In theory, with new systems like the Shrike, the SAMs could be destroyed, but reality proved much more difficult.[28]

In 1965 the Shrike was new, and only a few A-4s had been modified with the specialized gear needed to launch it [29] Navy pilots launched only twenty-five preproduction versions of the missiles before military leadership decided to stop using them so they could build up their stock. But the presence of the radar-tracking missile had already impacted the North Vietnamese: they shut down their radars if they thought a Shrike was nearby, making the SAMs less effective. Pilots armed only with dumb bombs could sometimes trick the enemy into shutting down their radar by maneuvering as if they were about to launch a Shrike.[30] Throughout the war both sides developed an endless series of equipment and tactics to counter the others' missiles and aircraft, a cat and mouse game that continues in combat to this day.

During his first cruise Willie also became VF-191's landing signal officer. There was no formal LSO training aboard the carrier, so Willie shadowed another LSO for several weeks. A senior LSO then supervised him for about two more weeks. The LSO stand, large enough to hold a half-dozen people, was a platform on the port side of the carrier. At a minimum a yeoman accompanied Willie on the platform to record comments about each recovery in a notebook. Pilots and other personnel also came out to observe recoveries, hoping to improve their skills or learn more about carrier operations. The stand held a waist-high panel with lights, instruments, and a camera that Willie could use to help monitor each approach. His most important piece of equipment was the "pickle switch," a button on top of a small wand. If an approach became too hazardous or the deck was fouled, he pushed the pickle button and the lights on the glideslope flashed as Willie called, "Wave off, wave off, wave off," to tell the pilot to go around and try again. If things got really dangerous, everyone on the LSO stand jumped into a large safety net off the side of the ship.

Willie preferred standing on the flight deck next to the stand. He wanted to focus on the approaching aircraft and not be distracted by the lights and instruments on the panel. He held the telephone handset for talking on the radio in his left hand while his right clutched the pickle switch, both connected to the panel by long cables.

LSO duty was usually routine; Willie didn't have to say anything to most pilots as they approached and landed. But sometimes a pilot needed him. A pilot sometimes got behind the airplane, or a pilot might be confused from exhaustion. Turbulence and low visibility played havoc with even the most experienced pilots. If a pilot had trouble, Willie intervened with comments and suggestions. "Don't climb," "Watch your glideslope," "A little low in the middle," or "Check your lineup."

Willie loved being an LSO. At only twenty-four he had an awesome responsibility, supervising pilots in twenty-five-ton airplanes hurtling toward the flight deck. He also got to know all the carrier pilots, not just the ones in his squadron. Each LSO primarily did duty for his own squadron, but the LSOs had to fly as well, so they took turns covering other squadrons. Sometimes pilots from the other squadrons invited him to imbibe their contraband alcohol.

LSO duty had one downside: pilots sometimes got mad at him over a landing grade. The yeoman on the LSO platform wrote down Willie's comments and which wire the tailhook caught. Each recovery was debriefed in the Ready Room, which had a "Reddy-Greeny Board" mounted on a wall. The board listed the squadron pilots' names down one side, from the skipper on down. Next to each name was a series of boxes, one box for each landing, filled in with a color, the wire caught, and the recorded remarks. Green meant a recovery with no LSO assistance and no remarks. No color meant a fair landing, one that required some intervention by the LSO. Red was a "cut," in which a pilot could have crashed without LSO intervention. To a carrier pilot, a cut was like a knife through the heart.

A glance at the Reddy-Greeny Board told a lot about a pilot: all greens and threes were best, followed by pilots with greens and a few numbers other than three. Too much of no color or more than a few reds was cause for concern. Too much red, and a pilot might lose his carrier qualification or even his wings altogether. Even pilots in no danger of being grounded sometimes argued about grades as a point of pride. When that happened, Willie pulled up his evidence: film from the PLAT—the Pilot Landing Aid Television. The camera captured every burble and minor correction a pilot made, and Willie usually won the arguments. The PLAT also made it much easier to tell a higher-ranking and more experienced pilot that he had made a lousy approach.

One day during LSO duty, Willie watched an A-3 approach. The A-3, officially the Skywarrior, had an unofficial nickname: the "Whale." It was the largest aircraft that routinely landed on a carrier. The A-3 pilot that day couldn't get stable on his approach. Too high. Too low. Willie pushed the pickle button.

"Wave off! Wave off! Wave off!"

The A-3 thundered above Willie on the go-around. He called out the dangerous approach to the yeoman: "Give that guy a cut!"

Willie looked to his right. Everyone on the stand, including the yeoman, had disappeared. A dozen frightened eyeballs stared back at him from the safety net.

Through the summer and into the fall, the carnage from carrier operations and combat increased. On September 12 Satan's Kittens lost yet another young pilot, Lt. (Junior Grade) Jerry Green. Green crashed into the sea about a mile southwest of the *Bonnie Dick* as he returned from a mission. The Crusader sank into three hundred feet of water. An initial helicopter search came up empty, although a destroyer later spotted an oil slick and found the F-8's nose cone and wheel. Green's body was not found.[31] During the next two weeks the *Bonnie Dick* lost three more pilots: an A-1 pilot and an A-4 pilot died when they crashed in South Vietnam, and a pilot from Willie's rival squadron died when his F-8 crashed into the sea shortly after taking off at night.[32]

The mounting deaths took their toll on the aviators. They mostly stuck to themselves, even eating separately. Willie and the other pilots often wore their flights suits all day. Much of the ship was off-limits to them when they were in their flight suits, as if the clothing carried the stench of fear and death. To eat in the Ward Room with tablecloths and stewards required a tan summer dress uniform. Most aviators eschewed the Ward Room for the Flight Suit Mess next door.

To eat in the Flight Suit Mess, a pilot went through a cafeteria-style line and carried his tray into a separate room filled with cast-off office furniture. There were no tablecloths or stewards, but the room was a cocoon where aviators let their guard down and vented about things only they knew or cared about. Willie put on a coat of armor before he flew in combat. As he preflighted his aircraft each day, he rammed the fear that rose back inside. He faintly hoped he might find some small thing wrong with the jet that would keep him from flying. Then he felt guilty if he didn't fly the mission because it meant someone else had to. He sometimes had to fly for someone else, so in theory it all evened out. The lost pilots, whether from combat or accidents, added up. Willie began to wonder if every launch would be his last. Surely, his luck couldn't hold out forever. He was despondent before a mission, elated after surviving, then full of dread at knowing he had to do it again in a few hours or the next day. In the Flight Suit Mess, Willie discovered he wasn't alone. Most of his fellow pilots put on the armor too, returning as frightened young men, confessing and crying. Occasional trips to staterooms with well-stocked bars helped as well.

Amid the misery were moments for celebration. On October 26 Lt. (Junior Grade) Rick Millson was on a bombing run in one of the A-4s that had been modified to kill SAMs with Shrikes, when he felt a jolt and heard an explosion. The Scooter flipped upside down.

Millson called, "I've taken a hit and am heading for the water."

"You've got a hole in your left wing," his flight lead called.

Millson managed to roll the Skyhawk right side up, but something was wrong—he needed both hands to hold the control stick all the way to the right to keep the jet from rolling to the left and upside down again. His left leg pushed hard on the rudder pedal to keep the nose straight.

The A-4 cockpit was located too far forward of the wing for Millson to see the hole in his airplane: it was twice the size of a manhole cover and took out one-third of the left wing near the fuselage. But a SAM hadn't clobbered the SAM hunter, ironically. A 37 mm cannon AAA shell had bounced off an external fuel tank before smashing into the bottom of the wing. The fuel inside the wing exploded and ripped the hole through the bottom and top of the wing. The metal looked like a sardine can lid peeled partway back. Fuel sprayed from the bottom of his wing, and as he turned toward the coastline, his flight lead was sure that a fireball had consumed the little jet.

The fuel ran out quickly, and the fire disappeared, but Millson had another problem: he didn't have enough fuel to return to the *Bonnie Dick*. Luckily, he was only a few miles inland; within minutes he found an A-4 "buddy tanker" orbiting over the water right offshore. The buddy tanker, laden with an external fuel tank to use in an emergency just like Millson's, was flown by a squadron mate, Mike Allum.

Millson hooked up to the tanker, and Allum led him toward the carrier floating more than one hundred miles away. The A-4 had a switch in the cockpit that sent the fuel Millson took on board directly into a small fuselage tank behind his seat and then into the engine. Without that switch the fuel would have flowed out the damaged left wing.[33]

Alerted that a battle-damaged aircraft was inbound, Red Shirts manned the fog foam stations, hoses that hooked into firefighting foam stored in a gigantic tank in the bowels of the carrier.[34] Capt. William McClendon, the *Bonnie Dick*'s commanding officer, happened to be on the flight deck: he had just finished directing the ship's 75,000th accident-free catapult launch.[35]

Plugged into the tanker, Millson couldn't see a thing. He relied completely on Allum to get him to the carrier; they had practiced the emergency refueling many times.

Allum called, "Gear." Millson dropped his landing gear.

"Flaps."

"Hook."

The A-4 was ready to land.

Allum called, "You're on the ball," and pulled up and away.

Millson looked up and saw the carrier right in front of him, the ball perfectly aligned.

Other than being a little fast and flying with the crossed controls—full right stick and full left rudder pedal—the landing was normal. He even caught the three wire.

Millson taxied the A-4 over to the island, shut down the engine, and climbed out. He nearly fainted when he saw the size of the hole. It was big enough that he could crawl into it, and he did just

FIG. 17. Rick Millson with his damaged A-4. (Courtesy Willie Sharp)

that later in the day. Navy photographers snapped several pictures of Millson and Allum standing inside the hole (fig. 17).

In spite of Millson's heroics, the LSO gave his trap a grade of "OK, 3, fast in close."

An LSO himself, Millson thought the grade should have been

simply "ok, 3." He argued, "I wasn't really fast because any slower the airplane would have stalled." He lost the argument.

The last time Millson saw the battle-damaged a-4, it was chained to a barge sailing to a naval repair facility in Japan.[36]

The day after Millson's happy ending, a Satan's Kittens pilot, Lt. Dennis "Denny" Moore, departed the *Bonnie Dick* for a simple job: fly straight and level at thirty-three thousand feet above an overcast over Laos, keeping an eye out for MiGs. There were no MiGs, but the North Vietnamese were getting better at operating their sams: about forty miles southwest of Hanoi, an sa-2 tore the tail off Moore's f-8. The Naval Academy graduate ejected from his tumbling jet.[37]

Willie and other pilots were in the Ready Room when another pilot entered and said, "We lost an f-8."

The pilots fell silent. Then someone asked, "Is he alive?"

"He had a good chute."

A search and rescue mission was underway, but it was futile: the pilots didn't know it, but Moore had landed just outside a village and was captured immediately.

Willie felt a pain in his stomach, an uneasiness and foreboding he hadn't felt when the other pilots died. Denny was a damned good pilot; how could this have happened to him? Was Willie's time running out too? If he got shot down, was it better to die or to be taken prisoner? No one knew how the North Vietnamese were treating pows, but Willie had to assume that the fake pow camp wasn't for nothing.

Two days after Moore's shoot-down, the *Bonnie Dick* headed to Subic Bay for replenishment and then to Hong Kong for R&R. For five days Willie and the other pilots ate at Jimmy's Kitchen and the Parisian Grill and bought flight jackets, belt buckles, and red sport coats adorned with their squadron patch. The *Bonnie Dick* arrived back at Yankee Station on Monday, November 15.[38]

6

The Mission

THE GULF OF TONKIN WAS INKY AT 3:00 A.M. ON NOVEMBER 10, 1965. Lt. Tommy Saintsing and his UH-2 helicopter crew skimmed two hundred feet above the black water. The weather was terrible; twenty-five-foot waves rose and merged with the dark sky into a black hole. Saintsing relied on his instruments to keep the helicopter upright. His copilot, Lt. (Junior Grade) Jim Welsh, scanned the approaching shoreline for an A-1 pilot. He was out there somewhere.[1]

Lt. Cdr. Paul Merchant had been hit by ground fire during a night reconnaissance mission over North Vietnam. As his damaged engine gradually lost power, Merchant flew toward the Gulf. He ditched the Spad about a mile offshore and climbed out and got into his raft.

The race to find the pilot was on. Saintsing was up against two North Vietnamese fishing boats. Enemy forces on the beach fired at the approaching helicopter.[2] Blue streaks filled the sky.[3]

An enlisted crew member called over the intercom, "Lieutenant, what are those things?"

"Those are tracers." Saintsing didn't add the obvious: they're trying to kill us.

No one on the helicopter had been shot at during a rescue before. They didn't even wear flak jackets. Their armament consisted of two Thompson submachine guns tossed aboard almost as an afterthought. The crew's orange flight suits were designed for easy spotting in friendly territory. They would be a deadly target if the men crashed into the water.

The helicopter won the race. As the Seasprite approached the downed pilot, Welsh used the loud hailer, a loudspeaker mounted to the side of the helicopter, to tell Merchant to leave his raft and get ready for the pickup. Merchant reluctantly slipped into the water and watched his raft drift away. Then Saintsing realized he had made a mistake: he had approached with a tailwind, and the helicopter wouldn't be able to hover. Welsh called Merchant again and told him to get back in the raft. Saintsing flew past the pilot and turned around so the Seasprite was headed into the wind. Merchant abandoned his raft a second time and waited as the helicopter came to a hover above him. The two enlisted crew members, Airman James Hug and Petty Officer 3rd Class John Shanks, lowered the rescue sling to Merchant and reeled him aboard through a door in the right side of the helicopter.

Dangerously low on fuel, Saintsing turned back toward the uss Gridley, the guided missile frigate they had departed from earlier. Before they took off, he knew the Seasprite wouldn't have enough fuel to fly the more than two hundred–mile round trip from the Gridley, so he asked the ship's crew to steam toward the coast so it would be closer when they returned. It worked, barely. Just before Saintsing touched down, about 4:15 a.m., a light illuminated in the cockpit. The helicopter was nearly out of fuel.[4]

Exactly how Saintsing and his crew came to be aboard the Gridley to rescue Paul Merchant that dark night is lost to history, but someone in the navy had the idea to put helicopters on board guided missile frigates. The small, maneuverable ships could operate much farther north and closer to shore than lumbering aircraft carriers. The frigates were already part of the carrier's flock and were equipped with radars and surface-to-air missiles that could shoot down enemy aircraft. The frigates also tracked friendly aircraft with their radars, vectoring pilots to targets and helping coordinate and control SAR operations.

The UH-2 was chosen for the new mission, probably because the navy already knew it was small enough to fit on a guided mis-

FIG. 18. The USS *Gridley* with the first UH-2 aboard, June 1964.
(Courtesy Naval History and Heritage Command, U.S. Navy photo)

sile frigate's fantail, a flat area at the rear of the ship. More than
a year earlier, in June 1964, a Seasprite from the carrier *Constellation* had landed on the *Gridley*'s fantail. A navy public affairs
release dated July 6, 1964, began, "If you're a lost helo pilot looking for a place to roost USS *Gridley* (DLG-21) has a home for you
and your helicopter." On a more serious note, the press release
stated that UH-2s from the *Constellation* were making several trips
a day to the *Gridley*, carrying passengers, mail, and spare parts
(fig. 18). The demonstration proved that helos could operate from
the smaller ships, but the innovative delivery concept apparently
went by the wayside when the shooting war in the Gulf started
a month later.

The Seasprites weren't designed for combat: the helicopter had
only a single engine with limited horsepower, no armor plating,
and no guns for self-protection. During normal operations the
UH-2s were used for mundane tasks such as carrying mail and
returning sailors who fell overboard to their ships. The aircraft

also flew plane guard during carrier operations in case a pilot ejected or crashed during launch or recovery.

By late October several Seasprite crews back in the United States were training for combat operations in UH-2s that had been modified with armor and an engine with more power. But as combat operations in the Gulf grew, commanders began to ask more from the unmodified Seasprites already in the theater. On November 8 a UH-2 from helicopter squadron HC-2 was sent to wait on the guided missile frigate USS *Turner* as a last-ditch backup for an overland CSAR mission that had kicked off on November 5 after an air force F-105 crashed. Two A-1s and a CH-3 helicopter were shot down during the rescue attempt, and another helicopter, an SH-3, crash-landed on a four thousand–foot mountain after running out of fuel. The desperate task force commander dispatched the only helicopter he had left, the UH-2 sitting on the *Turner*. Arriving at the mountaintop, the underpowered helicopter struggled with the high altitude but pulled two of the four downed aircrew aboard. An air force helicopter arrived later to rescue the remaining two crew members.[5]

The UH-2 on the *Turner* had been staged forward as a desperate measure for a single mission. To really test the frigate-helicopter combo, someone sent a Seasprite from the *Oriskany*'s squadron HC-1 to the *Gridley*. Saintsing and Welsh, along with Hug and Shanks, were the guinea pig crew. The same day the *Turner* Seasprite made its rescue, the *Oriskany* crew ferried a UH-2, call sign "Angel 43," to the *Gridley*.

They landed on a spot barely big enough for one helicopter, in the middle of a twenty-five-foot circle pained on the *Gridley*'s fantail. The cruiser's captain, Albert Sackett, at least a dozen years older than the aircrew, was in charge of everything on his ship. But deferring to the aircrew's expertise, he greeted the newcomers with "I know nothing about helicopters. You're going to have to tell me what to do and how to do it."[6]

Saintsing and Welsh barely knew what to do themselves, with limited rescue experience and no time in combat. Saintsing had only rescued one pilot, a month earlier. He retrieved a marine

FIG. 19. Tommy Saintsing with his UH-2 Seasprite crew on October 17, 1965; that night he made his first rescue. (Courtesy Tommy Saintsing)

corps pilot who ejected after he hit the back of the *Oriskany*'s ramp while trying to land at night in poor visibility and rough seas. The weather and waves made for a tricky recovery, but the crew handled it with aplomb (fig. 19).[7]

The junior pilot, Welsh, had four rescues under his belt. His first rescue was on May 25, when he piloted a Seasprite to pick up three of four crew members from an A-3 that dribbled off the *Oriskany*'s deck and into the sea after a catapult mishap. With ten-foot waves, three survivors with broken bones, and limited space in the UH-2, Welsh decided to leave the uninjured last survivor in the water along with one of his enlisted crew; they were picked up a few minutes later by a destroyer.[8]

Once aboard the *Gridley*, Saintsing and Welsh didn't wait long for some action. Weather closed in the second day of their stay. Waves tossed the smaller ship about in ways the helicopter crew had not seen on a carrier. Plates slid around the table during dinner, and they pulled up guardrails to keep from being tossed from their bunks. About 2:00 a.m. someone woke the crew and sent them to retrieve Paul Merchant. Between the *Turner* UH-2 rescue and Merchant, the helicopter-frigate concept had already proved its worth. It would soon be needed again.

November 17 was the navy's worst day since the beginning of the war, in terms of pilots and aircraft lost. Three *Oriskany* aircraft went down while attacking a bridge east of Hanoi. Two of the pilots were killed; the third, a marine corps F-8 pilot, limped back to the Gulf and found the *Bonnie Dick*, but he ran out of fuel before he could land.[9] A *Bonnie Dick* helicopter picked him up.[10] Adding to the *Oriskany*'s troubles, a young marine corps F-8 pilot hit the back of the carrier's ramp on his recovery. The aircraft was a total loss, but the pilot survived.

Later that day Robert Chew, the commander of Willie's rival F-8 squadron, ejected into the water after attacking the same bridge that had just felled the *Oriskany*'s three aircraft. Chew refueled three times in a vain attempt to reach the *Bonnie Dick*. An HU-16 pulled him out of the Gulf and flew him to Da Nang, where he waited for someone to pick him up and return him to the carrier. As he waited, personnel onboard the *Bonnie Dick* made plans against an enemy that seemed to be getting the upper hand. They would strike again the next day.

At the beginning of November, an Albatross crew from Da Nang had earned Silver Stars for a rescue under fire (fig. 20). Capt. Dave Westenbarger and his copilot, Capt. Dave Wendt, had been almost ready to return to Da Nang at the end of their shift when an air force F-101 was shot down. Two *Oriskany* A-1s orbiting with them headed for the downed pilot, Norman Huggins. He had landed in the water but was close to an island and went ashore. North Vietnamese spotted him and chased him back into the water. While he used his .38 pistol to keep his attackers from coming closer, the Albatross arrived.

The HU-16 carried external fuel tanks, which still contained fuel. The crew had to jettison the tanks before they could land. But the left tank didn't drop away. Given Huggins's dire situation and the lack of a nearby helicopter, Westenbarger and Wendt decided to land with the tank anyway. As they turned toward the pilot, they

FIG. 20. An A-1 Spad from the USS *Oriskany* escorting an HU-16 Albatross
back to Danang after a rescue on November 1, 1965. The rescue earned the
HU-16 crew Silver Stars; note the missing drop tank from the wing pylon.
(Courtesy David Wendt)

lowered their flaps and slowed down, and the tank fell off. Two
sampans fired at the HU-16, and Westenbarger asked the A-1s to
take out the lead boat. The Spad pilot launched several rockets,
and the sampan exploded; wooden debris flew into the air. The
HU-16's propellers made a sickening sound as they shredded the
debris, but the Albatross emerged unscathed. The second sampan turned around and left.

After chasing away another enemy swimming toward them, the
HU-16's PJ, Airman 1st Class James Pleiman, went into the water
and pulled Huggins to safety. Once aboard, dripping with seaweed,
Huggins yelled, "Those sons of bitches shot me down!" Westenbarger and Wendt delivered him to Da Nang, where the grateful
pilot bought drinks for everyone.[11] Four months later Pleiman was
killed during an attempt to rescue an F-4 crew from the Gulf.[12]

On Thursday, November 18, an HU-16 Albatross crew in Da
Nang woke at about 3:00 a.m. and had breakfast.[13] During their

flight briefing they learned their orbit station for the morning: about sixty miles east of Vinh, North Vietnam, about one hundred miles north of the seventeenth parallel. The USS *Strauss*, a guided missile destroyer, call sign "Fleet Fox," controlled all aircraft in the Gulf that day. The *Gridley*, carrying Angel 43, steamed a few miles from the *Strauss*.[14]

Just before dawn, the Da Nang Albatross, call sign "Crown Alpha," arrived at the orbit point. They were about twenty miles south of the *Gridley* and the *Strauss*. Two *Bonnie Dick* Spads with "Milestone" call signs joined with the Albatross. The A-1s throttled back their engines to match the slower speed of the Albatross. The formation settled in about fifteen hundred feet above the water, beneath a layer of clouds. They waited for anyone who needed help during the morning strikes.[15]

Aboard the *Gridley*, the Seasprite crew scattered after breakfast. Saintsing went to his room, while Hug and Shanks headed to the fantail for small arms practice. Jim Welsh found a chair in the Combat Information Center (CIC), where he listened to the strike operations over the radio. If a pilot got into trouble, he would be among the first to know.

Willie woke at dawn and had breakfast in the *Bonnie Dick*'s Flight Suit Mess. A few weeks earlier he had turned twenty-five and also recently had been promoted to lieutenant (junior grade). He had survived exactly one hundred combat missions during his nearly six months at sea, each mission carefully inscribed in a logbook by a yeoman.

After breakfast Willie and the other pilots headed to Air Intel. The target was a railroad yard, specifically boxcars sitting to one side in the yard. The boxcars appeared to be disabled, but U.S. intelligence officers suspected they were being used to store supplies en route to Viet Cong down the Ho Chi Minh Trail. The railroad yard was about five miles inland, near the foothills of mountains, and was expected to be partially obscured by clouds. The weather forecasters believed the cloud deck was at least fifteen hundred feet above the ground, giving the attackers enough room to maneuver. Willie took a few notes, marking the target location on the map he carried on his kneeboard. But the weary pilot wasn't really paying that much attention; still a wingman, he just followed his flight leader and did what the leader directed.

Six A-4s, three each from attack squadrons VA-192 and VA-195, would drop five hundred–pound bombs on the boxcars. The two F-8s, including Willie, would provide flak suppression, attacking any AAA that might be lurking about. The CAG, John Tierney, led the mission, flying one of the A-4s.

The gaggle in Air Intel split up for their individual squadron Ready Rooms. The F-8 flight leader that day was "Cactus Jack" Buckley; Willie had flown with Cactus Jack before and was comfortable with him. He readily agreed with Cactus's plan to go to opposite sides of the target and orbit while the A-4s attacked the boxcars. That way they could quickly respond to AAA activity regardless of where it was. The pilot closest to any action could attack first; by the time he finished his run, the second pilot would have maneuvered into position for another attack.

Willie donned his G suit, survival gear, ejection seat harness, and pilot spurs. He removed the Ruger from his helmet bag and slid it into the left pocket of his survival vest. He and Cactus Jack checked out the Ouija Board. Willie was pleased to see that he was flying his favorite airplane, Feedbag 108.

Willie walked around Feedbag 108, inspecting for leaks and checking tire inflations and emergency equipment, along with checking the security of the wing and fuselage racks holding the Zunis. As always, everything with Feedbag 108 was fine. He handed his helmet bag to the plane captain, climbed up small openings in the fuselage that served as steps, and peered at the ejection seat he would occupy in just a few minutes. Using a checklist strapped to his knee, he surveyed the cockpit. All looked good to go—ejection handle in place, shoulder harness fittings not frayed, emergency oxygen bottle full.

Satisfied Feedbag 108 was ready, Willie mentally checked off the items in his survival vest. Mark C3 floating gear, flares, radio, all attached. Willie climbed into the Crusader's cockpit and clipped his harness and spurs to the ejection seat. The plane captain handed him the helmet bag. He pulled out the navy-issued .38 revolver, the first two rounds removed for safety as ordered by the CAG, and slid it into a holster around his waist. Nina's Ruger was fully loaded.

Willie finished strapping in, donned his helmet, hooked up his radio and oxygen, and stashed the helmet bag behind his seat. The plane captain removed a safety pin with a red REMOVE BEFORE FLIGHT banner attached and handed it to Willie. The seat would now fire if he pulled the ejection handle. He stashed the pin with the helmet bag, and the plane captain climbed back down to the flight deck.

Willie monitored his radio for the command to start. Once the jet's engine was running, he unfolded his wings as he taxied toward the catapult.

At 8:53 a.m. the *Bonnie Dick* changed course to a southeast heading and sped up to twenty-seven knots to account for the morning's light winds. At 8:59 jets in Willie's strike package began launching.[16]

As the Americans prepared for their mission, a fisherman in a village by the Gulf of Tonkin woke up. We don't know much about this fisherman, except that he was young and about average size for a Vietnamese man, which means he was small by Western standards, perhaps five foot four, and slender. He was the captain of a sampan, a small boat that fished using nets in the salty Gulf waters. The fisherman was probably barely literate but well schooled in the Buddhist and Vietnamese traditions that centered life in his village.

After a breakfast of noodle soup, the fisherman retrieved his AK-47 and walked out the door of his bamboo cabin. A few months earlier, when the Americans had increased their attacks, North Vietnamese soldiers had stopped by the village and issued AK-47s to any fisherman willing to carry one. The gun would help them capture American pilots who ejected into the Gulf. The fisherman had likely heard rumors that he could expect a bounty for capturing an enemy pilot.

After meeting with his first mate, the two talked about the day's plan, which entailed fishing farther offshore than normal. But with light winds and smooth water, the risk in the small boat was low.

Perhaps the first mate, who didn't have a weapon of his own, said something like "Maybe you'll get to use your gun today. The Americans seem to be flying a lot more lately."

"I heard a pilot landed just offshore a few nights ago, but a helicopter picked him up."

"They can't escape so easily in the day."

"I heard the helicopters don't have guns. And there's two of us."

The two fishermen launched the sampan into the Gulf, dreaming of nets full of fish and perhaps the biggest fish of all, an American pilot.

John Tierney, call sign "Rocket 88," must have been pleased that the launch and join-up went smoothly—getting eight functional jets into the air within a few minutes wasn't always easy. After joining up, the aircraft cruised toward the target, more than one hundred miles northwest of the *Bonnie Dick*. Clouds obscured the Gulf waters below them. Willie, flying off Cactus Jack's wing, had only a vague idea where they were.

About twenty minutes after joining up, the clouds disappeared, and the aircraft arrived over the target. Cactus Jack and Willie split up and entered their orbits, one to the east of the rail yard and one to the west. Tierney's plan was for the first three A-4s to drop their bombs running from south to north, followed by the second three attacking from north to south, then head back to the carrier.

A simple plan, if the enemy cooperated.

The first three A-4s delivered their weapons. There was no enemy fire. The second three approached the target, and the North Vietnamese unleashed a barrage of AAA. Tierney ordered the F-8s to hit the flak site. Some armchair warriors might question that decision—half the bombs had found their targets, the second set was seconds away, and the jets could have easily bolted for the carrier. But in the heat of the battle, in which fractions of an inch and decisions made in a single heartbeat can make the difference between victory and defeat, Tierney was probably just reacting to his years of training and experience. It would not have occurred to either F-8 pilot to question the order.

Cactus Jack, flying Feedbag 104, dropped toward the direction of the ground fire.

Willie followed. He fired two Zunis at the AAA site. He pulled up and turned Feedbag 108 around for another pass. Then he spotted another AAA site to the west. It fired even more furiously than the first one.

Willie radioed the new site to Cactus Jack, adding, "I'll take it."

He pointed his nose down at the second site and got hit.

Willie called over the radio: "Cactus, I'm hit. I don't know how bad it is."

"I'll come take a look."

In the *Gridley*'s CIC Jim Welsh heard Willie's radio call. He phoned Saintsing's stateroom. A minute later Saintsing arrived in the CIC, and Welsh left to get the UH-2 ready. As he dashed away, he heard Willie's distress call, "Mayday, Mayday, Mayday . . . I'm on fire."

While Saintsing confirmed Willie's position, Shanks and Hug tossed two submachine guns into the Seasprite. Saintsing arrived, and the crew strapped into their seats. One minute later they got the go-ahead to launch. Less than five minutes after Willie got hit, they were airborne (fig. 21).

Crown Alpha and the RESCAP Spads also heard Willie. The pilots knew about where the strike aircraft were; the formation turned northwest to start closing the distance. The speedier A-1s pushed up their throttles and broke away. The Albatross could catch up to make the pickup, but there would be no pickup to make if Willie was killed or captured first.

Two *Bonnie Dick* A-1s on another mission apparently also heard the emergency radio transmissions and decided to turn toward Willie as well. One of them was an AE-1F Queer Spad, call sign "Robinson 7," often shortened to "Robbie 7."

More than thirty miles from Fleet Fox, Willie didn't know if he

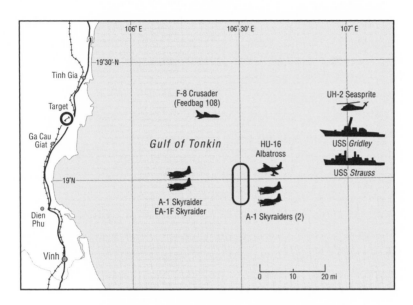

FIG. 21. Map of players and locations during Willie's rescue.
(Courtesy Erin Greb Cartography)

was over water or land, but every airborne rescue aircraft within fifty miles now converged on him.

Willie shot upward through the sky, strapped to his ejection seat. When he had pulled his ejection handle, a complex choreography of timers and tubes released the canopy. The slipstream yanked the canopy away.

The pilot spurs snapped Willie's legs tightly against the seat.

With Willie's hand no longer on the stick, the jet's nose skidded to the right.

A fraction of a second later, the seat rocketed him away from the mortally wounded Feedbag 108.

The windblast wrenched his left arm back so hard he thought the limb was gone. It was like driving five hundred miles per hour down a highway and accidentally sticking his arm out the window.

Willie's right hand still clutched the face curtain. He couldn't see anything, but the curtain helped cocoon him from the violence of the ejection. It kept him from going into shock.

Circling above Willie, Tierney called out his position, "Okay, Mayday, Mayday, Mayday. Pilot's at three-four miles, two-seven-eight from Fleet Fox. Three-four miles, two-seven eight from Fleet Fox." Willie was about thirty-four miles west of the *Strauss* and the *Gridley*.

A few seconds after leaving Feedbag 108, a weighted slug tugged a small drogue parachute from the top of the seat. The drogue chute popped opened. The seat slowed. Willie still couldn't see his arm. He imagined blood gushing from the socket like a fire hose.

Am I going to bleed to death before I hit the water?

In the next twenty seconds he fell through six thousand feet. Then a timer released the main parachute. The canopy blossomed above and yanked him from the seat. The only bits left of Feedbag 108 were the emergency oxygen bottle, the face curtain, and the seat pan with survival gear.

A survival school instructor's admonishment to never throw anything away came back to Willie. He tucked the face curtain between his harness and his abdomen. He had no idea what he might do with it, but the canvas fabric might come in handy.

He looked up at the parachute canopy. It looked good. Willie looked left and realized his arm was still there, dangling and useless but fully attached.

As Willie rejoiced, Cactus Jack called, "Okay, Fleet Fox, this is one-zero-four. Pilot's in the chute. Descending. I'm orbiting over him."

A few seconds later "Buffalo Joe" Tully, flying the lead A-1, reported in: "Roger, this is [Milestone] 611 on the way in."

A few seconds after Buffalo Joe checked in, the HU-16, scrambling to catch up, called, "Crown Alpha to follow."

"Crown Alpha, this is Fleet Fox. We are launching Angel at this time. Over."

Angel was the Seasprite from the *Gridley*; the controller aboard the *Strauss* now tracked all of Willie's potential rescuers.

The RESCAP Spads couldn't see Willie yet; he was still too far away and above the clouds. Voices filled the air as controllers tried to steer pilots toward Willie.

Willie was cut off from radio contact. He fell through the sky at about one thousand feet a minute. He had about five minutes to get ready for his landing. First, he inflated the flotation gear built into his survival vest. If he landed in the water, the gear would keep him alive even if he was knocked unconscious.

Next, he had to get the rest of the survival gear away from his body. Otherwise, it could injure him if he had a hard landing. The gear was in the seat pan, attached to his harness with two fittings. Using his good arm, he released the left fitting. The seat pack swung down to reveal a zippered pouch. He opened the zipper, pulled out a yellow lanyard, and hooked it to his harness. He released the right fitting, and the pan fell away. All his gear, including his life raft, now dangled ten feet below him. If it looked like he might land in a tree, he could still unhook the lanyard to get rid of the gear. Otherwise, the lanyard kept everything near him. But he wanted that raft even closer. With his right arm he inched the lanyard back toward him until he grabbed the raft and inflated it.

Willie gripped the raft under his good arm. His seven flight mates circled about, some saluting him with their middle fingers. While Willie's peers taunted him, his flight leaders tried to be helpful. Cactus Jack called, "Pilot's still descending over a thousand foot overcast."

"This is Rocket 88. I'm directly overhead him now, squawking emergency." With Feedbag 108 gone and no longer transmitting to tracking radars, Tierney had switched to the emergency code. Willie's position still bloomed brightly on the controllers' screens.

A few seconds later one of the young A-4 pilots called: "This is Chippy 3. I have twenty mike-mike in this bird. Want me to go down with him and keep an eye on him?" The Skyhawk pilot had two twenty-millimeter cannons on his airplane, each carrying one hundred rounds.

Two hundred rounds could wreak a lot of havoc, but Tierney waved off his eager subordinate: "Ah, we've got a couple of Spads coming in."

For the next forty-five seconds, pilots and controllers exchanged a rapid fire of bearings and distances. It was anyone's guess as to where Willie would break out of the overcast.

"Feedbag, this is Milestone six-zero-seven. What's our bearing from Fleet Fox?"

"Feedbag one-zero-four, roger, my bearing's two-seven-five."

"Crown Alpha's two-seven-five at three-two."

"Thirty-four miles now, still over the ship."

Then, "Hey, a lot of fishing boats out there."

The fishing boats were a mix of sampans and junks. By the navy's definition a junk was a boat wide enough that a water buffalo could stand on it from side to side. If a water buffalo had to stand in some other position or didn't fit at all, the vessel was a sampan.[17] The definition didn't really matter: at least one person on a boat of any size might be heavily armed.

An anxious Spad pilot called, "Has he passed through the overcast yet?"

"This is one-zero-four. That is negative. He is still descending on top of the overcast."

Saintsing checked in: "Angel four-three, we're heading two-three-five at this time."

Thirty seconds later Rocket 88 called out, "Pilot's now in the clouds."

"Six-one-one, I'm down under. I'll watch for him."

With Buffalo Joe in place, Tierney and Cactus Jack remained above the clouds, along with trigger-happy Chippy 3. The remaining four A-4s from the attack mission returned to the ship to keep the finely tuned launch and recovery schedule moving. Flying back to the *Bonnie Dick*, Rick Millson must have missed the radio call about the boats—he figured Willie's biggest threat would be a shark.

Willie emerged from the clouds facing north. He looked around.

On his left, land, and on his right, water, filled with fishing boats.

Willie had ejected about thirty miles offshore, but the sight of land and the presence of so many boats created the illusion he was much closer to the coastline, almost on top of it.

Only a thousand feet of altitude remained. Willie dropped the raft, grabbed the parachute risers above him, and tried to steer farther out over the water and away from the boats.

Perhaps no one had seen him yet.

In accordance with the Law of Armed Conflict, as a parachutist from a disabled aircraft, no one was supposed to shoot at Willie until he landed. After landing, he was supposed to have the opportunity to surrender. But most irregular North Vietnamese combatants had probably not heard of the Law of Armed Conflict, let alone planned to follow it.

Willie splashed into the gentle swells of the warm Gulf waters. A sampan floated about thirty yards away. Other boats lurked about a mile away. Thirty miles from shore, he had come down in the middle of a fishing ground. At least he wasn't on land.

Two flicks of his fingers over metal fittings released the parachute from his shoulder harness, and it collapsed onto the sea.

With some effort he pulled the raft over and hung onto the side with his right arm. He still couldn't move his left arm; the limb floated next to him, buoyed by the water.

Maybe, he thought, everyone had been too busy fishing to notice him. If he kept his head down, perhaps he could hide long enough for a pickup. Fleet Fox knew where he was, and he expected to see rescue aircraft any minute.

At the trough of a swell, the fishing boats disappeared. They likely couldn't see him either. But at the top of each swell, the boats reappeared. After a few undulations, the sampan nearby turned toward him.

As the boat pulled closer, a man shouted something in Vietnamese and fired his AK-47. The burst hit the water near Willie. Before he could think what to do, the gunman shouted and fired again. It was obvious he wanted Willie to get on the boat. The Vietnamese motioned at a net hanging over the side of the sampan. In no position to argue, Willie surrendered his hold on the raft. Still buoyed by his life vest, he swam over using his good arm.

Bruised from the violent ejection, legs bleeding from his shrapnel wounds, and weighted down by his soaked flight gear, Willie's right foot slipped through the netting. He lost his balance, crashed into the side of the boat, and slid underwater. Holding his breath, he struggled underwater for about thirty seconds until he gripped a rung of the net with his left boot. He pulled himself up with his good arm and, back above water, dragged himself up the remaining three feet of net. Despite Willie's obvious injuries, the Vietnamese continued to shout, apparently annoyed by his captive's slow progress.

Willie grabbed the sampan's railing to pull himself onto the deck. The fisherman smashed Willie's face with the butt of the AK-47. The blow stunned him, and he yelled, "God damn," as he rolled onto the deck. The Vietnamese stopped swinging, and Willie stood up. With his right arm he raised his left over his head in surrender.

The pilot of the Queer Spad spotted Willie.

"This is Robbie 7 overhead. They have him standing up. Not too far ahead."

With that news the air filled with incoherent squeals and cut-off transmissions as more than one pilot tried to talk at once. Finally, a loud, exasperated tone rose above the others: "So much chatter, I can't hear *Barry*."

It's not clear who Barry was, but the frustrated voice knocked radio sense back into the other aviators, and the jumble of excited calls died down.

On the sampan the Vietnamese fisherman looked bewildered at his catch. The six-foot, two-inch Willie towered over his captor. In his flight gear, with a small strobe light flashing on his harness, Willie must have resembled an alien from outer space. His heart pounded harder than if he'd just run a mile at top speed. His world shrank to the deck and the man holding the gun. He thought this would be the last world he would know.

A man he took to be the first mate stepped over and removed Willie's .38 revolver. The man retreated under a tarp in the middle of the boat and trained the weapon on his prey. The fisherman with the AK-47 moved near the front of the boat to keep the captive between them.

Willie didn't see any escape.

Three young men, who under different circumstances might have been friends having a beer, stared at each other, wondering what to do next.

Buffalo Joe and another A-1 pilot circled above. With Willie so close to the enemy, the Spad pilots didn't dare fire at the boat. But Buffalo Joe had an idea.

With his attention riveted on the AK-47, Willie barely noticed the A-1s, until one of them suddenly turned and headed straight for the sampan. Buffalo Joe descended to just a few feet above the water, so low that his propeller left a small wake as he approached. Willie stepped back to brace himself.

The A-1 screamed a few feet above the sampan, so low that the fuel smell and hot wake from the propeller and engine washed over Willie. He knew the Spad wouldn't hit him, but the fisherman with the AK-47 dropped face down onto the deck and curled up.

His captor didn't move, and Willie saw his chance. Maybe he could retrieve the Ruger. But other things were stashed in the pocket. What if the ejection had moved the pistol and he couldn't find it right away? And if he did find it, the weapon normally took two hands to cock—how would he fire it? Would it still work after being in the water?

The Vietnamese still hadn't moved.

Willie unzipped his pocket, and the first thing he touched was the gun's handle.

He pulled the weapon out, rested it on his left kneecap, and, ignoring the searing pain in his left arm, braced the handle with his left index finger and thumb.

He pulled back on the spring, and the Ruger cocked on his first try.

Willie's motion or the cock's snap caught his captor's attention. He looked at Willie holding the pistol and then at his first mate. Confusion was on his face as if to say, "Hey, you took the pistol, but he's standing here holding a pistol."

The fisherman started to get up and turned the AK-47 toward Willie. Willie looked into his captor's eyes and saw that the other man realized it was his day to die, not Willie's.

Willie knew he had to pull the trigger. He had no hesitation.

Willie didn't know that only 15 to 20 percent of soldiers in World War II fired their weapons, even when they could see the enemy right in front of them. The inhibition to take another person's life is so ingrained in our DNA and social norms that many people find it impossible to kill another human. After World War II, improved training led to firing rates as high as 95 percent in Korea and Vietnam, but as a pilot, Willie didn't have that training.[18]

It didn't matter. The boy who mourned the death of a sparrow became part of the 15 to 20 percent.

The reluctant warrior pulled the trigger.

Again.

And again.

Three loud pops, three bullets, seemingly in slow motion, hitting the other man in the face.

One.

Two.

Three.

The fisherman crumpled to the deck.

The horror of what he had done replaced Willie's elation at being alive. He watched, mesmerized, at what looked like dentures sliding from the man's mouth. How could someone this young have dentures, he wondered, before realizing it didn't matter.

By then the first mate had recovered enough to squeeze the .38's trigger. With the first two rounds empty, nothing came out. The startled Vietnamese dropped the revolver onto the deck and leaped overboard.

Willie put the Ruger safety back on and returned it to his survival vest. He jumped into the water and swam back to the life raft still attached to him by the yellow lanyard.

The episode on the sampan felt endless to Willie, but only two and a half minutes after the Queer Spad spotted Willie on the boat, Buffalo Joe called, "The pilot's okay—he's in his raft."

Eight minutes had passed since Willie's ejection. He knew more help was on the way, but plenty could still go wrong. Several of the junks headed toward him.

Buffalo Joe's wingman called, "Hey, there's a lot of boats over there."

"Yeah, I'm going to give them a little of this." A little of this was the Spad's gun.

Clinging to his raft, Willie heard Buffalo Joe's cannon firing into the water not far away. With the Spads protecting him, he relaxed a bit. He didn't think at all about the remaining fisherman, who was probably clinging to the side of the sampan, hoping that the Spads didn't finish him off.

Saintsing checked in, and a controller relayed that the helicopter was now about eighteen miles from Willie. But he added: "You'll probably be aborted. We have Crown Alpha on site."

The Albatross had finally found Willie. With his pickup imminent and Spads protecting him, Cactus Jack and Chippy 3 returned to the *Bonnie Dick*. John Tierney remained to watch over his charge.

The fishing boats continued to threaten, but Buffalo Joe assured everyone, "They're not coming any further as of right now."

Willie spotted the Albatross heading toward him. He would be safe in another minute or so.

Crown Alpha's copilot pressed a button to jettison the external fuel tanks so they could land. But something went wrong.

Crown Alpha's pilot sounded in pain as he called: "Ahhhhh, I tried to blow my fuel tanks, but only the left one went. I'm unable to get the right one off. How far out is the helicopter?"

Fleet Fox called, "Approximately ten miles."

"Bring 'em in and let them make the pickup. I'll continue to see if I can shake this fuel tank loose."

With the A-1s keeping the boats away, Willie wasn't in immediate danger, so there was no need to risk a landing as long as the helicopter could make the pickup. The Albatross crew dropped a smoke light to guide Saintsing and show which way the wind blew to help him with the hover. Crown Alpha circled overhead Willie to keep an eye on him while its pilot tried to shake the recalcitrant tank.

Willie pushed himself and the raft over to the smoke. He could see that only one tank had fallen off the Albatross and assumed that was why the amphibian didn't land. While he waited, he pulled a flare from his survival vest and lit it, figuring that more smoke would help everyone keep him in sight. He still assumed that someone was coming to get him. It was dinnertime in California, but Willie was too busy to think about Nina and what she might be doing, with no inkling her husband was floating in the Gulf of Tonkin.

Tierney continued his vigil above the clouds. With drop tanks not dropping and a slow helicopter inbound, the commander fretted about the activity he couldn't see below the clouds.

Tierney called, "Hey, Joe, you see any more action from those boats?"

"No, ah, one of them fired a tracer, but that's about it."

"Well, if he fires at you, you can let him have it. This is 88."

"I saw about four or five. I don't know which one it was though."

"You say they were firing at ya?"

"One tracer came up at me. They're not moving any closer though." The last transmission seemed to satisfy Tierney; his radio fell silent.

Apparently thinking Saintsing and Welch were closer than they were, a controller called, "You should have the pilot in sight."

His helicopter still about five miles from Willie, Saintsing's North Carolina drawl boomed onto the airwaves: "We have something in sight up here. We don't know what it is. There's several junks in the area."

Someone called, "He-lo, there's a smoke light in the water; you should be able to spot him."

"I think I have him in sight."

Still flying inbound, another ninety seconds passed while Saintsing, the *Gridley*, and Fleet Fox negotiated radio frequency changes. The constant chatter and delays must have been driving Tierney crazy, but trusting the pilots below the clouds, he stayed off the radio.

Saintsing called, "We have the smoke in sight . . . we're approximately two to three miles."

About thirty seconds later: "Crown Alpha, this is Angel four-three. Y'all expect to pick up? I'm one mile now."

During Saintsing's radio call one of the A-1s must have given Crown Alpha a scare because instead of answering, the amphibian's pilot called: "Six-zero-three, we've got a drop tank on the right that hasn't gone. It may go at any time, so I wouldn't get too close."

Saintsing, sounding confused and a bit irritated, called, "Do you want me to make the pickup?"

"Roger, affirmative."

The helicopter crew still hadn't found Willie. Another minute passed before someone called, "Pilot's to the west of the white smoke."

Saintsing and Welsh spotted Willie's raft from about one hundred yards. With the helicopter closing in on him, Willie lit another flare. He didn't want to take any chances.

Already pointed into the wind, Saintsing began a slow descent as Welsh dumped fuel so they would be light enough to hover.

When the Seasprite was about thirty yards away, Welsh called over the loud hailer, "Clear the raft." Willie pushed the raft away.

Saintsing came to a hover about ten feet above Willie. The wake from the rotor wash churned the sea like a mini-typhoon. Shanks and Hug dropped a "horse collar" that resembled a giant teardrop with a hole into the water. Saintsing thought Willie looked fine, so he told Hug not to descend to the water to help.

The best way to get into the collar is to stick your head and both arms through the hole and then pull the cable around to the front. Willie found that impossible with his bad arm. He stuck his right arm through the opening, thinking he would pull the cable around and try to put his head and maybe his left arm through. Shanks and Hug thought Willie had a good enough grip, that he had simply entered the collar backward; they'd seen other downed aircrew do the same thing. They started to reel him in. Attached only by his right arm, Willie wasn't about to let go, even if he had to hold on with his teeth.

7

Recovery

THE DEAD VIETNAMESE FISHERMAN WALKED TOWARD WIL-
lie. Willie gasped and stopped pushing the shopping cart filled
with Christmas presents. Then he realized he was mistaken. It
was not the same man. Shaken, he hesitated as he tried to regain
his composure. But he couldn't fool Nina.

"What's the matter?"

Willie didn't say anything. Three years after his rescue, he had
still not told anyone about the shooting, except for the flight surgeon, his skipper, and his executive officer. He hadn't let it slip to
his closest friends or his roommates, even during alcohol-fueled
confessional bouts. It wasn't a topic that came up in conversation, and the time never seemed right.

Willie pushed the cart out of the store, Nina following. He
couldn't hold it in anymore. Tears streaming down his face in a
Kmart parking lot in Pleasanton, California, the story spilled out.
He hadn't just been rescued; he had killed someone—someone
who looked just like the man in the store. He couldn't bring himself to describe details; he had yet to reconcile the monster who
fired the Ruger with the gentle soul he imagined himself to be.
He knew he had probably killed people on the ground with his
rockets and bombs, but those people had been invisible to him or
indistinct blobs actively firing AAA or SAMS. The fisherman had
somehow been different. Willie hadn't really wanted to kill him,
but he thought he had no choice.

Nina understood. Willie's tears told her everything she needed to know, and she wrapped her arms around her husband as he cried.

Willie resolved that the killing would not take over his life. The first time I interviewed him, he told me, "I just wanted to put that in a shoebox and wrap it with duct tape and pile it into a closet and fill the closet with bricks and then nail the doors shut, plaster over that and paint it, and then it would always be there and I'd never have to think about it again."

His joy at being rescued and the business of family life initially overshadowed thoughts of the killing. But the memory of the fisherman lay dormant, like a seed waiting to sprout and lay claim to the surrounding land. More than two decades later, the seed in Willie began to grow.

A deafening silence reigned for more than a minute as the Seasprite hovered over Willie. John Tierney couldn't stand it any longer. "Crown Alpha, Rocket 88. What is the progress?"

"Helicopter's making the pickup now."

"Roger, if you'll inform me when they pick up, I'll relay word back to the carrier."

Twenty seconds later Crown Alpha called, "Helo's made the pickup, has the pilot aboard now."

With Willie safe, Tierney and the Spads departed, while the Albatross accompanied the helicopter back toward the *Gridley*.

Soaking wet, Willie sat on the chopper's floor and looked up at one of his excited rescuers, a young enlisted flyer clad in his requisite orange flight suit. He shouted over the din of the helicopter, "Are you okay, sir?"

"I'm okay," Willie shouted back, meaning, in aviator speak, I'm not about to die.

Hug and Shanks helped Willie stagger to his feet. Out of the water, his left arm once again hung uselessly. Putting any weight on his right heel hurt, and he realized for the first time that his legs were bleeding.

He admitted, "I need to see a doctor."

Despite his pain, Willie jumped around and shouted with joy

at being alive. He poked his head into the cockpit to thank Saintsing and Welsh, but Welsh elbowed him back—the pilots still had to land on the *Gridley* before they could claim success. Hug and Shanks helped Willie out of his soaked flight gear and draped a blanket around his shoulders.

He felt as though he could float from happiness. He had come so close to a much worse end. In the water he had been reacting without time to think. Realizing he was safe, he felt a huge sigh of relief, as if he had studied hard for a test and aced it.

So much had gone wrong—the hit, the fisherman, the other boats, the Albatross that couldn't land. But so much had gone right—the F-8 that held together, the ejection over water, the Spads to protect him, the Ruger, the .38's empty chambers, the helicopter that seemed to appear out of nowhere. Willie didn't know his rescuers had come from the *Gridley*, that his rescue was part of a successful experiment.

The enormity of what had happened came over him, the decisions he had made and the results of those decisions. All his training, all his life experiences, every fiber of his existence, had somehow combined to help him make the best decisions.

Willie didn't think at all about the dead fisherman.

While Willie contemplated his survival, Saintsing called Fleet Fox to discuss the return trip to the *Gridley*. "The pilot says he needs to see a doctor. Do you want us to drop him off and go pick the doctor up and come back?"

A brief delay, then, "This is Fleet Fox, affirmative, over."

Seconds later, "This is Fleet Fox, doctor's aboard Willow." Willow was a nearby destroyer, the USS *Tucker*.

"Roger, we'll drop the survivor off at *Gridley*, then go to Fleet Fox and pick up a doctor, return to *Gridley*."

"Negative, negative, go to Willow to pick up doctor and return to *Gridley*."

With the *Gridley* only two minutes away, Saintsing challenged this new direction. "Where is Willow at this time?"

"Zero-five-four, fourteen miles from me." Well past the *Gridley*.

After a quick mental calculation, Saintsing pushed back. "Zero-five-four, fourteen, I think we let this pilot off, let him get in some dry clothes before we pick up the doctor."

Fleet Fox caved. "Concur, let pilot change clothes."

Two minutes later, twenty-six minutes after Willie's ejection, Angel 43 was cleared to land.

Saintsing set the helicopter down on the *Gridley*'s fantail. Willie dropped a couple of feet to the ship's deck and crouched as he moved away from the still-whirling rotors. He turned around and watched Angel 43 take off to collect the doctor.

Willie, by tradition, saluted the *Gridley*'s "ensign," the ship's flag. An officer clasping his bridge cap to his head with one hand to keep it from blowing away came up to Willie.

"Follow me, sir."

Willie limped to a hatch held open by an enlisted sailor, who saluted Willie and said, "Welcome home, sir."

Inside the *Gridley*'s sick bay, Willie exchanged his wet flight suit for a dry bathrobe. The doctor arrived, sutured the cuts in his legs, and decided the shoulder injury was a severe dislocation. His left arm in a sling, Willie's next stop was Captain Sackett's quarters. As Willie entered the stateroom, the captain looked up from his desk and asked, "Scotch or bourbon?"

"Yes and yes," Willie replied.

Sackett laughed and motioned Willie to sit. The older man poured scotch into two glasses and handed one to Willie.

"Tell me everything that happened."

After Willie related his story, Sackett gave him a tour of the ship. The crew ran a missile onto a launch rail above the deck so Willie could see the U.S. answer to the SAMs the North Vietnamese had shot at him.

Willie stayed overnight and the next day on the *Gridley*. The dead fisherman crowded his thoughts before exhaustion took over. The second evening, at dinner, Sackett made Willie an honorary crew member, and a controller from the CIC presented him a reel with a tape recording of the radio transmissions during his rescue. Someone had appended a short explanation to the twenty-nine-minute tape that concluded with, "In addition to your destroyer qualification sheet presented by Captain Sackett this evening, this tape of the history of your first punch out with the compliments of the uss *Gridley*, take this and may it be a memento and perhaps conversation piece in your ripe old age."

Saintsing and his crew flew Angel 43 back to the *Oriskany*. Before departing the *Gridley*, Saintsing handed Willie a business card that read, "Know ye that William D. Sharp having been rescued from the clutches of the Denizens of the Deep and removed from the Peril of spending Eternity in Davey Jones' Locker by a Hutron One Helicopter on 18 November 1965 is hereby required to mark this date and pay annual homage to the officers and men of the Pacific Angels." The card was signed by Tom Saintsing as the "Retrieving Angel." Willie understood that the "annual homage" meant a bottle of alcohol.

At nearly midnight on Willie's second evening aboard the *Gridley*, he began hopscotching his way back to the *Bonnie Dick*. The *Gridley* was connected by a highline to the oiler the uss *Neches* during a refueling. The highline transferred supplies, mail, and, that evening, Willie, sitting in a small cage. He had not expected his celebrity status to continue, but the oiler's xo invited him to stay in his private quarters. Like Sackett, the commander wanted to hear about the adventure. The xo also asked a favor: sailors on oilers don't get many pats on the head; could Willie write a letter that the xo could read to the crew? Willie agreed to do so.

The next morning Willie highlined to the uss *Hornet*, another aircraft carrier. After lunch a helicopter flew him back to the *Bonnie Dick*. He did not complete his knock "and a threesie" on the Ready Room wall for the mission on November 18. Instead, he spent another night in the sick bay before being cleared to fly again. Before flying, there was paperwork to fill out and conversations to be had with his skipper and xo. He told them, "I left my revolver back there," and explained what happened. As part of the loss report, Willie filled out a questionnaire about the ejection and how well his survival equipment had worked. For the question "Did you have any problems with the use of survival equipment? Please explain," Willie wrote, "My thirty-eight (.38) pistol was lost during the ejection and survival radio did not work (it was the old model)." He could not bring himself to write in the report the real reason for losing the gun. In a different answer he dropped a hint that something involving a pistol might have happened. For the question "Do you have any recommendations related to survival equipment?" he wrote, "Highly recommend carrying two pistols—the .38 with tracers for signaling, a .22, etc., for survival." He then seemed to have second thoughts and added, "Or one light, accurate pistol to do both duties."

Willie didn't say anything about the killing to anyone besides his superiors. He wrote Nina a letter explaining only that he had ejected and been rescued. He didn't add any details.

The yeoman who maintained Willie's logbook wrote, "A/C lost at sea," in the "Remarks" column for November 18. He noted that Willie made one catapult shot that day but no landing.

Willie still had most of his flight gear, and he easily replaced the items he had lost. Only four days after his ejection, he rode a small carrier-based cargo aircraft into Cubi Point. He spent the night and then returned to the *Bonnie Dick* the next day in an F-8.

With his injuries Willie could have returned to the safety of the United States, but he couldn't stand the thought of leaving his friends behind on the carrier. To him it seemed cowardly to go home when he didn't have to. If he left the *Bonnie Dick*, the enemy would have achieved the same result as if they had killed him. He decided to stay. He flew twenty more combat missions, including three on Thanksgiving Day.

On November 28 the first Seasprites equipped with armor plates and navy crews specifically trained for the CSAR mission arrived in the Gulf of Tonkin. For the rest of the war, detachments of CSAR helicopters were stationed on guided missile frigates.[1]

At 11:16 p.m. on Thursday, December 16, the *Bonnie Dick's* deck log noted, "Completed recovering aircraft; this completes the operation of aircraft from the USS Bon Homme Richard (CVA-31) against enemy forces in Vietnam for the year 1965." Three minutes later the carrier headed south, arriving back in San Diego on New Year's Eve.

A few days after Thanksgiving, Satan's Kittens lost one more pilot to the war: the XO, Cdr. Howie Rutledge, was captured after being shot down. The squadron had lost one-fourth of its sixteen pilots during the cruise: two killed and two captured. Willie had narrowly escaped being the fifth. During 1965 more than 150 U.S. airmen were killed in action in Southeast Asia, and 55 became prisoners; at least 20 POWs were naval aviators.[2] No one yet had any idea where the POWs were or how they were being treated. That would soon change.

As Willie returned to a life of domesticity, his acquaintance from the recruiting office, Dieter Dengler, embarked on what is likely the wildest survival of the Vietnam War. Dengler's aviation dreams had also come true: the German immigrant had become a Spad pilot. A-1 pilots at the time had an abbreviated training course, and Dengler received his gold wings about one month before Willie. Hard times in postwar Germany helped Dengler become a legend at the survival course: he escaped three times from his "guards." With his scrounging skills, he even gained weight during the week, unheard of for an experience in which just about everyone lost weight.[3]

As the *Bonnie Dick* steamed home, Dengler was heading to Vietnam. His cruise didn't last long: he was shot down on February 1, 1966, while attacking a target in Laos.[4] Dengler had customized his survival gear with a High Standard .22 semiautomatic pistol, extra food, extra medical supplies, fake IDs, and even one hundred–dollar bills hidden inside the tongues of his boots. He never got to use any of it: he was quickly captured by Pathet Lao troops.[5] He escaped, was recaptured, and then was turned over to North Vietnamese soldiers, who took him to a POW camp in Laos that housed six other Americans.[6] After being moved to another camp, the Americans escaped on June 29. Dengler paired up with 1st Lt. Duane Martin, an air force pilot who had been shot down and captured the previous September. Martin was killed during an encounter with villagers, but Dengler slipped back into the jungle. Near death, he was finally rescued on July 20, 1966, after surviving nearly six months of torture, starvation, and evasion.[7]

Dengler's escape and rescue became a media sensation.[8] He spent two months recovering in the navy's hospital in San Diego.[9] Willie went to visit one afternoon and asked, "Can I bring you anything?"

"I want to get out of here and go eat!"

The navy was tightly monitoring its hero's recovery; he couldn't just waltz out of the hospital. That evening Willie returned carrying a long coat over his arm. When he entered Dengler's room, the other pilot was dressed in civilian clothes, including brown shoes. He donned the long coat and added a bridge cap to his outfit. He looked like any naval officer. The pair of aviators walked nonchalantly out of the hospital. Joined by Nina, they drove to a nearby Italian restaurant. After two hours of drinking and dining, Willie returned the thoroughly lubricated Spad pilot to his hospital bed. Apparently, no one missed him that evening, although he reportedly drove navy officials crazy with several other "escapes" during his recovery.[10]

Despite Dengler's antics, the navy awarded its now famous pilot the Navy Cross, but it refused to send him back to combat. Instead, he learned to fly A-4s and spent the next eighteen months in a stateside assignment before leaving the navy.

Not long after Willie took Dieter to dinner, it was time for him to return to Vietnam, this time on a different carrier. Earlier in the year Satan's Kittens and Carrier Air Wing 19 had been reassigned to the USS *Ticonderoga*, usually shortened as "*Tico*." A half-dozen F-8 pilots arrived from East Coast bases to replace Kittens who left the navy or moved to other assignments. The new pilots were eager to get into combat, as if it were a lark, the same thing as strafing targets on the Yuma training range. Willie found their attitude naive as well as insulting to the squadron mates he'd lost during his first cruise. He had been eager for his first combat tour as well, but that was early in the war, before the handful of retaliatory raids grew into a relentless killing machine. Hardly an elder warrior himself, he tried to counsel the younger pilots, to warn them of the ugliness he had seen, a counseling he wished he had heard before his first tour.

In October 1966 the *Tico* left San Diego to join the *Oriskany* and other carriers at Yankee Station. On October 27, 1966, a fire on board the *Oriskany* claimed forty-four lives.

As the one-year anniversary of his shoot-down approached, Willie planned to honor the annual homage required by Saintsing's card. Per tradition, each rescuee sent his rescuers a bottle of their favorite adult beverage. Willie dispatched a note to the *Oriskany* asking what Welsh and Saintsing wanted. The answer came back that there would be no need: both pilots had died in the fire. The news crushed Willie. His coat of armor had kept the killing in the recesses of his mind, but the anniversary brought the gruesome images forward. He was happy to be alive, even celebratory, but still horrified by what he had done. Paying homage to the angels who had saved his life might have been some small atonement for the killing. Now even that small gesture was gone, another human connection ripped from him, like so many others.

On the *Tico* Willie roomed again with Lee and a third experienced pilot, Bill Worley. The trio occupied a four-man stateroom four levels below the flight deck. They turned the extra space in the relatively quiet room into an entertainment center that included the reel-to-reel recorder from the first cruise. Willie, who had started his first cruise as a rule-following rookie, was now one of the old hands. He saw nothing wrong with adding a well-stocked bar, including a blender. A steward even brought ice if they asked. A porthole in the room made it easy to get rid of the evidence—mostly empty bottles—that accompanied their contraband.

The new squadron xo had a reputation for being straitlaced, but during his first meeting with the pilots he said, "If I don't see any evidence of drinking, it's not happening." Willie and his roommates took the comment as at least a yellow light, if not a green one, to keep stocking their liquor locker. A few days later, after flying was over for the day, Willie made a martini, and Lee poured a scotch on the rocks. Before they could take a sip, they heard a knock on the bulkhead.

"Just a second!" Willie called. Lee scrambled to hide the drinks.

Willie opened the curtain to the hall. "Oh, hi, Commander Aldern."

The xo stepped into the stateroom and looked around. "Nice space you've got here. Air-conditioned."

Willie and Lee stood at attention and mumbled, "Yessir."

"I've been told you have some liquor down here."

Willie and Lee grimaced at each other. They couldn't lie; getting caught in a lie would be worse than getting caught with alcohol. Lee stepped over to the locker and opened the door. The contents looked like they had burglarized a liquor store.

The xo stared at the alcohol for a long time, as if considering an appropriate punishment.

Finally, "Is that Glenfiddich?"

Three hours later Willie and Lee carried the xo back to his stateroom.

Aldern was the sort of leader Willie could get behind, but he soon learned that the new CAG, a self-proclaimed "world's greatest fighter pilot," was no John Tierney.

One night when Willie was the LSO, already stormy seas roughened to the point that two pilots finishing a "FORCE CAP" combat air patrol mission barely made it aboard the carrier. Willie called Pri Fly and asked to speak to the CAG.

"Hold on a sec. We gotta get him out of the movie."

About three minutes later Willie heard a rough voice say through the receiver, "CAG."

"Willie Sharp, LSO. Sir, I recommend we shut down the FORCE CAP due to the deteriorating weather." Willie expected immediate agreement and perhaps a compliment for his good judgment.

The CAG inhaled sharply. "One, the weather isn't that bad. Two, don't ever call me again in the middle of a movie."

One night at the Cubi Club, Willie witnessed the new CAG being taken down a peg. A legendary fistfight broke out between the CAG and a "Caspar Milquetoast" intelligence officer. The world's greatest fighter pilot ended up with a black eye. The next day a collection of junior officers, Willie included, blackened their eyes with soot and stood at attention in two lines, saluting the humiliated CAG as he passed between them to board a helicopter.

On March 3, 1967, the CAG committed his worst sin, in Willie's opinion. The CAG was leading three F-8s, one flown by Willie, during an attack on a bridge in North Vietnam. As Willie pulled away after dropping his bombs, he felt a thump, like the AAA hit that led to his ejection. He couldn't see any damage, and nothing in the cockpit indicated a problem, but he couldn't be sure. He asked the CAG to come take a look. Just then, the third pilot lost one of his hydraulic systems. Willie considered the loss of one hydraulic system a relatively minor emergency; the checklist had a standard set of procedures to follow, and the aircraft could easily be landed back on the carrier. But the CAG seemed to think otherwise.

"I'd better get this guy back."

Willie, astonished, didn't say anything.

The CAG added, "We'll wait for you feet wet."

Willie assumed the other two pilots would speed ahead to the Gulf and wait for him to catch up. Once over the water, Willie didn't find the pair, but he assumed the CAG would return for him after escorting the other pilot back to the carrier. The CAG landed instead.

Willie was furious at being abandoned. He knew Tierney would have never left him. Fortunately, the damage was relatively minor: the round had only sliced an eighteen-inch hole in the front of his left wing, and he had no problems catching a wire. But he knew how much worse the hit could have been, and he couldn't forgive the CAG.

On the *Tico* Willie also experienced his only loss as an LSO. One afternoon, with no combat operations and good weather prevailing except for a gusty wind, he expected a routine LSO tour. A little past one Lt. Chester Nightengale approached in an A-4. The Scooter was easy to land compared to most carrier aircraft, but Nightengale was in trouble. He reduced power because he was too high, then got too slow and added too much power. He kept cycling back and forth, too much power, then too little.

As the A-4 neared the ramp, Willie decided Nightengale couldn't touchdown safely. He pressed the pickle button and shouted into his handset, "Wave off, wave off!"

Despite the insistent flashing glideslope lights and Willie's pleas, Nightengale settled toward the ramp instead of climbing away.

The A-4 slammed into the top of the ramp at the fantail. The jet rolled inverted and veered toward the LSO stand. Willie dove into the safety net as the A-4 sheared all the equipment off the platform, fell into the water, and sank. Even though searchers knew exactly where the airplane had gone down, the only thing they recovered was the pilot's helmet.[11]

For days afterward Willie had trouble falling asleep. He saw the jet hit the back of the carrier again and again. He wasn't at fault, but guilt weighed on him. Should he have called for a wave off sooner? Had Nightengale not heard him? He'd monitored hundreds of successful traps, but the single failure made him feel useless.

Willie's second combat tour was his last. For the two tours combined, the navy awarded him a Distinguished Flying Cross, fifteen Air Medals, and two Navy Commendation Medals, along with the Purple Heart for his injuries on his first tour. During more than three hundred combat missions, he never once saw a MiG, let alone had a chance to shoot one down. He wasn't alone; of the hundreds of pilots who flew the F-8 during Vietnam, only nineteen were credited with killing an enemy aircraft.

After returning to San Diego, the navy assigned Willie to Kingsville, Texas, where he trained other officers as LSOs. Although he never mentioned the killing, he passed his combat experiences on to the younger pilots—he wanted them to understand that they would see death and loss during their combat tours and that they might die or be taken prisoners themselves. The war had become increasingly unpopular in the United States and around the world. Willie no longer believed a victory in Vietnam was worth the price being paid. But even if he no longer believed in the war itself, he wanted to help others survive their combat tours.

By moving to Texas, Willie got away from the CAG whom he hated, but he still couldn't get away from death. His *Tico* roommate, Bill Worley, had joined the Blue Angels demonstration team. He called just before Christmas in 1967 and said he would come to Kingsville in January to pick up an aircraft for the team. But the reunion never happened. On January 14 Worley died in a crash during a practice session near El Centro, California.[12]

Willie completed his five-year commitment to the navy in the summer of 1968. He had never really thought about making the navy a career, and the ever-expanding airlines beckoned. United Airlines hired him. The family, now with a second daughter, settled into a house in Pleasanton, about an hour from the San Francisco airport. A third daughter followed.

For a quarter century Willie lived the ordinary life of an airline pilot with a wife and kids in the suburbs. He was gone a lot, but his trips were a few days at a time, not the navy's months-long deployments. Nina kept the household going during his absences. Every few years Willie moved up to another aircraft in the 700-series Boeing airframes, flying the 727, 737, and 757. Every move up meant more pay. Eventually, he was promoted to captain, flying in the left seat and in charge, as he had been in his F-8 decades earlier.

In the early 1990s Willie began waking up in the middle of the night feeling afraid, with a sense of foreboding. At first he chalked the sleep disruptions up to growing older. But during a layover in Philadelphia, he had a full-blown nightmare: he saw the bullets hitting the fisherman in the face, and he woke with a start, disoriented by the darkness of his hotel room. It was daytime when he fired the shots; why was it now dark?

After a few seconds of confusion, he realized he was not in Vietnam. He was a fifty-something airline pilot who had to get up in a few hours and fly a load of passengers across the country.

The nightmares continued. If he awoke at home, the slumbering form beside him disoriented him further and he thought, what is Nina doing in Vietnam?

The terrors didn't come every night but often enough that Willie began to dread falling asleep; he sometimes lay awake for hours. Not wanting to jeopardize his career, he told no one about the bad dreams.

According to the book *On Killing: The Psychological Cost of Learning to Kill in War and Society,* by Lt. Col. Dave Grossman, it would have been just about impossible for Willie's killing of the fisherman to stay packed away.

The nature of most combat provides psychological protection for individuals: orders to shoot from a higher authority, the safety of a group, and the inability to see distinctly the enemy killed. Aircrew members, who rarely see their victims during an air or ground attack, have very few psychological problems from combat.[13] Even soldiers who can make out the enemy standing across a field or a street are protected by killing as part of a group: with so many people shooting, you have plausible deniability that one of your bullets actually killed someone. Many combat veterans claim they have never killed anyone.[14]

Willie's kill, which Grossman terms a "personal kill," had none of these protections. Although he was obliged to try to avoid capture, no one had ordered him to shoot. He could not deny that he had shot the Vietnamese man, and he had made a personal connection, not only seeing his victim's face but looking into his eyes. Grossman says that only about 2 percent of the population can survive a personal kill like this without becoming a psychiatric casualty.[15]

Willie was not part of that 2 percent.

About twenty-five years ago someone rear-ended me on a freeway as I slowed to avoid an accident. The violent collision shoved my car forward; I bounced off a concrete divider and spun around, before coming to a rest. Except for a minor scratch and extreme soreness for several days, I wasn't injured. But for weeks afterward I had trouble falling asleep. I kept hearing the collision over and over again as I tried to think about other things. After the accident I was nervous about driving on freeways for a couple of years. Brake lights in front of me sent waves of panic coursing through my body, and I looked obsessively in my rearview mirror to make sure no one was bearing down on me. I sometimes forgot about the traffic in front of me and had to slam harder on my brakes when I looked forward again. The collision intruded on my thoughts for several months before eventually fading away. I rarely think about the accident any longer, and when I do, it no longer triggers any emotion. The freeway panic also faded.

In terms of trauma my accident was almost nothing, yet it took my mind several months to let go. What if I had been a nineteen-year-old soldier who witnessed her best friend blown to bits by an improvised explosive device? Or a young marine who survived a dozen firefights while fellow marines died around her? These circumstances, unimaginable for most of us, burn into a person's soul.

I hesitate to even use the word *trauma* in relation with my accident. My experience was more like a scratch that heals within a week or two; the scar might remain longer, but it eventually disappears. Much combat trauma is akin to the deep thrust of a knife; the external scar can perhaps be covered with clothing or makeup, but the internal damage remains, hidden away.

A decade before the term post-traumatic stress disorder (PTSD) was introduced to the American public, the Vietnam Veterans against the War (VVAW) decided to do something about combat trauma. In 1967 a band of six Vietnam veterans marched together in a peace demonstration and afterward formed the VVAW. Three years later the VVAW began to hold "rap groups" to help those among them who struggled with war trauma.[16] In 1980 the American Psychiatric Association recognized PTSD as a disease by entering it into its *Diagnostic and Statistical Manual of Mental Disorders.*[17]

The Veterans Administration (VA) describes PTSD as "a mental health problem that some people develop after experiencing or witnessing a life-threatening event, like combat, a natural disaster, a car accident, or sexual assault." The VA estimates that about 30 percent of Vietnam veterans have suffered from PTSD during their life. Current VA treatments for PTSD focus on psychotherapy and medication.[18] At first, however, the condition was largely misunderstood and poorly treated. Many people even brushed off the idea of PTSD, considering its victims as weak or perhaps damaged prior to their traumatic experiences; some still do. Once, when I related Willie's story to a group of pilots, a couple of them opined that Willie was simply overthinking his experience. They were sure that they would not have had the same reaction as Willie. I tried to convince them that they had no way of knowing their reaction since they didn't have the experience, but I gave up.

John Miller, a retired U.S. Army lieutenant general and Vietnam veteran, belongs to a growing number of veterans and therapists who believe PTSD should not be treated as only a mental health problem but instead as a "moral wound." All humans have a moral dimension, whether they are religious or not; morals are what form us as human beings. No matter our religious beliefs, it is not normal to kill people and destroy property; moral wounds occur even if killing and destruction are done legally, as in wartime.

Once someone has a moral wound, they want to heal and move back to their life as it was before the injury, but that isn't possible; the scar from the wound is now a permanent part of the person. Amputees are taught to mourn the loss of their limb or limbs and to focus on the new person they are and the capabilities that they still have. We don't encourage those with moral wounds to do the same.[19]

Dr. Edward Tick, a psychotherapist who has worked with veterans since the 1970s, believes that calling moral wounds a mental health "disorder" focuses on the treatment of symptoms rather than the healing and restoration that returning warriors require from their communities.[20] From Tick's perspective our entire country suffers from PTSD because our modern society no longer takes a collective responsibility for war.[21] Ancient and traditional societies embraced a warrior class, whose members went through rituals of initiation, restoration, and return that involved their entire community. Warriors told their stories of combat trauma in public, and the community accepted the responsibility for those traumas since they were not the ones who had to fight.[22] Poetry and prayer were common expressions for trauma, including the *Iliad* and the *Odyssey*; many of David's Psalms in the Bible are anguished cries for the redemption of his many sins on and off the battlefield.[23]

Although Tick acknowledges that PTSD related to trauma exists, he believes that combat trauma is in a separate category from that created by other forms of trauma such as car accidents and sexual assault, especially when a veteran has been involved in killing. When it comes to combat trauma, Tick suggests that PTSD should be renamed "post-traumatic social disorder" or "post-traumatic soul distress," names that more accurately reflect that combat trauma is not a disease to be medicated and counseled until it recedes into the corners of an individual's mind but, rather, a disorder that must be set right by our entire society.[24] What we now call PTSD has been given many names in past conflicts: soldier's heart during the Civil War, shell shock during World War I, and combat fatigue during World War II.[25] Soldier's heart may be the best term for what happens to warriors who have faced combat and killing; it implies more than a wound or injury and conveys that the wound is honorable and must be carried for life.[26]

A common myth endures that World War II veterans don't suffer from PTSD because that war was viewed as "honorable." Many World War II veterans came home, took advantage of the GI Bill to attend college, and became part of the American dream. Like Willie's uncles, most World War II veterans talked little about their war experiences, although many who served clearly endured much trauma.[27] Some of them retreated completely inside themselves, like Willie's reclusive neighbor in Dinuba. But as many veterans who had been silent reached retirement age, they suddenly found themselves confronted with nightmares similar to Willie's and began to seek treatment at VA hospitals.[28]

I've sometimes wondered if one of those "silent vets" was one of my paternal great uncles, Robert Kubly, who was captured in the Philippine Islands in April 1942. He endured the Bataan Death March and more than three years of internment in Japan.[29] After he returned from the war, my uncle married a nurse he met during his recovery in his home state of Wisconsin. They had a daughter and moved to Southern California, where the daughter died while still an infant, yet another soul-searing trauma. The only other child, a son, disappeared as a teenager during the 1960s. My uncle had very little contact with my father and his relatives. I was vaguely aware that my grandmother had a brother, but I don't remember hearing about him during annual visits to Wisconsin as a child. One day in the mid-1990s, after I told my mother about a Bataan Death March reenactment and memorial that takes place at White Sands Missile Range every year, she mentioned that my great uncle was a March survivor. Incredulous that I had never heard the story, I pressed her and my father for details. They said nothing that pointed to any reason for my uncle to be estranged, except that perhaps my great-grandmother hadn't liked the nurse he married. I speculated that war trauma made him want to start a new life when he returned, or maybe he had a hard time fitting back into rural life after seeing more of the world. Perhaps he felt ashamed or embarrassed by his captivity—a few POWs I have talked to thought not only that had they not done anything special but that they had screwed up by getting captured in the first place. They felt embarrassed when people fawned over them and called them heroes. My father declined to speculate whether his uncle might have suffered from his war trauma. I didn't try to find Uncle Robert for another decade, and after a bit of internet sleuthing, I learned he had died in 2004. I also learned of a haunting coincidence: his daughter was buried in a cemetery in Lancaster, California, a town where I spent much time when I was stationed at nearby Edwards Air Force Base. Newspaper articles told me that my uncle had apparently led an ordinary life in California. Late in life he had talked some about his combat experience: an article featured the story of his captivity, and the details matched what my father had told me. I made some half-hearted attempts to find my uncle's son but gave up after a few tantalizing leads slipped away. Like many World War II veterans, my uncle's warrior spirit has vanished.

David Morris, an embedded reporter in Iraq from 2004 to 2007, knows about silence from veterans. In *The Evil Hours: A*

Biography of Post-Traumatic Stress Disorder Morris bemoaned that
he could not talk about his experiences. Nonveterans often didn't
give him a chance to tell his story about being nearly blown up
before interrupting with their views on the Iraq War or with racist
comments about Arabs.[30] When interviewing military veterans,
even those who were never in combat, I, too, have seen this dis-
connect with society. After interviewing someone, I always thank
them for their time. I'm always amazed at how many say something like "No, I want to thank you for *your* time. It's so nice to talk
to someone who understands me. I haven't told these stories for
decades because I have no one to talk to. Thank you for bringing
back these memories." Other than a slide presentation arranged
by his in-laws to about twenty people in a tiny California town,
Willie told no public stories when he returned from Vietnam.

Simply thanking veterans for their service is not enough, and
many veterans tire of the phrase. Tick instead prescribes multiple actions to help heal moral wounds and restore warriors to
their rightful place in society: as elder warriors who act as a cau-
tion against war and mentor younger members as they are initiated into the brotherhood and, increasingly, sisterhood of the
warrior class. He suggests we must restore meaning and respect
to Memorial Day and Veterans Day, instead of viewing them as
excuses for sales and a day off from work. We should invite veterans to share their stories with civilians through appearances
at libraries, schools, and cultural centers. Older veterans should
mentor younger veterans when they return from combat, and veterans should be encouraged to express themselves through cre-
ative arts such as literary essays and paintings that become part
of our society.[31] Only when we do these things can we heal as a
nation and embrace the sacrifice of our warriors.

PTSD among warriors is not destiny; in fact, it may be unique
to the American way of waging war. Vietnamese soldiers, many
of whom endured decades of battle, report few PTSD symptoms
such as flashbacks and failure to reintegrate into society. These
Vietnamese soldiers may have been largely protected from PTSD
because they saw themselves as defending their country from

invaders trying to take away their families, homes, and children.[32] Willie understood this dynamic. When he first related his story about killing the fisherman to me, he said: "A lot of people say, 'Good, you shot the little prick,' but I say, he's North Vietnamese, he's in North Vietnam, defending his country, and I'm the invader here. Who's really the bad guy? I didn't hate him. I didn't want to do that. When I celebrate surviving on the eighteenth [of November], I always feel grief for him. He had to have brothers and sisters, mom and dad, maybe a wife and children, who knows. I took no pleasure in that at all. He was defending his country. He wasn't doing anything wrong."

The family of the fisherman whom Willie killed would likely have viewed their relative's death as honorable. As members of a communal, largely Buddhist society, they are probably at peace with their loss. They would not have blamed Willie.[33]

Willie continued to fly for United until he reached the mandatory airline pilot retirement age of sixty in late 2000. By then he was flying Boeing's newest airframe, the 777. After retirement Willie's nightmares continued. Nina encouraged him to go to the VA for treatment, and Willie finally agreed. After much paperwork, he saw a VA counselor, who suggested he sleep with a nightlight to reduce the confusion of waking in the dark. The counselor also told him to talk about the incident, which he started to do with anyone who would listen. He joined a therapy group, in which he could discuss his experience with other veterans. Slowly, the trauma began to heal, but like other veterans, Willie will always have soldier's heart. Even Vietnamese veterans suffer at times from prolonged grief, melancholy, and disappointment; these reactions are inevitable for those with a moral wound.[34]

Willie also instinctively adopted some of Tick's other suggestions, such as giving back to his community and becoming an elder warrior as a way of creating meaning from his wound.[35] Mentoring younger aviators when he returned from his first combat tour provided an early means to channel his warrior spirit. After retiring from United, Willie answered an ad for a literacy project. He started out helping older people who had never learned to read and then, realizing that many immigrants struggled with English, got his certificate to teach English as a second language (ESL). His ESL classroom had a nursery to make it possible for those among his twenty students who had kids to attend. Willie loved the diversity of his classes: about half his students were Latino, and the rest were a mixture of Korean, Chinese, Indian, and the occasional Japanese. He began every new class by telling his students to think of themselves as strands in a cable, woven together to make the cable flexible and strong, like his shipmates and fellow pilots from decades earlier. Over the years he accompanied sixteen students to their citizenship ceremonies.

In 2010 Willie returned to Vietnam, along with Nina and another couple. The group took a short cruise to see the karst limestone formations in Halong Bay, a part of the Gulf of Tonkin. While riding a bus to the cruise embarkment point, they passed a power plant sporting a new smokestack alongside an older one. Willie remarked to Nina and his friends that he had flown on the raid that had knocked down the original smokestack. Their tour guide, a man in his early twenties, caught part of Willie's comment and asked him to repeat it. When Willie did so, the young man said, "Oh." He had no memory of the war, and he didn't hold Willie or anyone else responsible for destruction to his homeland. The knowledge that an entire country had moved on helped give Willie permission to move on as well.

More recently, Willie became a docent on the USS *Hornet*, the Essex-class carrier similar to the *Bonnie Dick* where he spent a few hours on his journey back to his ship after being rescued. The *Hornet* has been transformed into a museum docked in Alameda, the town where Willie took the first steps toward fulfilling his aviation dreams. Much of his Vietnam era flying gear—flight suit, harness, pilot spurs—adorns a mannequin on display inside the carrier. He gives tours to visitors, along with relating his personal experiences (fig. 22).

The United States continues to struggle with combat trauma in returning war veterans, and now a new class of trauma is

Fɪɢ. 22. Willie as a docent on the USS *Hornet*. (Photo by the author)

emerging, trauma that occurs in operators of remotely piloted aircraft (RPA) and the intelligence analysts who digest the live video
streams of targets and combat collected from thousands of miles
away. RPA operators and analysts often observe a human target
for days and weeks, during which time they may learn intimate
details about the person's family and life. When a strike takes

place, the killing is much closer to a personal kill than a bomb dropped on a faceless target. The resulting trauma suffered by some RPA operators bolsters the idea that it is the killing that produces a wound in the killer, not the combat itself. RPA operators and analysts are not in combat and do not fear being killed. Remoteness may in fact aggravate the trauma: when someone is in a "fair fight," in which they can be killed themselves, killing an enemy can be morally justified. But what happens when you are in a sterile environment halfway around the globe and at the end of your shift you get a text message from your spouse asking you to do some ordinary errand such as pick up a gallon of milk on your way home?[36] We have yet to answer this question.

The VA is trying new approaches to PTSD, such as surfing, horseback riding, and other activities. Teams of veterans approach and counsel other veterans in distress.[37] In addition, a drug originally developed for heart patients, propranolol, can help veterans and other victims forget or deal with their trauma. But forgetting trauma or making it manageable raises a dilemma: if inflicting trauma no longer carries consequences, do we risk becoming a society more willing to wage war or use other violence?[38] Propranolol remains a controversial drug, not a miraculous solution to a wound that carries a moral aspect. Until U.S. society recognizes the unique nature of moral wounds and the culpability of society writ large, we may doom our returning warriors to trauma for life.

8

Never Forget

THE LINGERING OREGON SUMMER SUNLIGHT MADE IT EASY to find the sculpture—the robed hands clasped in prayer, the shock of white against a backdrop of red bricks. Carol Leitschuh had learned about the Praying Hands Memorial just minutes earlier that evening in 2016, from a priest at dinner. As she drew closer to the sculpture, she began to see engraved names in bricks that made up a broken wall. Eighty names in all, memorializing students from the University of Portland who had died serving their country from World War I through the Gulf Wars. Sixty-nine names came from World War II, including the name Carol had come to see: her uncle John H. Carroll Jr., whom she had never met.

A few days later Carol showed photos of the memorial to her aunt Jeanne, John's younger sister. Jeanne stared at the photo of the brick with the name of her only brother, who had died seventy-two years earlier. The university's class of 1948 had built the memorial, but somehow its existence had escaped her and the rest of the Carroll family. Her voice tinged with sadness, she said, "That's the only marker we have for John."

John H. Carroll Jr. seemed destined to become a renaissance man: in high school he lettered in football; was president of his sophomore class; and was a member of the physics, chemistry, and drama clubs. He learned to ski without a chairlift, climbing to the top of a mountain in the Cascades and skiing down. After graduating from high school, in 1940, he began studying for an engineering degree at the University of Portland, where his father John H. Carroll Sr. worked as a purchasing agent. The next year John attended a civil pilot training course in Portland, entering a pool of ready candidates who the military could call upon if needed. The senior Carroll had received a Purple Heart in World War I and was reluctant to let his only son enlist in the military, but after the attack on Pearl Harbor, he finally gave his blessing. John hated the war but wanted to serve and fulfill what he thought was his duty to help keep America safe. He left school to enter the army air force in March 1942 and received his commission and air force pilot wings on January 7, 1944. He returned to Portland to marry Violet Law five days later and then left for the South Pacific, where he would fly B-25 bombers.

John wrote regular letters home to both Violet and his parents. He told his parents that he continued to attend Catholic Mass and Adoration regularly and that he found great comfort in these rites. He looked forward to having the war behind him. He ended each letter with "Sending lots of love, Your son, Johnny."

On November 12, 1944, Japanese antiaircraft artillery fire hit John's B-25 during a raid in the Dutch East Indies. One of the other pilots in the formation saw the back part of John's bomber engulfed in flames. The nose of the crippled aircraft pitched up, and the plane stalled, spun into the ground, and exploded. The aircraft had been flying too low and too fast for the five crew members to have any chance of bailing out. An army Catholic priest went to the site of the crash the next day on tiny Pegun Island and celebrated Mass. Only two bodies were recovered; neither body could be identified. They were buried as x-1 and x-2.

For reasons that aren't clear, the army was slow in notifying the Carroll family of John's death. He wrote his last letter home two weeks before he died, and his parents and wife struggled to understand why they suddenly stopped hearing from him. Then one day Violet received a shipment containing his belongings, although the army still didn't confirm or deny his death. She finally received a telegram with the official notification on December 15, 1944.

John's body was not recovered. The family's deep faith and a letter from the priest who performed the Mass provided comfort: he assured the family that no one was better prepared to meet God than John.

After the war ended, the military tried to identify as many remains as it could but, given the technology at the time, had a low success rate. Sgt. Charles Lunsford was the only one identified from the five crew members aboard John's B-25. A letter to Violet in 1950 expressed sympathy for the situation: "Realizing the extent of your grief and anxiety, it is not easy to express condolence to you who gave your loved one under circumstances so difficult that there is no grave at which to pay homage."

John's older sister, Patricia, Carol's mother, tended to wounded soldiers as a flight nurse; Patricia and her mother were prolific letter writers, and her mother's greatest sorrow was that she could no longer also write to John. Despite her grief, John's mother put her arms around the family and led them in moving on. The family continued to work, attend Sunday Mass, and do all the things that families do: dinners, birthdays, Christmas celebrations, going to the movies. The Holy Cross Fathers on the university campus regularly offered Masses for John. John Sr. passed away in 1948. Violet remarried.

Carol grew up hearing stories about her uncle and seeing pictures of him. Every year on Memorial Day, the family headed to a local cemetery that contained the graves of ancestors dating back to the 1800s. While the boys clipped the grass around the headstones, other family members decorated graves with flowers plucked from their garden. There was no grave to decorate for John.

Since the discovery of the Praying Hands Memorial, Carol Leitschuh has a place to decorate with flowers for John. She would like to thank the students in the class of 1948 who built the memorial, but she has no idea how to find them.[1]

In the summer of 2018 Carol received a letter from the army asking for a DNA sample. A follow-up letter acknowledging receipt of her DNA noted, "The request for DNA sample does not imply there are recovered remains associated with your loved one." But a letter in April 2019 indicated that the U.S. government has not given up on John Carroll. The second body found on Pegun Island is interred in a mausoleum in the Philippines; the Defense POW/MIA Accounting Agency (DPAA) plans to disinter the remains for possible identification. The letter also discussed possible plans to visit Pegun Island to search for the other three missing airmen from Carroll's B-25. However, it may be several years before the DPAA will receive permission from the Indonesian government to conduct its search.[2]

It is possible that John Carroll will be found, but the chances are very low. Many of the nearly eighty-three thousand personnel missing from World War II, Korea, Vietnam, and other conflicts will never be found and are remembered only by their families and other loved ones or by an inscription on a memorial. Words that adorn the Tomb of the Unknown Soldier at Arlington National Cemetery, which houses unknowns from both world wars and Korea, also pay tribute to the fallen who have not been identified: "Here rests in honored glory an American soldier known but to God."[3]

The Carroll family continues to have faith that John is with God, who takes good care of him. Words that John's mother wrote to his sister not long after his death speaks for many with a relative who will never make the journey home: "All we can possibly do is have the Faith and Courage which will help us carry along . . . The 'Irish prayers' will carry him and us through and John is safe and happy wherever he may be, we know that. It is just that it seems impossible and that we keep talking about someone else."[4]

Many families find peace in knowing that a missing loved one has been returned for burial or accounted for. Nearly 125,000 U.S. personnel from the Mexican War and the first and second world wars are buried in overseas cemeteries.[5] The U.S. government has no intention to bring these fallen warriors home. But at least the families of those buried overseas know where their loved one lies. They had something to start the grieving process.[6] A family with enough resources could even visit the grave. The families of the missing have no such closure.

For thousands of years armies have tried to recover their war dead, although the ethos has been unevenly applied. In the *Iliad* one of the themes centers around the desire to recover the fallen so the enemy does not dishonor the victim by mutilating the body; on the other hand, in the *Odyssey* Odysseus has no qualms about leaving dead soldiers behind to save himself and other survivors.[7]

Nearly all cultures memorialize their war dead, but the United States stands apart with our obsession to "leave no man behind," especially after the end of a conflict. The ethos, while not codified in any official military doctrine, is a relatively recent phenomenon, driven largely by families of the missing. But we also have the resources and technology in the United States to recover our lost warriors. In 2017 the Department of Defense (DoD) spent $131 million searching for and identifying the remains of the dead from past wars. That amount of money might be unaffordable for many countries, but it's a round-off error in what we spend on the U.S. military, a sum that currently hovers around $700 billion each year. The VA receives another $200 billion each year.

The advent of DNA technology has enhanced our ability to identify our war dead even decades later. Previous identification techniques included dental records and the proximity of official and personal possessions, such as ID cards and dog tags. But DNA can be extracted even from small bits of remains. In fact, we have gotten so good at DNA identification we will likely never have another service member to place in the Tomb of the Unknown Soldier. The remains of the Unknown from Vietnam were interred on Memorial Day in 1984. But questions lingered about the possibility that the Vietnam Unknown might be identified. After much controversy the remains were exhumed in 1998 and identified through DNA analysis as air force 1st Lt. Michael J. Blassie, who was shot down in 1972. The crypt that contained Blassie will remain vacant.[8]

Part of the U.S. obsession in rescuing personnel and repatriating our war dead surely stems from our ability to afford the people, training, and equipment that can make it happen. And once we can make something happen, it often becomes an imperative, the way expensive cancer treatments are. But while most wealthy countries maintain CSAR capabilities, no country expends the resources that we do on recovering remains. Perhaps the answer to our obsession can be found in a U.S. culture that embraces the recovery and redemption exemplified in the Bible's parable of the lost sheep. We rejoice more over the one we have searched for and found than the ninety-nine who were never lost and whom we may put at risk to search for the lost one.

However, U.S. government policy on searching for the missing was slow to develop. The impetus for change initially came from several wives of Vietnam POWs, who pushed to make public the plights of their husbands.

The U.S. military instructed the families of early Vietnam POWs and MIAS to tell no one except immediate family members about their husbands' status. The official stance was born from legitimate concerns that the North Vietnamese might react negatively to publicity and take it out on the POWs or might use information gleaned from the press against their husbands.[9] As a result, the American public knew almost nothing about those captured and missing during the 1960s.

But it was impossible for the tightly knit community of military families to stay completely quiet. Neighbors and close friends inevitably learned of a man's POW or MIA status and wanted to help his family. As the population of the captured and missing grew, families found each other to provide mutual support. Navy POW/MIA families were clustered on the West Coast, mostly near San Diego, and on the East Coast, mostly near the Tidewater area in southern Virginia. Air force POW/MIA families were more scattered, but as the war dragged on, many families moved to the area surrounding Eglin Air Force Base in the Florida Panhandle. Many of the early air force POWs and MIAS belonged to the special operations community, which makes its home at nearby Hurlburt Field, so the area may have reached a critical mass that made it a magnet for others. It's also a nice place to live, with mostly warm weather, good schools, and good facilities at Eglin.

My family moved to the area in 1968, when my father returned from his second trip to Vietnam. By the time I entered high school, in 1971, many of my classmates had fathers who were POWs or MIA. The four boys across the street from my house had lost their father early in the war.

Jane Denton, the wife of Cdr. Jeremiah Denton, an A-6 pilot who was captured on July 18, 1965, stayed quiet initially. However, she waged a behind-the-scenes campaign to put pressure on the U.S. government regarding information about the POWs and plans to bring them home. Within one month of her husband's capture, she made two trips to Washington DC to meet with government officials and the American Red Cross. One of President Johnson's liaison officers assured her the government was doing all it could but warned her against expecting any results too quickly.[10]

On May 17, 1966, Jeremiah Denton appeared from captivity in a short film broadcast on television in the United States. During his interview with a Japanese reporter, Denton repeatedly blinked the word *torture* in Morse code. Apparently, no one in the American media or public picked up on the code, but naval intelligence officials did. It was their first indication of the conditions being endured by the POWs.[11]

The week before Denton's appearance, Sybil Stockdale, the wife of Cdr. James Stockdale, whose A-4 had been shot down the previous September, made a trip to Washington to meet with a naval intelligence officer and the State Department. She learned that the State Department, not the Pentagon, was handling the POW issue because the action in Vietnam was not an officially declared war. The Pentagon and the State Department didn't talk much; the intelligence officer asked Sybil to tell him what she had gleaned from State. The visit was for naught; officials at State refused to disclose any details regarding their work on the POWs, citing security concerns. Sybil left frustrated and lost confidence in the Johnson administration's ability to deal with the POW issue.[12]

Several months later Sybil invited about a dozen POW/MIA wives to a luncheon, where they shared what little information they had and vented their frustrations with the government's slow and opaque processes and protocols.[13] Some family members began to question the need to keep quiet. As antiwar sentiments in the United States began to build, Sondra Rutledge, the teen-age daughter of Willie's captured executive officer Howie, began a telephone campaign to remind the public, regardless of how they felt about the war, to not forget the plight of POWs, MIAS, and all those serving in Vietnam. By the end of 1967 a group of thirty-three POW/MIA wives in the San Diego area formed the League of Wives of American Vietnam Prisoners of War; Sybil Stockdale was the group's leader. In 1968 the group banded together with a looser network of POW/MIA wives on the East Coast and changed its name to the League of Families.[14]

That October, Sybil gave up on the slow progress of POW negoti-ations and lack of response to reports of torture and other Geneva Convention violations. She worked with a reporter at the *San Diego Union*, which ran an article describing the abuses endured by the POWS and introducing the world to the League of Families.[15] The league and its advocacy efforts began to grow, and in 1970 the group incorporated in the District of Columbia. An MIA wife, Mrs. Michael Hoff, designed the stark black-and-white POW/MIA flag that went into production in 1972. To encourage use of the flag to raise public awareness of the POW/MIA issue, the league chose not to apply for a copyright or trademark.[16]

In 1969 two college students in Los Angeles came up with a wildly popular way to remember the plight of POW/MIAS and their families: bracelets. The idea grew from a meeting between the wives of three missing pilots and Carol Bates Brown and Kay Hunter, members of a student group called Voices in Vital Amer-ica, or VIVA. The wives hoped VIVA might do something to help draw attention to the POW/MIA issue. At first the students con-sidered sending petitions and letters to Hanoi to demand better treatment. Then they noticed television personality Bob Dornan wearing a metal bracelet given to him by a Vietnamese tribes-man. The idea for bracelets engraved with the names of individ-ual POWS and MIAS was born. Kick-started with a donation from their adult advisor's husband, the students produced twelve hundred bracelets; nickel-plated ones sold for $2.50 and copper ones for $3.00. The official POW/MIA bracelet campaign began on Veterans Day in 1970 with a press conference in California. The public response was overwhelming: VIVA got more than twelve thousand requests for bracelets on some days. Profits from the bracelets went for additional publicity for the POW/MIA issue in the form of bumper stickers, buttons, and other advertising. By the time VIVA disbanded in 1976, the organization had distributed nearly five million bracelets.[17] The bracelets were ubiquitous in the halls of my high school in Florida, and when I first entered the air force in 1980, many military members still wore them.

Amid stalled peace talks in the spring of 1972, Pres. Richard Nixon decided to force North Vietnam back to the negotiating table. In April he resumed the long-halted bombing of Hanoi; a month later he ordered the mining of Haiphong Harbor.[18] Antiwar protesters sprang into action, but the community near Eglin Air Force Base demonstrated in favor of Nixon's actions. On May 12 more than sixteen thousand people marched a mile across a bridge and down the main drag, Eglin Parkway. The school superintendent excused students who wanted to support the event, so I marched, along with my mother and three sisters. After the march, local police escorted a delegation to Eglin, where they boarded a Southern Airways jet and flew to Washington to deliver a "Pledge of Support to the President" with more than twenty thousand signatures.[19]

It took a second series of bombings in late 1972 to force the North Vietnamese back to negotiations that finally resulted in the end of the war a month later.[20] In February 1973 POWs began returning in the order of their capture. With his early shoot-down, Bob Shumaker was one of the first to return; although he never again flew the F-8, he retired as a two-star admiral.[21] Dennis Moore and Howie Rutledge, Willie's former *Bonnie Dick* squadron mates, also returned in the first group of released POWs. Moore retired with the rank of commander; Rutledge retired as a captain and died in 1984, cancer claiming what the North Vietnamese could not. Edward "Dean" Brown, the first Satan's Kitten killed in 1965, after being shot down in South Vietnam, and Jerry Green, who crashed into the sea, are both still listed as missing in action: "Killed in action, body not recovered."[22]

With the return of the POWs, the League of Families turned its attention to the nearly eighty-three thousand Americans still missing from World War II on. The League of Families works closely with legislators and the Department of Defense to advocate for a full accounting of those still missing. Other activities, such as National POW/MIA Recognition Day, help keep the issue in the minds of the public. In 1994 Pres. Bill Clinton began thawing the U.S. relationship with Vietnam, making it easier to search for the twenty-five hundred Americans missing from that war.[23]

The DPAA has a straightforward mission: "To provide the fullest possible accounting for our missing personnel to their families and the nation." This accounting includes "determining the fate of the missing and where possible, recovering them alive or recovering and identifying the remains of the dead."[24] The DPAA's six hundred employees view their work as a "sacred obligation, if not moral imperative." In addition to providing laboratory services and conducting archaeological digs, DPAA personnel coordinate with officials in hundreds of locations around the world every year in their quest for remains. In 2018 alone the DPAA identified the remains of two hundred formerly missing personnel.[25]

In 2015 the DPAA excavated the crash site of Pete Crosby, the first casualty of the *Bonnie Dick*'s Vietnam cruise fifty years earlier. In 2017 analysis matched DNA from Crosby's sister to a bone found at the site. He was buried May 28, 2017, in San Diego with full military honors.[26]

The DPAA continues its quest to return as many loved ones as possible to their families. The missing may be gone, but groups like the League of Families ensure they will never be forgotten. Yet no matter how much we search, we are unlikely to find all our lost sheep: the DPAA believes that only about thirty-four thousand of our nearly eighty-three thousand missing may be recoverable.[27]

Although most of the rescued and recovered are military men, some are civilians, women, or both. A small number of civilian

Red Cross nurses are missing in Vietnam, and some flight nurses and female ferry pilots are missing from World War II.[28] During the First Persian Gulf War in 1991, two women became POWs and were later released. With increasing numbers of women service members in harm's way, "leave no man behind" has morphed into "leave no one behind." The ethos is now embedded in the air force's Airman's Creed ("I will never leave an Airman behind") and the army's Soldier's Creed ("I will never leave a fallen comrade"). In addition to the quest to find and identify remains of our missing, the ethos drives current and future DoD investments in what the military now calls "personnel recovery." The air force now considers CSAR a "combat task" only undertaken for combat operations, but it falls under the same umbrella of personnel recovery that includes other rescue operations such as civil search and rescue or humanitarian assistance.[29] In the meantime the air force hasn't abandoned the dream of some sort of self-rescue system: in May 2019 the service requested proposals for an unmanned, autonomous aerial platform, a "Personnel Recovery / Transport Vehicle" that can fly up to one hundred miles to recover up to four personnel.[30]

Current air force doctrine is silent on the original idea that personnel recovery is about doing the right thing and increasing the morale of those sent into combat. Instead, the doctrine focuses on a more strategic reason: not recovering "isolated" Americans can be an intelligence and propaganda bonanza for the enemy if those personnel are captured. An enemy can leverage detainees to influence national and political will, potentially turning public opinion against the war and impacting strategic objectives.[31]

A valid question remains regarding the resources, both dollars and human lives, involved in rescue and recovery. The enemy can use to their advantage the knowledge that U.S. personnel will return to recover lost warriors, whether dead or alive. Both the North Koreans and North Vietnamese used either real survivors or imposters pretending to be survivors on occasion to set traps for rescue forces. Although modern technologies and procedures have reduced the likelihood of our military falling into a trap, the threat still exists, and it takes additional resources and risks to develop the equipment, conduct the requisite training, and plan and execute combat rescues that take traps into account. On the other hand, an autonomous rescue vehicle like the one the air force recently asked for would significantly reduce the peril of a trap since there would be no rescue personnel at risk.

However, even the United States will not expend infinite resources or people to rescue someone. In 1972 military forces spent eleven days rescuing a single survivor from the shoot-down of an EB-66 electronic warfare plane. During those eleven days at least ten rescuers died in the crashes of an OV-10 airplane and two helicopters. In addition, the lives of South Vietnamese soldiers were endangered when air strikes to support their assault on Communist forces were diverted to keep the North Vietnamese away from the downed flyer. Brig. Gen. Richard G. Cross Jr., who was serving in Vietnam at the time, soberly noted, "As airmen or soldiers or sailors, we should expect that there are times when as one person, we must be sacrificed for the overall."[32]

A half-century had passed since the jungle swallowed up Richard Whitesides and his O-1 spotter plane in 1964. John Whitesides, now an attorney in Sacramento, received a phone call that delivered stunning news: a laboratory in Hawaii had identified his father's remains. John and his mother had no idea that the DPAA was even looking for his father.

The Whitesides family had long assumed that their only remembrance of Richard would be his engraved name on two memorials. In 1980 his name was one of the 2,504 names of Vietnam missing added to a staircase wall at the Honolulu Memorial in the National Memorial of the Pacific (fig. 23). When the Honolulu Memorial was dedicated in 1966, it had included the names of 18,095 Americans missing from the Pacific theater in World War II and 8,210 Americans missing from Korea.[33] Whitesides's name and the other Vietnam missing were also engraved on the Vietnam Veterans Memorial in Washington DC, which was dedicated in 1982.

FIG. 23. The Courts of the Missing in Honolulu.
(Courtesy American Battle Monuments Commission)

On July 29, 1999, a team of U.S. and Vietnamese officials traveled to Quang Tri Province, hoping to find more information on the Whitesides shoot-down.[34] The team visited A Ngo, a village near the probable crash site, and found two or three villagers who remembered a crash from 1964. The o-1 had impacted on a steep hillside, and the pilot had been thrown from the aircraft, still strapped to his seat. Some villagers climbed up to find the dead pilot. The villagers left his remains on the hillside; superstitions prevented them from touching his body.[35]

In 1999 several villagers took the search team to the site, now unrecognizable as a plane crash. Still, the searchers found a few metal scraps, which the Americans took back to the United States. Analysis showed that the scraps were consistent with metal used in the o-1. Between the metal and the eyewitness accounts from the villagers, U.S. officials concluded the site was likely the final resting place for Whitesides.

John Whitesides, who had no memory of his father, was thrilled to receive a detailed report later that year describing the search team's efforts and the conclusion that his father's crash site had been found. With no body and inconsistent stories from Floyd Thompson, the Special Forces officer who had survived the crash and been taken POW, he and his mother had always wondered what had happened. After his release in 1973, Thompson refused to talk with the Whitesides family, bewildering the survivors and brewing suspicions about the circumstances of the shoot-down. But now, finally, here was proof that Richard had been killed on impact, that he hadn't suffered. The family knew where he lay.

For John the 1999 report was good enough. Even though there was no body to bury, he was pleased with the effort by the U.S. and Vietnamese governments, along with the selfless villagers who took time from their busy days to lead the team to the crash site. The report said that the only way to learn any more information would be to excavate the site, and he assumed that, given the location, an excavation would be too expensive and difficult. Still, he and other relatives provided DNA samples in case anything turned up.[36]

John underestimated the DPAA's tenacity. In August 2013 a team returned to the site.[37] The excavation was a major effort: fifty team members from the United States and Vietnam. The team could only work during the dry season; once the rains came in the fall, the team packed up and returned in 2014. In June the team found aviator sunglasses frames and part of an ankle bone.[38] The bone was sent to the Armed Forces DNA Identification Laboratory in Hawaii, which matched the DNA to the sample provided years earlier by Whitesides's mother.[39]

John received the stunning phone call in October. Unaware of the excavation, he was completely unprepared. Shocked, he couldn't speak about the news for several days without becoming emotional.[40] He was grateful for the extraordinary effort put out by the government to find his father, an effort that defied any sort of standard cost-benefit analysis. He also felt a great deal of gratitude toward the Vietnamese villagers, who had nothing to gain from helping. They hadn't been paid and in fact had probably lost money from the time spent taking the teams to the crash site.[41] But the Vietnamese villagers likely understood better than most what it was like to lose relatives to war; there is a comradeship in loss.

In the spring of 2015 John's mother flew to Hawaii and accompanied Richard's casket to West Point for the funeral on May 1. John flew to West Point, and the army housed them in the distinguished visitors' quarters on the campus, right across from the chapel where Richard and Judith had been married in 1959. Although the funeral party could have easily walked across the street, the army insisted on a motorcade to keep everyone in the right order. Overwhelmed with emotion, John was relieved to not have to think about anything; he simply went wherever someone told him to go.

The air force had been unable to arrange a flyover, but at some point during the ceremony, a raptor flew overhead and let out a piercing cry that John took as a sign for his father. He was almost relieved there was no flyover; the gun salute, the flag folding and presentation, and then taps was so much, he wasn't sure he could have taken more.

John saw the relief in his mother's face during the funeral. Although he had been happy with the information in 1999, he thought his mother needed more. Uncovering the remains and holding the funeral, where she saw Richard's classmates whom she had met more than a half-century earlier, provided a closure that no report could.

John maintains a small memorial to his father in his law office in Sacramento. Richard's medals and insignia are encased in a display, along with his West Point diploma. A triangular box sits on a table below the display; it contains the flag the army presented to John at the funeral.[42]

The names of the Pacific missing who have been accounted for remain on the Honolulu Memorial. A small rosette is engraved beside their names to indicate that their final resting place is known. Richard Whitesides's name now has a rosette.[43]

Another lost sheep has come home.

Epilogue

THE F-8 LIVES ON IN MUSEUMS AND WEBSITES DEVOTED TO its legacy. No one knows what happened to Feedbag 108, the aircraft that stayed together long enough for Willie to eject over water. The Crusader likely rests at the bottom of the Gulf of Tonkin, perhaps acting as a mini-reef for ocean creatures, creating life instead of destruction.

Rick Millson, who recovered the A-4 with a huge hole in the wing, later became a Blue Angel, flying first the F-11 Tiger and then the F-4 Phantom. After leaving the navy, he continued to fly A-4s as a civilian aggressor pilot—a pilot who emulates enemy tactics to train fighter pilots.

Several decades after landing his damaged aircraft on the *Bonnie Dick*, Millson was walking through the San Francisco Airport when he ran into the landing signal officer who had downgraded the landing. Still mad, Millson accosted the LSO.

"George, it was an OK, three. Period."

The LSO shot back. "It was an OK, three, high, fast."

Millson didn't know it, but his damaged A-4 had been repaired in Japan after sailing away from the *Bonnie Dick*. Rather than return it to combat, the navy sent the little jet back to the United States, where it was apparently used as a trainer until about 1970. Decades later a warbird company pulled the Scooter out of the air force's aircraft boneyard near Tucson, Arizona, and restored it to flying condition in 2011.

At the time, Millson was still a check airman for A-4 Skyhawks;

the FAA relied on him to certify other pilots to fly civilian versions of the airplane. The chief test pilot for the warbird company that rebuilt the A-4 contacted Millson; the test pilot needed a checkout. Millson couldn't believe his ears when the pilot told him the navy's bureau number for the aircraft: his damaged Scooter hadn't just been repaired but had been resurrected once again.

Since the A-4 is a single-seat airplane, Millson couldn't fly with the test pilot in the A-4. He flew with him in a similar two-seat airplane, and then, standing at the end of the runway, he watched the pilot perform three takeoffs and landings in the A-4. Everything looked fine, and Millson signed him off. Then Millson climbed into the Scooter. As he strapped into the seat, he felt like he was putting on a favorite old shirt. Taxiing to the runway, he marveled that it was possible that the sturdy little airplane that had brought him back in one piece to the carrier had survived so much—an enemy shell, thousands of landings, and decades of desert storage. Before he pulled onto the runway for takeoff, he had to stop to wipe tears from his eyes.

Millson flew around the traffic pattern twice, making two landings. After the second landing, he taxied back to the ramp, climbed out of the cockpit, and said goodbye again to his favorite steed.

When Willie ejected, he became member number 826 in the Martin-Baker Tie Club (fig. 24). He bought a tie, but he doesn't wear it much, mostly because it's too short. Nina passed away in 2016, and Willie and their three daughters scattered her ashes in Kernville, California, where she grew up. His killing of the fisherman still haunts him today, and he wishes that he and the fisherman could have somehow talked their way out of things.

As I researched this story, one loose end bothered me. Although Jim Welsh was on the list of shipmates who died during the 1966 fire on the *Oriskany*, I could not find Tom Saintsing's name on that list or any list of Vietnam casualties. I thought Willie had spelled the name as *Saintsong*, and my extensive internet searches didn't find anyone in the United States with that last name. Ten minutes after getting the correct spelling, I located someone in North Carolina who I thought fit the bill and seemed very much alive.

Fig. 24. Willie's Martin-Baker Tie Club membership card.
(Photo by the author)

I passed along the phone number to Willie, and two days later I got an email: "I just called Tom Saintsing! We had a great conversation. He remembered picking me up."

Saintsing had left the *Oriskany* for a stateside assignment before the fire.

Nothing could resurrect the Vietnamese fisherman, but after a half-century of mourning, one of Willie's saviors had arisen.

NOTES

1. The Hit

1. Mouton et al., *Rescuing Downed Aircrews*, xii.
2. Mouton et al., *Rescuing Downed Aircrews*, xii.

2. Leave No Man Behind

1. vcgc Association, "Frank Hubert McNamara."
2. "Honours," 579; Cutlack, *Australian Flying Corps*, 59.
3. Garrisson, *Australian Dictionary of Biography*, vol. 10.
4. "Honours."
5. "Honours."
6. Garrisson, *Australian Dictionary of Biography*, vol. 10.
7. Ransom, *Air-Sea Rescue*, 23.
8. "Aircraft and the War," 1218.
9. "Aircraft and the War."
10. Meyer, *Introduction to Deployable Recovery Systems*, 7.
11. Meyer, *Deployable Recovery Systems*.
12. Doolittle, with Glines, *I Could Never Be So Lucky Again*, 78–79.
13. Doolittle, with Glines, *I Could Never Be So Lucky Again*.
14. "Caterpillar Club," https://www.irvingq.com/our-story/caterpillar-club/.
15. Lindbergh, *Spirit of St. Louis*, 6–7, 214–15.
16. Ransom, *Air-Sea Rescue*, 23.
17. Ransom, *Air-Sea Rescue*, 3, 23.
18. Ransom, *Air-Sea Rescue*, 2–3.
19. Ransom, *Air-Sea Rescue*, 42–43.
20. Ransom, *Air-Sea Rescue*, 2–5.
21. Ransom, *Air-Sea Rescue*, 48–49.
22. Hendrie, *Flying Cats*, 2.
23. Ransom, *Air-Sea Rescue*, 50.
24. Ransom, *Air-Sea Rescue*, 18.

25. Ransom, *Air-Sea Rescue*, 49.

26. Ransom, *Air-Sea Rescue*, 50.

27. Ransom, *Air-Sea Rescue*, 17, 48–49, 51.

28. Ransom, *Air-Sea Rescue*, 52.

29. Ransom, *Air-Sea Rescue*, 59.

30. Ransom, *Air-Sea Rescue*, 27.

31. Ransom, *Air-Sea Rescue*, 10–12.

32. Ransom, *Air-Sea Rescue*, 36.

33. Ransom, *Air-Sea Rescue*, 37.

34. Ransom, *Air-Sea Rescue*, 68.

35. Ransom, *Air-Sea Rescue*, 71.

36. Ransom, *Air-Sea Rescue*, 73–74, 77.

37. Ransom, *Air-Sea Rescue*, 77.

38. This account was taken from Ransom, *Air-Sea Rescue*, 78; multiple documents from Second Emergency Rescue Squadron; and "Wood River Man," 8.

39. Ransom, *Air-Sea Rescue*, 98–99.

40. Ransom, *Air-Sea Rescue*, 81.

41. "Nathan G. Gordon."

42. Kammen, *Operational History of the Flying Boat*, 7, 32, 43.

43. Kammen, *Operational History of the Flying Boat*, 35.

44. Kammen, *Operational History of the Flying Boat*, 57.

45. Kammen, *Operational History of the Flying Boat*, 41, 55.

46. Kammen, *Operational History of the Flying Boat*, 59.

47. Kammen, *Operational History of the Flying Boat*, 61, 111.

48. Kammen, *Operational History of the Flying Boat*, 116–24.

49. Ransom, *Air-Sea Rescue*, 81.

50. Pedretti, *Leonardo*, 34.

51. "New Aircraft at the Paris Aero Exposition," 190–91; "Sikorsky Aviation Company," 1757.

52. "First Helicopter to Fly a Circular Kilometer," 888–89.

53. Bane, "De Bothezat Helicopter," 645; "Successful Helicopter Trials at McCook Field," 97.

54. "Military Progress in Helicopter Presages Early Commercial Models," 12–13; Sikorsky Aircraft website, "s-47."

55. This account was taken from Dorr, "First Rescue," unless otherwise noted.

56. Harman interview, in *Sikorsky R-4 Hoverfly*.

57. Harman interview.

58. Ransom, *Air-Sea Rescue*, 71–72, 92, 97.

59. Ransom, *Air-Sea Rescue*, 98.

60. Ransom, *Air-Sea Rescue*, 58.

61. Ransom, *Air-Sea Rescue*, 17.

62. Ransom, *Air-Sea Rescue*, 21–22.

63. U.S. Congress, *Public Law 80-253*, July 26, 1947, "National Security Act."

64. Ike Skelton Combined Arms Research Library Digital Library, "Functions of the Armed Forces and the Joint Chiefs of Staff."

65. Ransom, *Air-Sea Rescue*, 98, 145–47.

66. Ransom, *Air-Sea Rescue*, 146.

67. Ransom, *Air-Sea Rescue*, 148–49, 152.

68. U.S. Air Force (USAF), Brig. Gen. Richard T. Kight official biography.

69. USAF, "Air Force Doctrine, Annex 3-50: Personnel Recovery," 3.

70. Ransom, *Air-Sea Rescue*, 152, 155, 157–58.

71. *Pilot Ejection*, video.

72. "It Is Reported That," 94.

73. Holloway, "Punching Out."

74. Martin-Baker Aircraft Company, "History and Founders."

75. Holloway, "Punching Out."

76. Ryan, *Sonic Wind*, 69 (Kindle ebook version).

77. Ryan, *Sonic Wind*, 64–65.

78. Ryan, *Sonic Wind*, 68.

79. Ryan, *Sonic Wind*, 82, 85.

80. Ryan, *Sonic Wind*, 86.

81. Ryan, *Sonic Wind*, 103, 119–20, 175.

82. Ryan, *Sonic Wind*, 175, 176.

83. Ryan, *Sonic Wind*, 176, 187.

84. *Pararescue*, 7–10.

85. *Pararescue*, 13–14, 39, 47.

86. *Pararescue*, 42–43.

87. Ransom, *Air-Sea Rescue*, 160–61.

88. Marion, *That Others May Live*, 1.

89. Marion, *That Others May Live*, 22.

90. Ransom, *Air-Sea Rescue*, 163–64.

91. Marion, *That Others May Live*, 3–4.

92. Ransom, *Air-Sea Rescue*, 170.

93. Ransom, *Air-Sea Rescue*, 172.

94. Ransom, *Air-Sea Rescue*, 171.

95. Marion, *That Others May Live*, 5, 12.

96. Marion, *That Others May Live*, 19–21.

97. Marion, *That Others May Live*, 1.

98. *Pararescue*, 86.

99. Marion, *That Others May Live*, 48.

100. Federal Aviation Administration (FAA), *Civil Aeronautics Board Accident Investigation Report*; National Park Service (NPS), National Historic Landmark Nomination; NPS, interviews with Andy Schlipp, May 6, 2014; and Bill Fay and David Shearer, July 8, 2014.

101. FAA, *Civil Aeronautics Board Accident Investigation Report*; "2 Airliners Crash with 128 Aboard," 1, 5.

102. "2 Airliners Crash with 128 Aboard."

103. Miles Burd interview, by the author, September 17, 2014; Daryl Strong interview, by the author, September 18, 2014; NPS, interview with Miles Burd and Daryl Strong, April 18, 2000.

104. NPS, interview with Burd and Strong.

105. NPS, interview with Burd and Strong.

106. Burd interview, by the author.

107. Lynch, "Little Has Changed," 19–24; "Sidelights on Air Tragedy."

108. Burd interview, by the author; Heatwole, "Only One of Heroic Crew Still at Luke," 10.

109. Lynch, "Little Has Changed"; "Hamilton Airman Spots Debris," 1, 5.

110. Strong interview, by the author.

111. Burd interview, by the author; NPS, interview with Burd and Strong; Prince, "Pilot Calls Crash Scene 'Terrible,'" 1.

112. NPS, interview with Burd and Strong; Heatwole, "Only One of Heroic Crew Still at Luke"; NPS, interviews with 1976 cleanup crew.

113. Burd, citation for Distinguished Flying Cross.

114. Burd interview, by the author; Strong interview, by the author; NPS, interview with Burd and Strong.

115. "Copters Head into Air Crash Scene."

116. Burd interview, by the author.

117. "Grand Canyon Disaster," 31–36.

118. "Grand Canyon Disaster."

119. "Grand Canyon Disaster."

120. Wren, "Gory Crash Scene," 1, 5; "148 Letters Recovered by Rescue Team," 5.

121. "Grand Canyon Disaster"; "Copter Lands at UAL Plane Debris," 1.

122. Hill, "Removal of Air Victims Starts."

123. "Grand Canyon Disaster"; Hill, "Removal of Air Victims Starts."

124. "Grand Canyon Disaster."

125. Hill, "Climbers Seeking Plane Wreckage"; "Helicopter Heroes."

126. NPS, National Historic Landmark Nomination.

127. NPS, National Historic Landmark Nomination.

128. L. David Lewis email, May 8, 2016.

129. "29 DC-7 Dead Identified"; Wayman, "United Identifies 29 of the 58 Who Died," 1.

130. "Grand Canyon Disaster."

131. NPS, interviews with 1976 cleanup crew.

132. "Grand Canyon Disaster"; Burd interview, by the author; Strong interview, by the author.

133. Lewis email.

134. Joseph Isenberg interview, May 1, 2016.

135. Federal Aviation Administration (FAA), "Brief History of the FAA."

3. Willie

1. Marolda, *By Sea, Air, and Land*, 53.

2. Futrell, *United States Air Force in Southeast Asia*, 27.

3. Futrell, *United States Air Force in Southeast Asia*, 30.

4. Futrell, *United States Air Force in Southeast Asia*, 35, 40.

5. Futrell, *United States Air Force in Southeast Asia*, 53; Schlight, *War Too Long*, 2.

6. Futrell, *United States Air Force in Southeast Asia*, 79.

7. Futrell, *United States Air Force in Southeast Asia*, 83.

8. Air Force Historical Research Agency (AFHRA), Anthis oral history interview transcript, vol. 1, (November 17, 1969); transcript, February 5, 1988, 2, 14.

9. Tilford, *Search and Rescue in Southeast Asia*, 39.

10. Tilford, *Search and Rescue in Southeast Asia*, 38.

11. Tilford, *Search and Rescue in Southeast Asia*, 34, 39.

12. Marion, *That Others May Live*, 48.

13. Tilford, *Search and Rescue in Southeast Asia*, 34, 38.

14. Marolda, *By Sea, Air, and Land*, 40.

15. AFHRA, Maj. Alan W. Saunders oral history interview transcript, July 1, 1964, 5–6; hereafter cited as "Saunders interview."

16. Tilford, *Search and Rescue in Southeast Asia*, 39.

17. Saunders interview, 16.

18. Saunders interview, 5.

19. Saunders interview, 5.

20. Saunders interview, D-1-G-1.

21. Saunders interview, 7.

22. Saunders interview, 9.

23. Saunders interview, 10–11.

24. Saunders interview, 17.

25. Saunders interview, 18–20.

26. U.S. Military Academy, *Howitzer* yearbook, 1959.

27. Library of Congress, "Statement of Military Service and Death of Richard Le Brou Whitesides," August 17, 1965, 153.

28. Saunders interview, 11.

29. Mutza, *Kaman H-43*, 56–62.

30. Saunders interview, 11.

31. Tilford, *Search and Rescue in Southeast Asia*, 50.

32. LaPointe, *PJs in Vietnam*, 52, 54.

33. Saunders interview, 13.

34. John Christianson interview by author, December 17, 2018.

35. Christianson interview.

36. Hobson, *Vietnam Air Losses*, 12.

37. Christianson interview.

38. Hobson, *Vietnam Air Losses*, 12; LaPointe, *PJs in Vietnam*, 67–68; Christianson interview.

4. The Crusader

1. Maj. Gen. Robert Behler, USAF, Ret., Speech at International Test and Evaluation Annual Symposium, December 11, 2018.

2. Tillman, *Migmaster*, 10–11.

3. John Glenn interview by author, May 22, 2015..

4. Glenn interview.

5. National Aeronautic Association, "Collier 1950–1959 Recipients."

6. Meixner, "Thompson Trophy Story."

7. Glenn interview.

8. Don "Frazz" Fraser interview by author, April 29, 2015.

9. Rabbi Jem Golden interview by author, May 7, 2015.

10. John Miottel interview by author, May 18, 2015.

11. Bob Shumaker interview by author, May 4, 2015.

12. Shumaker interview.

13. John Borry interview by author, May 6, 2015.

14. Shumaker interview.

15. Golden interview.

16. Hobson, *Vietnam Air Losses*, 9–11.

17. Tilford, *Setup*, 103.

18. Hobson, *Vietnam Air Losses*, 14.

19. Shumaker interview.

20. Townley, *Defiant*, 28 (Kindle ebook).

21. Futrell, *United States Air Force in Southeast Asia*, 266.

22. Clodfelter, *Limits of Air Power*, 51.

23. Tilford, *Setup*, 92.

24. Clodfelter, *Limits of Air Power*, 52.

25. Tilford, *Setup*, 106.

26. Tilford, *Setup*, 109.

27. Tilford, *Setup*, 115–20, 135.

28. "Professors Hold Vietnam Protest," 9.

29. Weintraub, "Vietnam Protest Blocks Fifth Ave.," 1, 4.

30. "Police Remove 40 in Vietnam Protest," 5.

31. Tilford, *Setup*, 109.

32. U.S. Navy, USS *Bon Homme Richard* cruise book and deck log 1965.

33. Hobson, *Vietnam Air Losses*, 22.

34. Anderson, *Project CHECO*, 61.

35. David Wendt interview by author, February 15, 2019.

36. Wendt interview.

37. Wendt interview.

38. Anderson, *Project CHECO*, 62.

39. Anderson, *Project CHECO*, 62.

40. Anderson, *Project CHECO*, 63.

41. LaPointe, *PJs in Vietnam*, 417–20.

5. Bonnie Dick

1. U.S. Navy public website, "USS *Bon Homme Richard.*"

2. U.S. Navy, "USS *Bon Homme Richard.*"

3. Tillman, *On Wave and Wing,* 198.

4. Tillman, *On Wave and Wing,* 197–198.

5. Tillman, *On Wave and Wing,* 198–99.

6. U.S. Navy, "USS *Bon Homme Richard.*"

7. USS *Bon Homme Richard* deck log.

8. USS *Bon Homme Richard* deck log.

9. NHHC, VF-191 Papers, Satan's Kittens stand-down ceremony at NAS Miramar on March 1, 1978.

10. USS *Bon Homme Richard* deck log.

11. USS *Bon Homme Richard* deck log.

12. USS *Bon Homme Richard* deck log.

13. "John M. Tierney," obituary.

14. "Carrier, Carrier Based Squadrons and Non-Carrier Based Squadron Deployments to Vietnam"; *Allowances and Location of Navy Aircraft,* OPNAV Notice P03110 (Washington DC: Department of the Navy, May 31, 1965).

15. Marolda, *By Sea, Air, and Land,* 70; Vietnam Center, *History of Task Force 77.*

16. USS *Bon Homme Richard* deck log.

17. Marolda, *By Sea, Air, and Land,* 78–80.

18. Library of Congress, "Report of Casualty, Crosby, Frederick Peter"; Hobson, *Vietnam Air Losses,* 21.

19. USS *Bon Homme Richard* deck log.

20. USS *Bon Homme Richard* deck log.

21. USS *Bon Homme Richard* deck log; U.S. Navy, *Annual Typhoon Report,* 1965.

22. USS *Bon Homme Richard* deck log.

23. *United States Navy in the Pacific,* 115.

24. *United States Navy in the Pacific,* 127.

25. *United States Navy in the Pacific,* 128.

26. *United States Navy in the Pacific,* 129.

27. *United States Navy in the Pacific,* 131.

28. *United States Navy in the Pacific,* 160.

29. Rick Millson interview by author, November 28, 2018.

30. *United States Navy in the Pacific,* 161.

31. USS *Bon Homme Richard* deck log.

32. USS *Bon Homme Richard* deck log.

33. Rick Millson interview.

34. USS *Bon Homme Richard* deck log.

35. "At Sea with the Carriers," 20.

36. Millson interview.

37. Hobson, *Vietnam Air Losses,* 37; USS *Bon Homme Richard* deck log.

38. USS *Bon Homme Richard* deck log.

6. The Mission

1. Tommy Saintsing interview by author, July 16, 2016.

2. Hobson, *Vietnam Air Losses*, 38–39.

3. Saintsing interview.

4. Saintsing interview.

5. Galdorisi and Phillips, *Leave No Man Behind*, 350–55 (Kindle book ed.).

6. Saintsing interview.

7. NHHC, *Rescue Report*, October 17, 1965.

8. NHHC, *Rescue Report*, May 25, 1965.

9. Hobson, *Vietnam Air Losses*, 39–40.

10. USS *Bon Homme Richard* deck log.

11. Wendt interview.

12. Hobson, *Vietnam Air Losses*, 53.

13. Wendt interview.

14. USS *Gridley* deck log.

15. USS *Gridley*, tape recording of rescue mission.

16. USS *Bon Homme Richard* deck log.

17. *United States Navy in the Pacific*, 44.

18. Grossman, *On Killing*, 34, 64–65 (Kindle book ed.).

7. Recovery

1. Galdorisi and Phillips, *Leave No Man Behind,* 356.

2. Galdorisi and Phillips, *Leave No Man Behind,* 356.

3. Henderson, *Hero Found*, 60–69 (Kindle book ed.).

4. Hobson, *Vietnam Air Losses*, 48.

5. Henderson, *Hero Found*, 87, 94–95.

6. Henderson, *Hero Found*, 166–80.

7. Henderson, *Hero Found*, 183–242.

8. "Navy POW Saved after 23-Day Trek," 1.

9. Henderson, *Hero Found*, 258.

10. Henderson, *Hero Found*, 260.

11. USS *Ticonderoga* deck log, 1966; Skyhawk Association, "VA-195."

12. "Pilot in Navy's Blue Angels Killed," 40.

13. Grossman, *On Killing*, 131.

14. Grossman, *On Killing*, 132–33.

15. Grossman, *On Killing*, 70.

16. Vietnam Veterans against the War, "VVAW: Where We Came From, Who We Are."

17. Tick, *Warrior's Return*, 96–97.

18. PTSD: National Center for PTSD.

19. Author interview with Lt. Gen. John Miller, U.S. Army (retired), October 8, 2018.

20. Tick, *Warrior's Return*, xviii.

21. Tick, *Warrior's Return*, xi, 36.

22. Tick, *Warrior's Return*, 88, 131–32.

23. Tick, *Warrior's Return*, 115.

24. Tick, *Warrior's Return*, 122, 144.

25. Tick, *Warrior's Return*, 99–100.

26. Tick, *Warrior's Return*, 148, 162.

27. Morris, *Evil Hours*, 133–35.

28. PBS, interview with Dr. Matthew Friedman.

29. "PFC Robert C. Kubly."

30. Morris, *Evil Hours*, 4.

31. Tick, *Warrior's Return*, 158–59.

32. Tick, *Warrior's Return*, 70.

33. Tick, *Warrior's Return*, 133.

34. Tick, *Warrior's Return*, 138.

35. Tick, *Warrior's Return*, 170–71.

36. Press, "Wounds of the Drone Warrior," 30.

37. Perry, "Navy Investigates Surfing," E1-E5; and Kuznia, "Veterans Helping Veterans," A3.

38. Morris, *Evil Hours*, 159, 220–21.

8. Never Forget

1. Carol Leitschuh interview by author, March 28, 2019.

2. Carol Leitschuh email, April 23, 2019.

3. Arlington National Cemetery website, "Tomb of the Unknown Soldier."

4. Leitschuh interview, March 28, 2019.

5. Wong, "Leave No Man Behind," 601.

6. Wong, "Leave No Man Behind."

7. Samet, "Leaving No Warriors Behind," 628, 633–34.

8. Arlington National Cemetery website, "Tomb of the Unknown Soldier."

9. Townley, *Defiant*, 51.

10. Townley, *Defiant*, 53.

11. Townley, *Defiant*, 91–93.

12. Townley, *Defiant*, 96–98.

13. Townley, *Defiant*, 99.

14. Townley, *Defiant*, 184–85, 239.

15. Townley, *Defiant*, 241–42.

16. National League of POW/MIA Families, "History of the POW/MIA Flag."

17. Brown, "History of the POW/MIA Bracelets."

18. Tilford, *Setup*, 227–33.

19. Weiss, "White House Gets Petitions," 1A.

20. Tilford, *Setup*, 253–64.

21. Bob Shumaker interview by author.

22. Defense POW/MIA Accounting Agency (DPAA) website, "Vietnam War POW/MIA List."

23. Sanger, "Clinton in Hanoi."

24. DPAA website, "Frequently Asked Questions"(hereafter cited as DPAA, "FAQS").

25. DPAA *Year in Review: October 2017–September 2018*.

26. DPAA.mil, "Navy Pilot Killed in Vietnam War Accounted For" (Crosby).

27. DPAA *Year in Review*.

28. DPAA, "FAQS."

29. USAF, "Introduction to Personnel Recovery," Curtis E. LeMay Center for Doctrine Development and Education, updated January 2, 2019, https://www.doctrine.af.mil/Portals/61/documents/Annex_3-50/3-50-D01-RECOVERY-Introduction.pdf.

30. Humphries, "U.S. Air Force Wants an Autonomous Rescue Aircraft."

31. USAF, "Introduction to Personnel Recovery."

32. Tilford, *Search and Rescue in Southeast Asia*, 119.

33. American Battle Monuments Commission, "Honolulu Memorial."

34. "Airman Missing from Vietnam War Accounted For (Whitesides)."

35. Fitzgerald, "After 50 Years, Stockton Hero Is Coming Home."

36. John Whitesides interview by author, July 9, 2018.

37. DPAA Release No. 15-022.

38. Whitesides interview.

39. DPAA Release No. 15-022.

40. Fitzgerald, "After 50 Years, Stockton Hero Is Coming Home."

41. Whitesides interview.

42. Whitesides interview.

43. American Battle Monuments Commission, "Richard Lebrou Whitesides."

BIBLIOGRAPHY

Archival and Unpublished Sources

Air Force Historical Research Agency (AFHRA), Maxwell Air Force Base AL
    Maj. Alan W. Saunders oral history interview transcript, July 1, 1964.
    Maj. Gen. Rollen Henry "Buck" Anthis oral history interview transcript (1969), vol. 1, February 5, 1988.

American Battle Monuments Commission, Arlington VA
    "Honolulu Memorial." https://www.abmc.gov/cemeteries-memorials /americas/honolulu-memorial.
    "John Lebrou Whitesides." https://www.abmc.gov/node/512243.

Arlington National Cemetery, Arlington VA
    "The Tomb of the Unknown Soldier." https://www.arlingtoncemetery.mil /Explore/Tomb-of-the-Unknown-Soldier.

Burd, Miles. Distinguished Flying Cross citation. Copy sent by Burd to the author.

Defense POW/MIA Accounting Agency, Washington DC
    "Frequently Asked Questions." https://www.dpaa.mil/Resources/FAQs/.
    "Vietnam War POW/MIA List." https://www.dpaa.mil/Our-Missing/Vietnam -War/Vietnam-War-POW-MIA-List/.

Federal Aviation Administration, Washington DC
    "A Brief History of the FAA." http://www.faa.gov/about/history/brief_history.
    Civil Aeronautics Board Accident Investigation Report. http://lessonslearned .faa.gov/UAL718/CAB_accident_report.pdf.

Ike Skelton Combined Arms Research Library Digital Library, Fort Leavenworth KS
Library of Congress, Washington DC
    "Report of Casualty, Crosby, Frederick Peter." Report no. 97780-A-1, June 2, 1965. *Post-Vietnam: Casualty Report.* 1965. MS / mixed material. https:// www.loc.gov/item/powmia/pw144003/.
    "South Vietnam, Statement of Military Service and Death of Richard Le Brou Whitesides." August 17, 1965. MS / mixed material. https://www .loc.gov/item/powmia/pw054083/.

National Park Service, U.S. Department of the Interior, Washington DC

Interviews with Andy Schlipp, May 6, 2014; and Bill Fay and David Shearer, July 8, 2014.

National Historic Landmark Nomination. https://www.nps.gov/NHL/news /LC/spring2011/GrandCanyonREDACTED.pdf.

Transcript of interview with Miles Burd and Daryl Strong, April 18, 2000.

Naval History and Heritage Command (NHHC), Washington Navy Yard, Washington DC

Allowances and Location of Navy Aircraft. OPNAV Notice P03110. Washington DC: Department of the Navy, May 31, 1965. https://www.history.navy .mil/research/histories/naval-aviation-history/allowances-and-location /allowances-and-location-of-navy-aircraft-1965/may.html.

"Carrier, Carrier-Based Squadrons and Non-Carrier Based Squadron Deployments to Vietnam." In *United States Naval Aviation, 1910–1995,* edited by Roy A. Grossnick et al. Washington DC: Naval Historical Center, 1997. https://www.history.navy.mil/content/dam/nhhc/research/histories /naval-aviation/pdf/app26.pdf.

Combat loss report for November 18, 1965.

Rescue reports for May 25, October 17, and November 18, 1965.

Second Emergency Rescue Squadron. Website. http://www.pbyrescue.org.

U.S. Air Force, Washington DC

"Air Force Doctrine, Annex 3-50: Personnel Recovery." https://www.doctrine .af.mil/Doctrine-Annexes/Annex-3-50-Personnel-Recovery/.

Anderson, Capt. B. Conn. *Project CHECO (Contemporary Historical Evaluation of Combat Operations) Report, USAF Search and Rescue in Southeast Asia (1961–66).* USAF Report DOPEC-66-03512, 1966. Defense Technical Information Center (DTIC), Fort Belvoir VA.

Brig. Gen. Richard T. Kight official biography. https://www.af.mil/About-Us /Biographies/Display/Article/106550/brigadier-general-richard-t-kight/.

U.S. Congress, Washington DC

"Airways Modernization Board." Public Law 85-133. August 14, 1957. https:// www.gpo.gov/fdsys/pkg/STATUTE-71/pdf/STATUTE-71-Pg349.pdf.

National Security Act. Sec. 208, USAF. Public Law 80-253. July 26, 1947. https://catalog.archives.gov/id/299856.

U.S. Department of Veterans Affairs, Washington DC

PTSD: National Center for PTSD. Website. https://www.ptsd.va.gov/understand /common/common_veterans.asp.

U.S. Military Academy, West Point NY

Howitzer yearbook, 1959.

U.S. Navy, Washington DC

Annual Typhoon Report, 1965. http://www.metoc.navy.mil/jtwc/products /atcr/1965atcr.pdf.

History of Task Force 77, 2 September 1964–17 March 1965. September 2, 1964–March 17, 1965, pt. 1, March 29, 1965, box 00, folder 01, Bud Harton Collection, Vietnam Center and Archive, Texas Tech University, Lubbock. https://www.vietnam.ttu.edu/virtualarchive/items.php ?item=168300010993.

USS *Bon Homme Richard* cruise book and deck log, 1965.

"USS *Bon Homme Richard*." Pacific Fleet Surface Ships. https://www.public .navy.mil/surfor/lhd6/Pages/history.aspx.

USS *Gridley* deck log, 1965.

USS *Gridley*. Tape recording of rescue mission, November 18, 1965.

USS *Ticonderoga* deck log, 1966.

VCGC Association. "Frank Hubert McNamara." Profile. https://vcgca.org/our -people/profile/116/Frank-Hubert-McNAMARA.

Vietnam Center and Sam Johnson Vietnam Archive, Texas Tech University, Lubbock

> *The United States Navy in the Pacific, 1965*. Report. Commander in Chief United States Pacific Fleet, Sedgwick Tourison Collection, 2860801001, n.d., box 08, folder 01. https://www.vietnam.ttu.edu/virtualarchive/items .php?item=2860801001.

Vietnam Veterans against the War (VVAW). "VVAW: Where We Came From, Who We Are." VVAW.org. http://www.vvaw.org/about.

Published Works

"148 Letters Recovered by Rescue Team." *Arizona Daily Sun*, July 4, 1956.

"2 Airliners Crash with 128 Aboard." *Rocky Mountain News*, July 1, 1956.

"29 DC-7 Dead Identified." *New York Times*, July 11, 1956.

"Aircraft and the War." *Flight*, December 18, 1914.

"Airman Missing from Vietnam War Accounted For (Whitesides)." Defense POW/ MIA Accounting Agency. Release No. 15-022, April 22, 2015. https://www .dpaa.mil/News-Stories/News-Releases/Article/586351/airman-missing -from-vietnam-war-accounted-for-whitesides/.

"At Sea with the Carriers." *Naval Aviation News*, January 1966.

Bane, T. "The De Bothezat Helicopter." *Aviation*, June 11, 1923.

Brown, Carol Bates. "History of the POW/MIA Bracelets." National League of POW/MIA Families. https://www.pow-miafamilies.org/history-of-powmia -bracelets.html.

Clodfelter, Mark. *The Limits of Air Power: The American Bombing of North Vietnam*. New York: Free Press, 1989.

"Copter Lands at UAL Plane Debris." *Logansport (IN) Press*, July 6, 1956.

"Copters Head into Air Crash Scene." *San Rafael (CA) Independent Journal*, July 2, 1956.

Cutlack, Frederic. *The Australian Flying Corps in the Western and Eastern Theatres of War, 1914–1918.* 11th ed. Sydney: Angus & Robertson, 1941. https://www.awm.gov.au/collection/RCDIG1069925.

Doolittle, Gen. James H. "Jimmy," with Carroll V. Glines. *I Could Never Be So Lucky Again: An Autobiography.* New York: Bantam Falcon, 1991.

Dorr, Robert. "The First Rescue." *Defense Media Network*, January 15, 2015. https://www.defensemedianetwork.com/stories/first-helicopter-rescue/.

DPAA *Year in Review: October 2017–September 2018.* Newsletter. https://www.dpaa.mil/Portals/85/Documents/Newsletters/YiR%20fy18%20final%20spreads.pdf.

DPAA.mil. "Navy Pilot Killed in Vietnam War Accounted For (Crosby)." DPAA Release No. 17-039, May 22, 2017. https://www.dpaa.mil/News-Stories/News-Releases/Article/1188950/navy-pilot-killed-in-vietnam-war-accounted-for-crosby/.

"First Helicopter to Fly a Circular Kilometer." *Aviation*, August 18, 1924.

Fitzgerald, Michael. "After 50 Years, Stockton Hero Is Coming Home." Recordnet.com, October 28, 2014.

Futrell, Robert. *The United States Air Force in Southeast Asia: The Advisory Years to 1965.* Washington DC: Office of Air Force History, 1981.

Galdorisi, George, and Tom Phillips. *Leave No Man Behind: The Saga of Combat Search and Rescue,* Minneapolis: Zenith Press, 2010.

Garrisson, A. D. "McNamara, Frank Hubert (Francis) (1894–1961)." *Australian Dictionary of Biography*, vol. 10. Canberra: National Centre of Biography, Australian National University, 1986. http://adb.anu.edu.au/biography/mcnamara-frank-hubert-francis-7430/text12933, December 9, 2019.

"Grand Canyon Disaster." *Army Aviation Magazine*, September 1956.

Grossman, Dave. *On Killing: The Psychological Cost of Learning to Kill in War and Society.* New York: Open Road Integrated Media, 2009.

"Hamilton Airman Spots Debris of UAL Plane in Air Disaster." *San Rafael Daily Independent Journal,* July 2, 1956.

Heatwole, Thelma. "Only One of Heroic Crew Still at Luke." *Arizona Republic*, June 30, 1957.

"The Helicopter Heroes." *New York Times*, July 11, 1956.

Henderson, Bruce. *Hero Found: The Greatest POW Escape of the Vietnam War,* New York: HarperCollins, 2010.

Hendrie, Andrew. *Flying Cats: The Catalina Aircraft in World War II.* Annapolis MD: Naval Institute Press, 1988.

Hill, Gladwin. "Climbers Seeking Plane Wreckage." *New York Times*, July 5, 1956.
———. "Removal of Air Victims Starts; Wreckage in Canyon Is Studied." *New York Times*, July 3, 1956.

Hobson, Chris. *Vietnam Air Losses: United States Air Force Navy and Marine Corps Fixed-Wing Aircraft Losses in Southeast Asia, 1961–1973.* Hinckley, England: Midland, 2001.

Holloway, Don. "Punching Out: Evolution of the Ejection Seat." *Aviation History*, June 13, 2018. http://www.historynet.com/punching-evolution-ejection -seat.htm.

"Honours." *Flight*, June 14, 1917.

Humphries, Matthew. "U.S. Air Force Wants an Autonomous Rescue Aircraft." *PC Magazine*, May 17, 2019. https://www.pcmag.com/news/368428/us-air -force-wants-an-autonomous-rescue-aircraft.

Irving Q. "Caterpillar Club." https://www.irvingq.com/our-story/caterpillar-club/.

"It Is Reported That." *Aviation*, September 1, 1916.

"John M. Tierney, 92, Decorated Navy Pilot Who Taught Astronauts." *Southside Daily* (Virginia Beach), September 21, 2016. Obituary. https://southsidedaily .com/obits/2016/09/21/obits-john-m-tierney/.

Kammen, Michael. *Operational History of the Flying Boat Open-Sea and Seadrome Aspects: Selected Campaigns—World War II*. Washington DC: Navy Department, 1959.

Kuznia, Rob. "Veterans Helping Veterans through Crisis in California." *Washington Post*, March 21, 2019.

LaPointe, Robert. *PJs in Vietnam: The Story of Air Rescue in Vietnam as Seen through the Eyes of Pararescuement*. Anchorage: Northern PJ Press, 2001.

Lindbergh, Charles. *The Spirit of St. Louis*. New York: Scribner, 1953.

Lynch, Dudley. "Little Has Changed." *Arizona Magazine* (*Arizona Republic*), June 27, 1971.

Marion, Forrest. *That Others May Live: USAF Air Rescue in Korea*. Washington DC: Air Force History and Museums Program, 2004.

Marolda, Edward J. *By Sea, Air, and Land: An Illustrated History of the U.S. Navy and the War in Southeast Asia*. Washington DC: Naval Historical Center, 1994.

Martin-Baker Aircraft Company. "History and Founders." http://martin-baker .com/about/history-founders/.

Meixner, Bill. "The Thompson Trophy Story." Society of Air Racing Historians. http://www.airrace.com/thompson_trophy_story.htm.

Meyer, Jan. *An Introduction to Deployable Recovery Systems*. Albuquerque NM: Sandia National Laboratories, 1985.

"Military Progress in Helicopter Presages Early Commercial Models." *Aviation News*, June 19, 1944.

Morris, David. *The Evil Hours: A Biography of Post-Traumatic Stress Disorder*. New York: Houghton Mifflin Harcourt, 2016.

Mouton, Christopher, et al. *Rescuing Downed Aircrews: The Value of Time*. Santa Monica CA: RAND Corporation, 2015.

Mutza, Wayne. *Kaman H-43: An Illustrated History*. Atglen PA: Schiffer, 1998.

"Nathan G. Gordon, Navy Medal of Honor Winner, Arkansas Lt. Governor Dies." *Mercury News*, September 14, 2008. https://www.mercurynews.com/2008/09 /14/nathan-g-gordon-navy-medal-of-honor-winner-arkansas-lt-governor-dies/.

National Aeronautic Association. "Collier 1950–1959 Recipients." https://naa
.aero/awards/awards-and-trophies/collier-trophy/collier-1950–1959-winners.

National League of POW/MIA Families. "History of the POW/MIA Flag." https://
www.pow-miafamilies.org.

"Navy POW Saved after 23-Day Trek." *New York Times*, July 23, 1966.

"New Aircraft at the Paris Aero Exposition." *Aviation*, February 12, 1923.

Pararescue: 50 Years Plus: A Commemorative History. Charlotte NC: Fine, 1996.

PBS. Interview with Dr. Matthew Friedman. "The Soldier's Front." *Frontline*,
October 7, 2004. https://www.pbs.org/wgbh/pages/frontline/shows/heart
/interviews/friedman.html.

Pedretti, Carlo. *Leonardo: The Machines*. Florence, Italy: Giunti, 1999.

Perry, Tony. "Navy Investigates Surfing as a Way to Counteract PTSD." *Washington Post*, March 13, 2018.

"PFC Robert C. Kubly." *Bataan Commemorative Research Project*. https://
bataanproject.com/Kubly_R.html, entry created May 14, 2019.

Pilot Ejection. Video. YouTube, October 12, 2016. https://www.youtube.com
/watch?v=FFAw76CIcq8.

"Pilot in Navy's Blue Angels Killed in California Crash." *New York Times*, January 15, 1968.

"Police Remove 40 in Vietnam Protest." *New York Times*, May 22, 1965.

Press, Eyal. "The Wounds of the Drone Warrior." *New York Times Magazine*,
June 16, 2018.

Prince, Phillip. "Pilot Calls Crash Scene 'Terrible.'" *Tucson Daily Citizen*, July
2, 1956.

"Professors Hold Vietnam Protest." *New York Times*, March 25, 1965.

Ransom, Frank. *Air-Sea Rescue, 1941–1952*. Maxwell Air Force Base AL: Air University, 1953.

Ryan, Craig. *Sonic Wind: The Story of John Paul Stapp and How a Renegade Doctor Became the Fastest Man on Earth*. New York: Liveright, 2015.

Samet, Elizabeth. "Leaving No Warriors Behind: The Ancient Roots of a Modern Sensibility." *Armed Forces & Society* 31, no. 4 (Summer 2005).

Sanger, David. "Clinton in Hanoi, Intent on Forging New Relationship." *New York Times*, November 17, 2000.

Schlight, John. *A War Too Long: The History of the USAF in Southeast Asia, 1961–1975*. Washington DC: Air Force History and Museums Program, 1996.

"Sidelights on Air Tragedy." *Centralia Daily Chronicle*, July 2, 1956.

Sikorsky Aircraft website. "S-47." *Sikorsky Product History*. SikorSkyArchives
.com. https://www.sikorskyarchives.com/S-47.php.

"Sikorsky Aviation Company." *Aviation*, December 1, 1928.

Sikorsky R-4 Hoverfly. Video. YouTube. https://www.youtube.com/watch?v=
o3o1SFeLJTY.

Skyhawk Association. "VA-195." Skyhawk.org. http://www.skyhawk.org/article
-unit/va195.

"Successful Helicopter Trials at McCook Field." *Aviation*, January 22, 1923.

Tick, Edward. *Warrior's Return: Restoring the Soul after War.* Boulder CO: Sounds True, 2014.

Tilford, Earl H. *Search and Rescue in Southeast Asia, 1961–1975.* Washington DC: Office of Air Force History, 1980.

———. *Setup: What the Air Force Did in Vietnam and Why.* Maxwell Air Force Base AL: Air University Press, 1991.

Tillman, Barrett. *Migmaster: The Story of the F-8 Crusader.* 2nd ed. Annapolis: Naval Institute Press, 2007.

———. *On Wave and Wing: The 100-Year Quest to Perfect the Aircraft Carrier.* Washington DC: Regnery History, 2017.

Townley, Alvin. *Defiant: The POWs Who Endured Vietnam's Most Infamous Prison, the Women Who Fought for Them, and the One Who Never Returned.* New York: St. Martin's, 2014.

U.S. Secretary of Defense. "Functions of the Armed Forces and the Joint Chiefs of Staff." Statement. April 21, 1948. Digital version, 2007. http://cgsc.cdmhost .com/cdm/ref/collection/p4013coll11/id/729.

Wayman, Ken. "United Identifies 29 of the 58 Who Died in Grand Canyon Crash." *Arizona Daily Sun*, July 10, 1956.

Weintraub, Bernard. "Vietnam Protest Blocks Fifth Ave." *New York Times*, May 16, 1965.

Weiss, Delores. "White House Gets Petitions." *Playground Daily New*, May 14, 1972.

Wong, Leonard. "Leave No Man Behind: Recovering American's Fallen Warriors." *Armed Forces & Society* 31, no. 4 (Summer 2005).

"Wood River Man Co-Pilot on Record Rescue of 17 Airmen." *Alton Evening Telegraph*, April 6, 1945.

Wren, Larry. "Gory Crash Scene Detailed by Larry Wren." *Arizona Daily Sun*, July 4, 1956.

INDEX

Page numbers in italics indicate illustrations